Corporate Sociopath Handbook

Don't get left behind:
The unethical path to success

Jonathon Grantham

Publishing Information

Corporate Sociopath Handbook
First Edition, 2025

Published by
Jonathon Grantham
12 John Princes Street
London W1G 0JR

ISBN 978-1-7637815-0-4

Printed worldwide via Amazon, IngramSpark and other print-on-demand services.

Contents

About the Author ---------- 9
Who should read this book? ---------- 10
Disclaimer and Warning ---------- 11
5 things this book will help you achieve ---------- 12
7 things that will help you get the most out of this book ---------- 13

Chapter 1: My Journey Begins ---------- 14

Chapter 2: Introducing the Corporate Sociopath ---------- 18
- What Exactly Is a Corporate Sociopath? ---------- 18
- How They Rise to Power ---------- 19
- The Spectrum of Sociopathy ---------- 19
- Sociopath vs. Psychopath ---------- 20
- The Sociopaths Among Us ---------- 20
- Beyond Sociopathy: The Dark Side of Humanity ---------- 21
- A Word of Caution: Diagnosing Your Colleagues ---------- 22
- The Sociopathic DNA of Corporations ---------- 23
- Your Place in the Corporate Machine ---------- 25
- Ethics: Guidelines, Not Rules ---------- 26
- Identifying a Corporate Sociopath: Wolves in Sheep's Clothing ---------- 27

Chapter 3: Deception and Manipulation Techniques ---------- 31
- Feigning Ignorance: Outsmarting Others by Playing the Fool ---------- 31
- Withholding Information: Silence as a Weapon ---------- 33
- Cherry-Picking Data: Your Version of Truth ---------- 35
- Misinformation: Controlling the Narrative ---------- 37
- False Consensus: Enforce Conformity ---------- 39
- Blame-Shifting: Making Your Problems Theirs ---------- 41
- Playing the Victim: A Well-Timed Tear ---------- 43

Fake Empathy: Winning Trust ---------- 45
Exaggeration and Overpromising: Selling Dreams ---------- 48
Triangulation: Pulling Strings ---------- 50
Creating Scarcity: Manufacturing Urgency---------- 52
Summary ---------- 54

Chapter 4: Undermining and Psychological Warfare ---------- 56
Microaggressions: A Thousand Cuts---------- 56
Subtle Undermining: Eroding Confidence ---------- 57
Invalidating Emotions: Crushing Self-Worth ---------- 58
Gaslighting: Rewriting Reality ---------- 60
Guilt-Tripping: Altering Motivation ---------- 61
Seeding Distrust: Growing Division ---------- 62
Spreading Rumors: Whisper Campaigns ---------- 64
Isolation Tactics: Out of the Loop---------- 65
Mocking or Ridiculing: Public Humiliation ---------- 66
Undermining Competence: Discrediting---------- 68
Undermining Authority: Chipping Away ---------- 69
Forced Compliance: Submission ---------- 70
Work-Life Balance: Disrupting Sleep ---------- 72
Intimidation: Fear---------- 73
Summary ---------- 74

Chapter 5: Divide and Conquer Strategies ---------- 75
Selective Sharing of Information: Misdirection ---------- 75
Inconsistent Communication: Keep Them Guessing ---------- 76
Playing Devil's Advocate: Stirring the Pot ---------- 77
Withholding Credit: Silence as a Weapon ---------- 79
Selective Promotion of Ideas: Picking Favorites---------- 80
Favoritism: Cultivating Jealousy ---------- 81
Encouraging Backchanneling: Secret Conversations---------- 83

Undermining Relationships: Seeds of Doubt ---------- 84
Instigating Minor Conflicts: Disputes to Distractions ---------- 86
Playing People Against Each Other: Divide and Conquer ---------- 87
Creating Factions: Building a Loyal Army ---------- 89
Double-Booking Tasks: Conflicting Agendas ---------- 91
Setting Contradictory Goals: Internal Strife ---------- 92
Encourage Competition for Resources: Compete! ---------- 94
Summary ---------- 95

Chapter 6: Exploiting Systems and Structures ---------- 97
Leveraging Bureaucracy: Exploiting Rules ---------- 97
Creating Red Tape: Introducing Procedures ---------- 99
Gatekeeping Information: Access Denied ---------- 101
Leveraging Organizational Silence: Silence is Platinum ---------- 102
Exploiting Loopholes: Gaps in Policies ---------- 104
Weaponizing Policies: Using Rules Selectively ---------- 106
Manipulating Reporting Lines: Control the Flow ---------- 107
Gaming Performance Metrics: Performance Indicators ---------- 109
Tokenism: Virtue Signaling ---------- 111
Hijacking Meetings: Dominating and Derailing ---------- 113
Circumventing Decision-Making Processes: Proper Channels ---------- 115
Exploiting Power Dynamics: Manipulate and Intimidate ---------- 116
Exploiting HR Processes: Removing Threats ---------- 118
Summary ---------- 120

Chapter 7: Social Engineering and Surveillance ---------- 121
Social Media Profiling: Stalking Made Respectable ---------- 121
Building Rapport: Faux Friendship ---------- 122
Pretexting: Plausible Lies ---------- 123
Impersonation: Wearing the Mask ---------- 125
Phishing: Net not Spear ---------- 126

Baiting: Lure of the Unattainable ---------- 128
Reverse Social Engineering: Problems to Solutions ---------- 130
The Honey Trap: The Sweetest Deception ---------- 131
Eavesdropping: Secrets Overheard ---------- 133
Shoulder Surfing: Take a Peek ---------- 135
Dumpster Diving: One Man's Trash ---------- 136
Tailgating: Slipstreaming Access ---------- 138
Data Mining: Diamonds in the Rough ---------- 140
Summary ---------- 141

Chapter 8: Cult of Personality and Charismatic Manipulation ---------- 142
Creating a Visionary Persona: Follow the Leader ---------- 142
Self-Promotion: I'm the Best ---------- 143
Charismatic Speaking: I had a Dream ---------- 144
Using Charm and Flattery: Smile and Switch ---------- 146
Performative Empathy: The World is Your Stage ---------- 147
Heroic Storytelling: Standing Tall ---------- 149
Mythmaking: Creating the Monster ---------- 150
Grand Gestures: Light the Beacon ---------- 152
Controlling the Narrative: Tell Them What to Say ---------- 153
Promoting a Cult of Loyalty: Protect the Leader ---------- 155
Creating Dependency: Aren't You Glad I'm Here ---------- 156
Emotional Manipulation: Understanding Drivers ---------- 158
Summary ---------- 159

Chapter 9: Legal and Financial Manipulation ---------- 161
Underreporting Income: Vanishing Profits ---------- 161
Tax Mitigation: Your Biggest Expense ---------- 163
Phantom Expenses: Life is Expensive ---------- 164
Insider Trading: First Mover Advantage ---------- 166
Kickbacks and Bribes: Greasing the Wheels ---------- 168

Financial Pressure Tactics: Squeezing ---------- 170
Fraudulent Contracts: Fine Print ---------- 171
Hidden Ownership: Owning Without Owning Up ---------- 173
Shell Companies: Perfect Disguise ---------- 174
Offshore Accounts: Hiding ---------- 176
Exploiting Bankruptcy Laws: Falling Upwards ---------- 177
Asset Stripping: Take the Gold ---------- 179
Ponzi Schemes: Get in Quick ---------- 180
Summary ---------- 182

Chapter 10: Sabotage and Subterfuge ---------- 184
Blocking Key Resources: Starve the Project ---------- 184
Deliberate Overloading: Drowning Your Target ---------- 186
Undermining Projects: Saboteur Within ---------- 187
Sabotaging Relationships: Breaking Bonds ---------- 188
False Allegations: Destroy Reputations ---------- 189
Fake Documents or Records: Rewriting Reality ---------- 190
Planting False Evidence: Framing Rivals ---------- 192
Data Tampering: Corrupting the Core ---------- 194
Technological Sabotage: System Failure ---------- 195
Disrupting Communication: Cutting the Lifeline ---------- 197
Equipment Sabotage: Grinding the Machine to a Halt ---------- 198
Destroying or Stealing Intellectual Property: Valuable Asset ---------- 199
Product Tampering: Success into Disaster ---------- 201
Summary ---------- 202

Chapter 11: Offensive and Defensive Strategies ---------- 204
Building a Loyal Inner Circle: The Trusted Few ---------- 205
Infiltration: Among Us ---------- 205
Controlled Transparency: Through the Looking Glass ---------- 207
Plausible Deniability: What? ---------- 207

Stonewalling: Nothing to See Here ---------- 209
Strategic Leaks: Drink Then Leak ---------- 210
Aggressive Lobbying: Join my Cause ---------- 211
Preemptive Strikes: Did we Start? ---------- 212
Character Assassination: Did you Hear? ---------- 213
Counterattacks: Return Fire! ---------- 215
Litigation as a Weapon: I'll Sue! ---------- 216
Hostile Takeovers: It's Mine Now ---------- 217
Shock and Awe Tactics: Bang! ---------- 219
Creating a Crisis: Fire Alarm Again? ---------- 220
Summary ---------- 221

Chapter 12: Ethical Defenses and Maintaining Integrity ---------- 223
Ethics Training: Knowing What's Right ---------- 223
Clear Conflict of Interest Policies: When to Declare ---------- 224
Encourage Ethical Leadership: Reward the Good ---------- 226
Transparency and Open Communication: Broadcast Depth ---------- 227
Building a Speak-Up Culture: Whistleblowers ---------- 229
Confidential Reporting Systems: I Heard Something ---------- 231
Whistleblower Protections: You Are Safe Now ---------- 233
Ethical Mentorship Programs: Sharing is Caring ---------- 235
Practicing Ethical Decision-Making: Practice Makes Perfect ---------- 237
Documenting Everything: Paper Trail ---------- 240
Independent Audits: Big Brother ---------- 242
Third-Party Oversight: Review Committee ---------- 244
Ethical Crisis Management ---------- 247
Summary ---------- 250

Final Thoughts ---------- 252

About the Author

From an early age, I've been driven by a pursuit of control, success, and power. This obsession led me deep into the darker corners of the corporate world. With degrees in computer science and an MBA, I started as a software developer and soon transitioned into management consulting. It didn't take long for me to realize that intelligence and hard work alone don't guarantee a rise to the top.

I discovered a group playing an entirely different game, one with unwritten and never spoken rules. Curious and determined, I chose a path of short-term contracts across various industries and roles; from accounting, IT, and marketing to politics, operations, and HR. My goal was simple: to understand every facet of business and how it intertwines with human behavior.

This journey exposed me to numerous corporate sociopaths, some dangerously influential. Imagine witnessing firsthand how a single manipulative tactic can dismantle a team's morale or derail a project's success. These encounters, coupled with my passion for psychological forensics, form the foundation of this book.

Through this work, I aim to reveal the tactics corporate sociopaths use. You've likely encountered some of these strategies without even realizing it. My motivation stems from seeing countless individuals suffer as unsuspecting victims of these hidden games. This book equips you with the tools to recognize and counter these strategies, so you don't become collateral damage.

I believe in truth and the uncensored exchange of ideas. Uncomfortable truths shouldn't be swept under the rug; acknowledging them is our duty and responsibility. We have one life, and we're all collectively responsible for the path humanity takes. Let's commit to growing, evolving, and sharing knowledge to improve life for everyone.

By understanding these covert tactics, you're not just protecting yourself; you're contributing to a more transparent and ethical corporate world. Together, we can navigate the shadows and bring these hidden strategies into the light.

Who should read this book?

Have you ever worked in a large corporation and suspect you have encountered a corporate sociopath? They're more common than you might think, and the higher up the ranks you go, the more prevalent they become. Corporations often encourage sociopathic behavior; the relentless drive for profit, efficiency, and innovation pushes people to climb over each other to reach the next rung on the ladder.

Whether you're already skilled at recognizing these individuals or you're tired of being blindsided by their tactics, this book is for you. The reality is, if you work for a large organization, corporate sociopaths are part of your daily life.

Are you exhausted from being pushed around? Do you work hard but feel like you're getting nowhere? Do you show up every day for years only to receive a mediocre paycheck? By understanding their strategies, you can break through that glass ceiling. After all, you have a much better chance of winning the game when you understand the rules.

Disclaimer and Warning

This book delves into strategies and techniques that range from morally questionable to outright illegal. Let me be absolutely clear: I am not encouraging you to break the law or engage in unethical behavior. In fact, I strongly advise against it. The goal here isn't to make you a corporate sociopath but to help you recognize their tactics and protect yourself.

The content is presented in a direct style, intentionally mirroring the mindset of a corporate sociopath. By understanding their thought processes, you'll be better prepared to navigate the corporate world. Remember, just because you can act unethically doesn't mean you should.

Karma exists not necessarily as a cosmic force keeping score, but in the way people respond to how you treat them. If you're cruel and manipulative, that behavior will come back to you. Show kindness, and kindness will find its way back. This isn't about hippie beliefs or religious doctrines; it's about the natural consequences of human interaction.

5 things this book will help you achieve

Awareness: First and foremost, I want you to recognize the signs of sociopathic behavior in the corporate world. By understanding these tactics, you'll be able to identify when they're being used against you. Pop culture loves to portray them as violent murderers, but the reality couldn't be further from the truth. I also hope you'll be able to spot the other personality disorders that circulate in corporate environments.

Resilience: It's easy to feel overwhelmed when you're being undermined or manipulated. This book is designed to give you the tools to stand your ground, protect your interests, and thrive despite the onslaught. It should also bring peace of mind knowing that these types of people are normal, common, and even necessary in some ways. If you're being attacked, it's not necessarily a bad thing it could be a sign you're making progress.

Strategic Thinking: Whether you use these strategies offensively or defensively, I hope this book helps sharpen your ability to think critically, outmaneuver rivals, and succeed in ways that are both ethical and effective. I also want you to develop the skill to recognize different strategies in play and predict the moves of those behind them.

Control: I want you to feel in control of your career trajectory. No longer a victim of corporate games, but an informed player who understands the rules and knows what options are available. Control is essential for success. You won't achieve it if you're constantly being tossed around by every challenge. Success comes from setting your own course and resisting resistance, your career should grow on your own terms.

Balance: While it's important to grasp the darker side of corporate life, I hope this book helps you find balance. You don't have to be ruthless to succeed. True strength often lies in knowing when to apply these strategies and when to choose a more honorable path. Balance not only brings corporate success but also success to the rest of your life. There's a difference between knowing what you could do and what you should do.

7 things that will help you get the most out of this book

Keep an Open Mind: The strategies and tactics discussed in this book are unconventional, and some may challenge your beliefs about right and wrong. Approach the material with an open mind, recognizing that understanding these behaviors is not the same as endorsing them.

Observe, Don't Judge: As you read, focus on understanding how these strategies work in practice, rather than passing moral judgment. The goal here is to give you insight into how corporate sociopaths operate, so you can better recognize and respond to these tactics.

Apply the Knowledge Thoughtfully: While the book provides tools to navigate and thrive in the corporate world, use this knowledge with care. You don't have to employ every strategy you learn knowing when and how to act is just as important as understanding the tactics themselves.

Adapt the Strategies to Your Environment: Not every technique will work in every situation. Think critically about how the strategies you learn can be tailored to your unique work environment and goals.

Stay Balanced: It's easy to get swept up in the power dynamics and cutthroat strategies discussed here. Remember that balance is key. While it's useful to know how to play the game, it's equally important to maintain your integrity and long-term career goals.

Self-Reflection is Key: Use the insights from this book to assess your own behavior and responses. Being aware of how you're perceived and how you react to others will help you navigate corporate dynamics more effectively.

Take Notes and Revisit: This book isn't just a one-time read. As you progress in your career, the situations and challenges you face will change. Come back to these strategies as needed and adjust your approach as you grow.

Chapter 1

My Journey Begins

In my early years, I dabbled in the darker domains of computer programming. No, I wasn't hacking into government databases or stealing credit card numbers. That's just foolish and orange jumpsuits wouldn't suit me. Why would I risk it when the real treasure was sitting there in plain view? I didn't have to break into anything. All I had to do was take it.

Picture the scene: 2007 Facebook was the all-knowing repository of social interaction, and online dating was no longer geeks and perverts; it was the digital revolution. Like drunks at a bar, people were sharing too much: sharing dreams, fears, and dirty secrets. "Big data" was the buzzword of the day, but most people didn't know a petabyte from a peanut. The world was clueless.

In the midst of this digital data deluge, I saw an opportunity to peel back the layers of the human psyche using the one source that is surprisingly more honest than anyone would think: online dating profiles. Why dating sites, you ask? Because it is the place where people do not hide but broadcast their desires. Can you think of anywhere else where strangers scream into the void about their need to control or be controlled?

The plan was simple: scrape 30 million profiles, feed them into the algorithm, and let it unravel the secrets buried in data. Simples.

Now, if you're in a university, you stick to the scientific method: hypotheses, predictions, analysis, blah blah. The problem is, you only find what you're looking for. I wanted to find everything. So, I wrote a statistical regression algorithm that grouped similar profiles. Everyone fits into a cluster, but some clusters were more statistically different than others. And oh boy, did I find one hell of a cluster. Three percent of the profiles sat on this statistical remote island. I didn't know what it was, but I knew these profiles were something else.

Who or more accurately, what were these people? I went undercover, posing as young, old, male, female whatever I had to be to start a conversation. Frustration set in. There was no clear pattern. Age, gender, race, religion none of it mattered. The only common thread? Their fetishes.

Ah, fetish a word that makes most people sweat. But the truth is, whether we like it or not, our fetishes strip us down to our rawest psychological drivers. They reveal more about us than we're comfortable admitting even to ourselves. When people hear "fetish," they think of leather, whips, and handcuffs. And sure, that's part of the show, but it's just the tip of the ice cube if you're into that. Here's some advice you didn't ask for: don't think of fetishes as just what people do behind closed doors. Think of them as windows into our deepest psychological desires. Some crave control, others long for comfort and safety; some get a kick out of danger and risk, while others seek connection. The desires we chase in our sex lives mirror the motivations that drive us in our everyday lives.

I know what you're thinking, "Easy, just target the people with the most extreme fetishes," and you're on the right track, but it's not that simple. Take water sports. Yes, I'm talking about urinating on your partner, try not to kink shame. For some, it's about dominance, humiliation, ownership like a dog marking its territory. But for others, it's the height of intimacy, an act of trust and sharing. Same action, different psychological driver.

The group we identified? They had a strong tendency toward sadism and masochism, the desire to inflict or receive pain. They also gravitated toward control fetishes, especially those involving power dynamics like master/slave relationships or bondage scenarios. But don't get beaten by the wrong end of the stick; this wasn't a catch-all group for anyone with a kinky streak. These fetishes were just more common here, not exclusive.

This isn't about voyeurism or the kinky underbelly of human sexuality. We're diving into the murky depths of human psychology, tearing off the mask to reveal what truly makes people tick.

When I stumbled across this statistically different group, I thought I'd hit the jackpot. The goal of the project was to develop a system that could sift through millions of profiles, interpret them, and sort them into neat little boxes for targeted marketing campaigns. Logical thinkers? Sell them a car with stats: fuel efficiency, 0-60 time, traction control tech. Emotional types? Sell them a dream on wheels, a ticket to freedom, ecstasy. It started as such a neat, tidy theory. But this group of outliers broke the model. Small, distinct, significant and for now, a mystery.

I started with the basics: I read the dating profiles. Nothing too weird at first glance, no red flags, no shocking declarations. They were, dare I say it, normal… at least for the world of kink. But the algorithm insisted otherwise. So, I went undercover. Multiple fake profiles male, female, young, old you name it. I messaged people. Conversations flew back and forth, but nothing. Just ordinary chit-chat. Emotional types, logical types, all just looking for a bit of fun.

Was my math wrong? Did I waste weeks chasing a ghost? Desperation is horrible. Before giving up, I decided to meet some in person, setting up a few coffee dates in Covent Garden. What could possibly go wrong?

First date: charming lawyer, sweet, charismatic. A true gentleman. He offers to pay for my coffee, hitting all the right notes with beautiful banter. I mirror his energy, playing the game. But after a few enjoyable but ultimately fruitless hours, I'm still empty-handed. Frustrated, and almost ready to give up, I suggest we order a bottle of wine.

I grew up in Adelaide, South Australia flanked by incredible wine regions. I do some of my best work with a drink in my hand. But my date? Not so much. A few glasses, and his tongue loosened. The conversation took a sharp turn into…more explicit territory. I kept up the act, matching his every move, encouraging him on, leading him deeper into his confession.

It got dark fast kidnapping fantasies, talk of rape, prolonged torture, and breaking someone psychologically. This wasn't just kink it was someone without a conscience. This is what happens when empathy is removed from the bedroom. It no longer matters whether the other person enjoys it... or even survives.

Disturbing, to say the least. Having found my answer, I made my exit as quickly as I could. After a few more dates with other members of this group, I confirmed my theory I hadn't just uncovered a marketing demographic. I'd built a machine that could identify one of the world's most elusive creatures: the sociopath.

Chapter 2
Introducing the Corporate Sociopath

What Exactly Is a Corporate Sociopath?

Imagine a sharp-dressed figure, social, smiling, and oozing with charm. Instantly likable. They seem genuinely interested in your weekend plans, your favorite hobbies, and even know your partner's name. But while people fall for their act, they're quietly gathering information, reading the room, waiting for the perfect moment to strike. Meet the Corporate Sociopath.

These aren't the headline-grabbing criminals of true-crime podcasts. They're not impulsive or emotionally driven. Quite the opposite. Behind that warm, friendly exterior lies a cold strategist, immune to empathy. They're not climbing the corporate ladder on talent alone though they probably have plenty of it; they're climbing using a well-stocked toolbox of manipulation, deception, and psychological warfare.

They play their role so perfectly that you never see it coming. Your closest friend, your ally, the colleague you trust most, slips the knife in just when you least expect it. And while you're standing there, still in shock, smiling, they push you in front of the moving train.

Psychopaths are the ones causing scenes and chasing the spotlight. Sociopaths? They're playing the long game, thriving, every move is deliberate and calculated. No recklessness, just precision. The last thing a sociopath wants is to be caught in a public spectacle or face a criminal charge. Why risk everything when there's a smarter, safer path to the top?

How They Rise to Power

How do these corporate chameleons make their way to the top? They don't play by the agreed morals and ethics like everyone else. While you're focused on perfecting your presentation skills and staying late to finish that report, they're playing a different game. Every interaction is a well-thought-out move, every colleague a potential tool, every situation a chance to get ahead. Think of the workplace as a chessboard: while you're planning your next move, they just bribed the referee.

Morals? Ethics? Empathy? Sociopaths left those behind long ago. They forge disposable alliances solely to seize opportunities. Today's friend is tomorrow's nothing. They cut through corporate red tape with surgical precision, exploiting every vulnerability, all without a flicker of remorse. Ever met someone who's always smiling, always 'on,' never slipping? That's them, all cute and fluffy with big hidden claws.

The Spectrum of Sociopathy

We need to set something straight: sociopathy isn't all or nothing; it's a sliding scale. And if you've made it to the upper echelons of a corporation, you've likely had to dip into that pool yourself. It's actually a prerequisite. Climbing the corporate ladder often requires making tough decisions, ones that demand a cold, objective view. Take firing someone, for example. It's never easy, especially when the person didn't see it coming. But you justify it to yourself. "It's just business," you say. Or, "If I don't do it, someone else will." These justifications aren't just excuses, they're justifications. They help you set aside empathy and focus on what needs to be done. And that, my friend, is a hallmark of a sociopath. Whether you're a full-fledged sociopath or just someone who knows how to navigate the corporate waters, one thing is clear: the ability to think like a sociopath isn't just helpful, it's essential.

Nodding along? Seeing a bit of yourself in this? Don't worry, it's normal. In fact, if you want to be successful it's required.

Sociopath vs. Psychopath

Definition time: "Sociopath" and "psychopath" are not the same, even though the terms are often used interchangeably. Psychopaths are the impulsive ones, thriving on chaos and reckless decisions, ignoring consequences. They don't care if their plans blow up; in fact, they enjoy the spectacle. Sociopaths, on the other hand, are more strategic. They plot, they plan, they stay three steps ahead, flying under the radar. While a psychopath might burn down the building for fun, a sociopath would quietly take control of it and everyone inside.

From a clinical perspective, psychopathy is often seen as more hard wired as a result of genetics or brain structure. It manifests early, with traits like impulsivity and a lack of fear. Sociopathy, however, is often thought to be shaped by environment and experience; it's a learned behavior. Both lack empathy, but while one reacts to impulses, the other is methodically planning to achieve their goals.

The Sociopaths Among Us

Think you can spot a sociopath in your office? Probably not. They are rarely obvious. More often than not, they're the ones smiling, laughing, joking in meetings, shaking hands in hallways, and gently pushing an agenda. They don't just survive in this environment; they yearn for it. The power struggle energizes them. When there are multiple sociopaths in the boardroom, they feed off each other, growing stronger. In the upper ranks of the corporate world, sociopathy becomes the norm.

If you've climbed the corporate ladder, you've probably tapped into your inner sociopath at some point. This isn't about judgment, it's just a fact. Corporate life demands a certain ruthlessness. Making tough calls, deciding whose careers will grow or shrink, determining which stakeholders you find a threat, constantly dodging and weaving all of this requires a certain level of emotional detachment. If you've ever justified a ruthless decision by saying, "It's in the business's interest," then you've already played the game. The trick is knowing when to lean into this mindset and when to pull back.

Beyond Sociopathy: The Dark Side of Humanity

Think sociopathy is the darkest trait in your office? If only it were true. Meet the Dark 5 personality traits. These aren't just psychological buzzwords; they are the blueprint for the nastiest people in history.

Let's break them down:

1. **Narcissism:** More than just vanity. A corporate narcissist craves constant admiration. They are always self-praising and likely to rewrite history to cast themselves in a better light. They see themselves as the center of the universe, with everyone else just orbiting around them.

2. **Machiavellianism:** Named after Niccolò Machiavelli, the author of The Prince, a piece we will explore in more detail further in this book. This trait is all about manipulation and cunning. They are ultimate strategists, always a few moves ahead and always using every opportunity to their advantage. They won't stab you in the back, they'll convince your best friend it's in their interest to do it for them.

3. **Sociopathy:** The theme of this book. Characterized by ruthlessness and a lack of empathy. They're rarely impulsive and see coworkers as tools, not people. Crush, kill, destroy. No remorse, no second thoughts, just another day at the office.

4. **Sadism:** Corporate sadists derive pleasure not just from success but from others' suffering. They enjoy psychological games denying promotions, public humiliations, and creating a toxic work environment just for fun. They thrive on power plays that make others squirm.

5. **Spitefulness:** The saboteurs of the corporate world. These individuals aren't just content with winning, they want others to lose. They're driven by grudges and never forget a slight. Spiteful colleagues go out of their way to create obstacles for those they feel have wronged them, no matter how small the offense. Expect them to undermine projects, spread rumors, and quietly revel in the downfall of their perceived enemies. For them, success isn't sweet unless it's bitter for someone else.

All five dark traits exist on a scale, and everyone possesses at least a small degree of each. There is a correlation between them: scoring high on one trait makes it more likely you will score high on the others. Successful executives often score higher in sociopathy and Machiavellianism, with moderate levels of narcissism (though this tends to be higher in American firms) and low levels of sadism and spitefulness. Scoring high in all these traits is not necessarily advantageous for a career.

A Word of Caution: Diagnosing Your Colleagues

Before you start seeing sociopaths everywhere, remember this: not every jerk in the office is a sociopath. It's easy to fall into the trap of armchair psychology, diagnosing everyone around you based on a few small examples. There's even a term for it: Medical Student Syndrome. When studying certain diseases or psychological phenomena, it is not unusual for medical and psychology students to start seeing these diagnoses everywhere, including in themselves. Just because someone exhibits a few dark traits doesn't mean they're a sociopath. These traits often cluster, but it's not a hard rule. A bit of narcissism or a touch of Machiavellian strategy doesn't automatically make someone a corporate villain.

Pro tip: Recognizing these traits gives you the upper hand. Spot the narcissist and fact-check their lies, identify the Machiavellian before they set you up for a fall, and learn the sociopath's playbook so you can stay one step ahead.

The Sociopathic DNA of Corporations

If you're looking for moral guidance in the corporate world, I'm sorry you've picked up the wrong book. Corporations are built to prioritize profit, not feelings. They don't have souls, they have shareholders, and that's their guiding principle. Everything else? Negotiable, flexible, and sometimes, utterly expendable. The role of morals and ethics in business is simply marketing.

All that said, don't jump to conclusions. Corporations aren't inherently evil or devoid of a moral compass. They operate within a framework defined by laws and regulations; in most countries, there will be a Corporations Act that mandates serving shareholders' interests. It isn't a "damn the rest" carte blanche instruction. Directors can be held accountable for failing to act responsibly or ethically. It's a balancing act juggling profit with public perception, legal obligations, and shareholder profit. But make no mistake: strategically, structurally, and legally, the first priority is the shareholder.

You can see how this might be appealing to a sociopath. Legally obliged to prioritize profit, they're not choosing ruthlessness; they're following the rules, fully justified in their actions. When companies make headlines for cutting jobs, dodging taxes, or bending regulations, they're not being unethical; they're doing what's expected. And when public outcry becomes too loud, this isn't a reflection on their business practices but merely a marketing problem. Behind every wellness program and diversity initiative, there's a strategy to keep the corporate machine running smoothly and efficiently.

I apologize in advance this might feel like the first time someone told you Santa isn't real. Have you ever wondered why big corporations are so focused on diversity and inclusion? It has nothing to do with treating people fairly or correcting historical wrongs. There are four reasons:

1. **Reduces Salaries:** The more diverse your workplace, the less likely employees are to support each other. Numerous studies

have shown that we are more likely to help and support people who are ethnically and culturally similar to ourselves. In a large corporation, this phenomenon results in significantly less industrial action in diverse workplaces. If you want to crush unions and decrease salaries, increase your diversity.

2. **Process and Replace:** One of the challenges of having a diverse workplace is that people will have a wider variety of ways to solve problems. To combat this, companies create more processes, structures, and management systems to ensure everyone does their job the same way. This creates consistency. The big advantage of consistency is it's the first step toward outsourcing or AI automation. If I can simplify and process map your role, I can outsource replacing you with cheaper staff or, better yet, a machine.

3. **Marketing:** By promoting diversity and inclusion, a company can tell the world it cares about people and believes in righting the wrongs of the past. This phenomenon is called virtue signaling. It's a way of telling customers you are more ethical than you actually are. When customers like what you stand for, they are more likely to buy your product, resulting in higher profits for shareholders.

4. **Increases Share Price:** An interesting mutation of the marketing phenomenon. Banks and financial institutions piggyback on the strategy of virtue signaling. They offer "ethical pension funds" currently about one-third of the financial fund market that only invest in companies meeting certain criteria, such as diversity and inclusion quotas. The biggest single thing a company can do to increase its share price is to meet these quotas and be seen as an ethical company.

If you are still unsure, Santa is not real.

"How's everything going?" asks your ever-smiling HR person. As I'm sure you've worked out, they're not there for you, they're there to protect the company. Wellness programs, open-door policies, feel-good emails they're all designed to keep you productive and compliant. It's not about caring; it's about minimizing risk. The company's priority isn't your happiness, it's your output.

Modern corporations have mastered the art of saying one thing and doing another. This isn't about being evil, it's about practicality. They know that being the "bad guy" for too long brings consequences, lawsuits, fines, regulatory scrutiny, and bad press. So, they adapt. They rebranded. They keep playing the game. It's not hypocrisy; it's strategy. If you notice your employer being "nice," the first thing you should do is ask why.

Your Place in the Corporate Machine

In the corporate world, you're replaceable. Easily replaceable. The system is designed that way on purpose. Job descriptions, key performance indicators, management systems, processes, and procedures are all there to make sure you are a standardized piece of the larger puzzle. Pieces are kept the same shape to make them easily replaceable. Why would any smart organization build an empire that could collapse if one person leaves or is incapacitated? They wouldn't. The corporate structure ensures that anyone and everyone can be replaced without a hitch. It's not a flaw; it's a feature.

This calculated replaceability keeps the wheels turning, no matter who's in which seat at any level. Think you're indispensable? It's hubris nothing more. The moment you become too costly, inefficient, or just don't fit anymore, you're out. It's not personal, it's business. Corporations don't cry when a cog breaks; they simply replace it.

A corporation is more than a machine, it's a living entity. It evolves, adapts, and grows. It has to because if it doesn't change while competitors do, it risks becoming obsolete. Corporations are constantly in survival mode, in an evolutionary arms race driven by market forces, consumer demands, and the threat of competition.

Ethics: Guidelines, Not Rules

Ethical principles guide and shape societies across all cultures, races, and locations. They don't exist as immutable rules that must be followed, but rather as perceptions that must be managed. Richard Dawkins discusses this in The Selfish Gene, where he highlights the evolutionary advantage of appearing altruistic while secretly acting in a selfish manner. It's not always the strongest or most powerful lion that gets to breed; sometimes, the sneaky lion's genes also get passed on. Ethical rules aren't set in stone; they're drawn in sand, shifting with the tides of culture, convenience, and self-interest. In a company, they change depending on who's in charge and what's at stake.

There are no ethical absolutes in business, just as there are no ethical absolutes in life. Ethics are a product of their time, place, and context. Two hundred years ago, slavery was common and generally accepted. Now, we find the concept abhorrent.

Even seemingly clear-cut ethical cases, like "do not kill people" a rule that appears in almost all religions and legal systems is often ignored in certain contexts. Take war, self-defense, euthanasia, or abortion; what seemed like an ethical absolute begins to crumble. The reality is, ethics aren't black and white; they never were; they only exist in a spectrum of grays.

A quick side note: Have you ever wondered what the driving force behind outlawing slavery was? Many have argued that it wasn't about humanity or equality at all; it was purely economics. Slaves have a high initial cost and require housing, food, healthcare, education, motivation, and entertainment. When the economics are adjusted and the books balanced, a slave workforce is more expensive and less efficient than a minimum-wage, free-market workforce. Apologies, I keep going back to money, it's just how I was trained.

Identifying a Corporate Sociopath: Wolves in Sheep's Clothing

How do you spot a corporate sociopath before it's too late? Simple. Read this book and learn to recognize the patterns. Everyone is a creature of habit, me, you, even the most cunning sociopaths. Look beyond what they want you to see and dig into their histories, relationships, and interests. Don't be dazzled by the glowing resume or LinkedIn endorsements. Dig deeper. Did they leave behind a trail of "strategic restructurings" that just so happened to align perfectly with their career moves? Red flag. Did they play the victim? Another red flag. Rapid promotions within the same organization? Yet another red flag. And what about those who constantly preach about ethics? The ones who won't stop talking about transparency and integrity? Be careful. The louder they shout about their virtues, the more they're likely hiding their vices. It's like a magician's trick: I wave my right hand, pocketing the ball with my left.

Here's a trick: if you suspect someone might be a sociopath, casually ask if they've ever been bullied. If they are, they'll likely use this as a chance to spin a sob story designed to tug at your heartstrings. But listen closely. These tales are often woven from half-truths. The person might be real, and the place may exist, but the drama and emotion? Likely fabricated on the spot. Take note of their answer, then ask the same question again in four weeks. Four weeks is enough time for them to forget their original response, forcing them to reinvent the emotional details. Both stories might be filled with vivid imagery and sound convincing, but they're likely to differ.

If you're really skilled, use that four-week gap to plant false psychological seeds. For example, if their story was about someone spreading a rumor to bully them, mention a similar but slightly different situation. Change a few minor details. You're implanting ideas now. If the event actually happened, they'll have a clear memory of it, and the story will remain consistent. But if it was fabricated, they'll struggle to separate the story they originally made up from the one you subtly suggested. Remember, it's much harder to keep two fictional tales straight than to recall a real event.

Always Trust Actions Over Words: words are cheap. Anyone can spin a story, but actions? They tell the real truth. So, ignore the pep talks and the grandstanding. Focus on what people do when no one's watching. Are they quick to take credit but slow to share it? Do they conveniently restructure teams to keep themselves on top? When there's news of a sudden shake-up, don't just ask, "What happened?" Ask, "Who benefits?"

You've surely noticed that politicians lie. Yet people still vote based on what they say, not on what they do. Always look at their past actions, ignore the rhetoric. Look at the recent UK elections (2024). The Conservatives claimed to be a right-wing party but governed with policies that seemed surprisingly left-wing, increasing government spending and expanding social rights and freedoms. Meanwhile, Labour portrayed itself as a left-wing party but adopted right-wing austerity measures, quoting Margaret Thatcher, reducing freedoms, and attempting to cut spending. When it comes to politics, watch actions, ignore words.

Always listen to gossip. It costs you nothing and can be much more than just a laugh around the water cooler. Gossip is a powerful strategic weapon. If multiple people whisper the same story about a colleague, there's likely some truth to it. But don't be fooled, cross-check the gossip against hard facts, look for patterns, motives, and the person's actions. Pay attention to the half-truths, those with just enough fact to be believable without glaring contradictions. Gossip is a tool of reputation damage and one of the most powerful weapons in a sociopath's arsenal.

Listening to gossip works to your advantage; speaking it works against you. Speak less, listen more. It's an old trick taught to senior leaders: stay quiet in meetings, and you'll hear more voices. Managers learn this to give quieter people a chance to speak up hopefully increasing the pool of ideas. Sociopaths are known to use it to their advantage, silently observing interactions and taking mental notes. Silence is a tool for observation.

As a side note, I've always thought that if you wanted to train the perfect spy, you'd teach them to talk nonstop about trivial things. Noise is distracting, and someone who constantly talks about unimportant topics would seem insignificant to a spymaster. I've never seen this strategy used in the real world, but I suspect that noise could be an incredible countermeasure.

Even the most seasoned sociopaths can't keep the mask on all the time. Look for the slip-ups. A flash of anger in a calm meeting, a joke that cuts a little too deep, or an offhand comment that's more revealing than they intended. Alcohol can be a useful tool where it lowers defenses and reveals true natures. But be warned: alcohol is a double-edged sword. Sociopaths will use it to lower your defenses, too.

Alcohol is a fascinating part of corporate culture. Despite efforts to curb drinking for health, inclusivity and ethical reasons, alcohol remains part of the business world. I've had several professional jobs where drinking alcohol at work was explicitly permitted in the employee handbook. Alcohol quickly creates bonds, trust, and relationships. In reality, there's little substance to these connections, but that's not how it feels in the moment. In a drinking culture, choosing not to drink can even lead to distrust.

When I was 21, I worked at a posh cocktail bar in Soho, London. Part of my job was to work the floor and encourage customers to spend more. One of the easiest ways to do this was to sit and have a drink with them. The problem? There is no way I could spend an entire 8-hour shift drinking shots. I would have died from alcohol poisoning. Not wanting to stand out by staying sober, I made a deal with the bar staff: whenever I ordered a particular obscure whiskey, they'd serve me a double shot of apple juice on ice in a fancy crystal whiskey tumbler. I'd drink liters of apple juice each night so much I would feel sick from the sugar. I cultivated a reputation as a drinking machine, but in reality, most nights, I was sober enough I could have driven home.

Here's another trick I learned early in my research: if you suspect someone might be a sociopath, try combining alcohol with a series of jokes. Start with safe topics, then gradually move to more controversial ones, touching on subjects like manipulation, torture, rape, and death. Laughter is like a sneeze, it's a reaction and almost impossible to fake. Pay attention to who laughs and when. It's a window into their psyche. Watch for the moment when dark humor stops being funny. Who gets uncomfortable? This can provide fascinating insights into a person's true nature.

Another thing to watch out for is social chameleons. Have you ever noticed someone who dramatically changes their personality to match whoever they're talking to? Observe them with ten different people, and you'll see ten different versions of them. A little flexibility is fine; you wouldn't talk to a three-year-old the same way you'd speak to an adult. But when someone goes out of their way to perfectly mirror another person, even when their original personality would have sufficed, it's a red flag.

Sociopaths are in a never-ending arms race. As people get smarter thanks to pop culture, internet, and tv they have to keep evolving, staying at least one step ahead. The general level of knowledge and awareness is rising fast. More people now understand the signs to look for and the strategies to defend themselves than ever before. Books like this one serve a dual purpose: they educate the wary on how to spot and counter sociopathic tactics, but they also act as a training manual for those who want to rise to the top. Just as learning a martial art for self-defense can also teach you how to strike first, understanding the handbook of a sociopath can both protect you and, for some, offer a roadmap to unstoppable success.

Chapter 3

Deception and Manipulation Techniques

Perception is more powerful than reality. Recognition and success often stem from manipulation and deception, not talent or effort. This chapter unpacks techniques to control information, shape narratives, and bend outcomes to your advantage.

You will learn how creating a false consensus can pressure others into conformity, how exaggeration and overpromising can cultivate an image of competence and confidence, how blame-shifting can help evade accountability, and how playing the victim can gain sympathy.

This chapter, like the rest of the book, is not solely focused on offensive strategies; it's also about recognizing when these techniques are being used against you. By understanding these tactics, you'll be better prepared to see through deception, resist manipulation, and protect your interests.

This exploration is not an endorsement of unethical behavior but an examination of the real dynamics at play in many organizations. By being aware of these methods, you can better navigate these complex and sometimes career-ending waters. Prepare yourself to dive into the nuanced strategies of deception and manipulation.

Feigning Ignorance: Outsmarting Others by Playing the Fool

Feigning ignorance is a classic tactic, one that aligns with Sun Tzu's concept from The Art of War: "Do not educate your opponent." By playing dumber than you are, you're likely to be underestimated, which can be a strategic advantage. This tactic involves pretending not to understand or know something, not to avoid responsibility, but to keep others in the dark about your true capabilities and intentions. By cultivating just enough confusion, you make others hesitant to confront or challenge you. After all, how can they blame you for something you "didn't know"?

A new policy has been introduced to tighten controls on resource allocation, directly hindering a project you've been pushing. Instead of confronting the policy head-on, you feign ignorance about its existence or relevance. When questioned about your project's budget exceeding the new limits, you respond with genuine surprise, "Oh, I wasn't aware the new policy applied to ongoing projects. I thought it was just for new initiatives!" This puts the policy's enforcers on the back foot, possibly buying you more time to continue as planned or forcing them to reconsider the application of the policy altogether. Your feigned ignorance here isn't a lack of knowledge but a deliberate move to sidestep a roadblock.

Feigning ignorance isn't about dodging responsibility; it's about evading obstacles while keeping your hands spotless. When new rules threaten, playing dumb keeps you in control without confrontation. It's not what you know, it's what they think you don't that seals the deal.

For instance, when a colleague implements a new process that you find obstructive, you might say, "I didn't realize we were expected to follow this new process so strictly perhaps we should revisit how it's impacting overall productivity." In doing so, you position yourself as being in favor of efficiency and progress while subtly undermining the new rule.

When it comes to unwanted tasks or responsibilities, a corporate sociopath doesn't simply avoid them, they redirect them. Instead of feigning ignorance to dodge a task, which could make you seem incapable, you position yourself to delegate the task to someone else while keeping the credit. "I think Sarah is better suited for this part, given her expertise, but I'd be happy to review the final version to ensure it aligns with our goals."

This way, the work gets done by someone else, but you retain oversight and authority.

Feigning ignorance is also useful in dodging tricky questions or avoiding a commitment to a stance, particularly in situations where taking a position could be risky. In a meeting, when pressed for an opinion on a controversial topic, you might respond, "That's a good question I'll need to look into that further," or "I think you're onto something; let me dig up some data to back it up." These responses not only deflect pressure but also position you as thoughtful and thorough, all while avoiding any potential pitfalls of taking an early stance.

The key to this tactic is balance. You must appear just uninformed enough to avoid action or scrutiny without raising doubts about your competence. A skilled practitioner of this tactic knows how to tread the fine line between feigned ignorance and genuine oversight, using it strategically when the stakes are high and the risks of exposure are worth the potential gain.

Like any strategy, feigning ignorance has its risks. Overuse can lead to perceptions of unreliability or manipulation. The art lies in using this tactic selectively and when it matters most, ensuring that when you do play dumb, it serves a higher purpose. Done right, feigning ignorance can help you navigate the corporate landscape with subtlety and finesse, steering clear of obstacles while appearing innocently out of the loop.

Withholding Information: Silence as a Weapon

Withholding information is a game of subtlety. Often branded as lying by omission, this strategy revolves around selectively holding back key details to manipulate outcomes and retain control. It's not the words that leave your lips, but the ones you swallow, that shape the story.

Imagine you're in a meeting discussing a new project. You're aware of a potential roadblock to a major system upgrade scheduled for the same timeframe but you keep this information to yourself. Why? Because by withholding it, you maintain an upper hand. When the project inevitably hits a snag, you can step in with the "hidden" knowledge and position yourself as the savior of the situation. Suddenly, you're not just a participant in the project, you're the person with the foresight and strategic mind to navigate the obstacles. Not only is withholding information useful in maintaining control, but when the time finally comes to share it, you can overwhelm others with a well-prepared, detailed explanation that showcases your expertise. This can give you even more control over the direction of the solution, as others will feel compelled to follow your lead.

Withholding information is the perfect sabotage tool. Picture this: a colleague preps a big report for senior management, and you know a vital update that'll render their data obsolete. Naturally, you 'forget' to share that little detail. As a result, your colleague's presentation is outdated, and they look ill-prepared. The fallout? You've subtly undermined their credibility, making yourself look more reliable and in-the-know by contrast.

The tactic isn't limited to sabotaging others; it can also be used to protect yourself. Let's say a competitor is about to launch a similar product to yours. You have insider knowledge about the flaws in their design, but you choose to stay silent. By keeping this information to yourself, you avoid tipping them off. Then, at the perfect moment such as during a live interview where your competitor is showcasing their new product you leak the information to the interviewer. What was intended to be a positive bit of press and marketing now turns into a damaging piece of negative press, catching your competitor off-guard and unprepared. Your silence becomes a strategic advantage, turning the tide in your favor.

Withholding information creates doubt, making others second-guess their own knowledge. They'll come to you for answers, cementing your control over the situation. If they know a key piece of knowledge is missing, you can subtly hint or suggest that they pursue a less effective path. This misdirection can make them look incompetent and waste valuable time, further consolidating your power and influence.

When done right, withholding information is not just about silence. It's about orchestrating that silence into a symphony of control, where every withheld fact or hidden truth plays a part in maintaining your influence and power. It's about knowing that sometimes, saying less is the most powerful move of all, allowing you to shape outcomes while others remain in the dark.

Cherry-Picking Data: Your Version of Truth

Cherry-picking data is one of my favorite strategies. If you have to lie, lie through numbers. By selectively presenting only the information that supports your agenda while conveniently ignoring anything that contradicts it, you can craft a version of reality that serves your needs. This tactic allows you to shape perceptions, control conversations, and build narratives all without ever telling an outright lie. In the hands of a skilled operator, cherry-picking becomes a powerful tool to bend reality to your will.

Imagine you're preparing a quarterly report, and your division's performance has been less than stellar. The overall sales numbers are down, customer satisfaction is dipping, and costs have risen. But buried in all that bad news is a small uptick in sales for one particular product line. Instead of dwelling on the negative, you spotlight this minor positive trend: "Sales for our new line have grown by 15%!" By focusing solely on this detail, you deflect attention from the broader downturn, creating an illusion of progress and success. If you're savvy, you might even compare the growth rate of the new line to the old, using it to predict a brighter future. And when someone challenges you on the overall decline, you can confidently argue that this uptick is a sign of things to come. Knowing your numbers and having a quick, confident response is crucial.

Cherry-picking is narrative control. You selectively parade the flattering customer reviews, quietly discarding the complaints. When discussing project timelines, the smooth stretches get a spotlight, while missed deadlines are conveniently buried in the shadows. The trick is in the editing.

This tactic is particularly effective in environments where people are overwhelmed with information and lack the time or inclination to dig deeper. By feeding them only the data points that align with your narrative, you create a powerful illusion of competence, success, or inevitability. Remember, if it doesn't support your story, it doesn't exist. And the numbers are only half the story presentation is equally important. Use bold colors, graphs, and traffic light indicators to convey your message from across the room. Green is good, yellow is a warning, red is bad, and blue is stable. The goal is to make the overall message clear at a glance.

Cherry-picking data isn't just for self-promotion; it's a double-edged sword for sinking rivals. When that colleague gunning for a promotion edges too close for comfort, you'll be sure to highlight their slip-ups while burying any hint of success. When speaking to decision-makers: "Yes, they closed that big deal, but wasn't it at the cost of the overall quarter's performance?" Missing information can also paint a picture. For example, if you're tracking when employees clock in for their shifts, deliberately omitting a clock-in time but showing the clock-out can create the impression they arrived late. Gaps in data can suggest incompetence without needing to lie outright.

As with all tactics in the corporate sociopath's handbook, there's a fine line between effective manipulation and overplaying your hand. If you're caught cherry-picking data too often, it can damage your credibility and lead to mistrust. People might begin to question the validity of everything you present, suspecting an agenda behind every statement.

The key is to be strategic selective but not blatantly deceptive. By carefully curating the facts you present, you can steer outcomes, shape perceptions, and maintain control. Remember, perception is often more powerful than reality, and with the right data, you can shape perception to your advantage.

Misinformation: Controlling the Narrative

Misinformation is a potent tool in the corporate sociopath's arsenal, a strategy that involves spreading false or misleading information to manipulate beliefs, perceptions, or decisions. Unlike withholding information or cherry-picking data, misinformation takes a more aggressive approach, aiming to distort reality entirely. When used effectively, it can create confusion, sow doubt, and lead people to act in ways that benefit the manipulator, often without them even realizing they've been influenced.

At its core, misinformation is about creating a narrative that aligns with your objectives, regardless of the truth. For example, imagine you're vying for a promotion, but a colleague stands in your way. You might start subtly spreading a rumor that this colleague is unhappy with the company and looking for opportunities elsewhere. "I heard they're interviewing with a competitor," you might casually mention over lunch. Even if there's no basis to this claim, the seed of doubt has been planted. The rumor spreads, and soon your colleague's loyalty is questioned. Meanwhile, you've positioned yourself as the more stable, reliable choice for the promotion.

Misinformation doesn't always mean outright lying. Exaggerations and half-truths are just as deadly. When a new policy starts threatening your position, you don't lie, you just dial up the fear factor. "This could cause massive layoffs," you warn, even when no such threat exists. By stirring fear and uncertainty, you derail initiatives that don't serve you.

Another effective use of misinformation is to create scapegoats. If you've made a mistake or failed to deliver on a project, you can use misinformation to shift the blame. You might imply that another department provided incorrect data or that a vendor failed to meet their obligations, all without any real evidence. By muddying the waters and creating competing narratives, you deflect attention from your own shortcomings and maintain your standing.

Misinformation can also be used to divide and conquer. By spreading false or misleading information about alliances, projects, or even personal intentions, you can create friction between colleagues, departments, or even external partners. For example, hinting that another team is planning to take over a project can sow discord and prevent collaboration, allowing you to step in and take control of the situation.

The effectiveness of misinformation lies in its ability to manipulate emotions, fear, uncertainty, doubt, and even hope. When people are emotionally charged, they're less likely to think critically and more likely to accept the narrative you're crafting. Misinformation taps into these vulnerabilities, exploiting the natural human tendency to seek simple explanations and clear villains.

Misinformation works best when it is fed to and spread by someone else. You don't want to be identified as the primary source. There are two key elements to avoid being detected: first, obscuring where the story started, and second, who it appears to benefit. The trick is to change both. Feed the story to someone and modify it so that the story appears to benefit them. This way, it looks like they not only created the story but did so for self-serving reasons. When misinformation is spread by a third party with a vested interest, it becomes far more believable, and you remain safely in the background.

If your falsehoods are exposed, the consequences can be severe, including damage to your reputation, loss of trust, and even disciplinary action. Therefore, it's essential to be strategic in your approach, use misinformation sparingly and always have plausible deniability. A well-placed rumor here, a misleading statistic there, these small deceptions can have a significant impact without exposing you to unnecessary risk.

False Consensus: Enforce Conformity

False consensus is a tactic that creates the illusion that everyone agrees with a particular point of view or decision, even when that's not the case. This strategy exploits the psychological phenomenon of groupthink, where individuals conform to perceived majority opinions to avoid conflict or stand out. Research shows that in settings like marketing surveys, people often align with the loudest opinion in the room, not necessarily because they agree, but because they want to fit in. In the hands of a corporate sociopath, false consensus becomes a weapon to silence dissent, sway opinions, and consolidate power.

Imagine you're in a meeting where a controversial decision is up for discussion. Instead of stating your strong stance outright, you begin with, "I think we all agree that..." and follow with your viewpoint. By framing your opinion as a collective agreement, you make it harder for others to voice opposition. Who wants to be the one to disrupt the supposed harmony of the group? This subtle manipulation taps into the powerful social norm of consensus if everyone else seems to agree, it must be right.

False consensus can be especially effective in hierarchical organizations where employees are conditioned to follow the lead of their superiors. By presenting your idea as the prevailing opinion, you create a situation where subordinates feel compelled to go along, either to avoid conflict or to align themselves with what they perceive as the majority or leadership's stance. "I've spoken to a few people, and everyone seems to be on board with this," you might say, even if your "few people" are just a couple of like-minded colleagues. The illusion of widespread support can quickly become a self-fulfilling prophecy, as more people fall in line with the perceived majority.

But corporate hierarchy isn't the only hierarchy at play. There are also dominance hierarchies rooted in human nature where traits like a deep voice, tall stature, and dominant body language can increase the odds of this strategy working. If you present your opinions assertively, utilizing physical presence and vocal authority, people are more likely to accept the implied consensus. Your dominance becomes another layer of persuasion, further discouraging dissent.

Another way to create false consensus is through selective reinforcement, a classic carrot-and-stick approach. In public settings, praise (the carrot) is more effective; you might publicly commend those who support your viewpoint while subtly ignoring or sidelining dissenters. "I really appreciate how Jane sees the big picture here," you say, making it clear which side you're on and nudging others to follow suit. In private, however, a more direct approach (the stick) might be more useful such as a private conversation suggesting that dissent is not well-received. Additionally, a selective name drop can reinforce your point: "I've spoken with Bob, the CEO, and he feels that this is the direction we should go." This aligns your viewpoint with authority, further cementing the illusion of consensus.

False consensus isn't just about creating agreement; it's about silencing disagreement. In meetings or discussions, you might subtly shut down opposing views by framing them as outliers. "I think most of us understand why this is the best path forward," you say, effectively marginalizing any dissenting voices. Those who disagree might feel isolated or reluctant to speak up, fearing they'll be seen as troublemakers or outsiders. Sometimes, more forceful tactics might be necessary to squash dissent, especially when multiple players are in the room. We'll explore strategies like public humiliation further in the book to handle these situations.

This tactic also works well in written communication. In an email to the team, you could say, "Based on our previous discussions, it's clear that the majority of us support this approach." Even if those discussions were limited or one-sided, framing it this way creates a perception of consensus that others may be hesitant to challenge. The power of false consensus lies in its ability to manipulate perceptions if people believe everyone else is on board, they're more likely to jump on the bandwagon.

False consensus thrives on illusion. If cracks show and dissent grows, you're exposed as manipulative and that's when the real trouble starts. Therefore, it's crucial to manage this strategy carefully, balancing it with genuine engagement and the occasional concession to dissent to maintain credibility.

Ultimately, false consensus is about crafting an environment where your viewpoint becomes the "norm," and deviations from it seem out of place. It's a psychological game, leveraging the human tendency to conform to perceived group norms. It is a powerful way to mold the organization's direction to their advantage, one subtle suggestion at a time.

Blame-Shifting: Making Your Problems Theirs

Blame-shifting: the fine art of slipping responsibility to anyone but yourself. In the corporate jungle, this tactic keeps your hands clean while others take the fall. It's all about survival and protecting your reputation at any cost. For the corporate sociopath, blame-shifting is about survival navigating a minefield of potential pitfalls without ever taking a hit. I once worked with a guy we called "Teflon Terry" because nothing ever stuck to him; no matter what went wrong, he always managed to slide out of trouble unscathed.

At its core, blame-shifting is about finding a scapegoat. When something goes wrong whether it's a missed deadline, a failed project, or a poor decision the goal is to ensure that the blame lands anywhere but at your own feet. Imagine you're leading a project that falls behind schedule due to a lack of proper planning on your part. Instead of owning up to it, you might say, "The team wasn't proactive enough in managing their tasks," or, "If only the IT department had fixed those technical issues sooner, we would be on track." By redirecting the blame to others, you deflect attention from your own shortcomings and create a narrative where someone else is at fault.

Blame-shifting thrives in sales, especially in industries like car sales. It's a classic maneuver: customers unknowingly sign away their rights, trapped by a small "error" the salesperson quietly fixes later. A contract is slipped into the stack, correcting the mistake without drawing attention. When the fallout hits, the blame lands squarely on the customer for "not reading carefully," while the salesperson walks away unscathed.

This tactic is particularly effective when combined with a grain of truth. Pointing out genuine mistakes or lapses by others can provide cover for your own faults. For example, "Yes, the client was unhappy, but that's because they didn't get the report on time, something that could have been avoided if the junior team had been more diligent." By mixing a valid critique with a shift in focus, you muddy the waters, making it harder for anyone to pinpoint exactly where the blame lies.

Another method of blame-shifting involves preemptively setting someone up as a potential scapegoat. This can be done subtly, by planting seeds of doubt or framing someone else as unreliable. If you suspect a project is likely to fail, you might casually mention in a few meetings, "I hope John is up to speed on this; he's had some trouble with deadlines in the past." When things inevitably go south, your colleagues are more likely to recall your earlier comment and attribute the failure to John's supposed incompetence, rather than any failings on your part.

Blame-shifting can also be accomplished through silence and omission. If you're aware of an impending problem but choose not to share it, you can later deflect blame by saying, "I assumed everyone was aware of the risks involved," or, "I thought the team leader would have communicated that issue to everyone." By withholding information, you set others up to fail and provide yourself with a convenient excuse when things go wrong.

This tactic is particularly potent in environments where accountability is diffuse, and roles and responsibilities are not clearly defined. The more ambiguity there is, the easier it becomes to shift blame. In chaotic or rapidly changing environments, blame-shifting can thrive, as people are less likely to have the time or resources to meticulously trace the root cause of a failure.

The key to effective blame-shifting is subtlety and plausibility. You must make the redirection of blame seem logical and not overly forced. A clever blame-shifter waits for the right moment a hallway conversation, a chat while walking to a meeting, or any informal setting rather than doing it openly in front of others, where the tactic is more likely to be noticed. By carefully framing the narrative and choosing your words wisely, you can make your version of events seem not only plausible but also the most reasonable interpretation of what happened.

Blame-shifting is about staying on top without ever being pinned down. It's a way to keep moving forward while others are left holding the bag, ensuring that no matter what happens, they remain untouchable.

Playing the Victim: A Well-Timed Tear

Playing the victim lets you deflect blame and soak up sympathy. It's not about fixing mistakes, it's about making sure the fallout lands anywhere but on you. In today's society, this tactic seems to be gaining popularity, but in the corporate world, where perceptions often drive reality, playing the victim can be a double-edged sword.

The essence of playing the victim lies in shifting the narrative from one of accountability to one of sympathy. Imagine you've made a costly error on a project, and it's about to come to light. Instead of owning up to the mistake, you might frame yourself as overwhelmed and under-supported: "I've been under so much pressure lately, and I haven't had the help I needed. It's no wonder something slipped through the cracks." By portraying yourself as struggling under difficult circumstances, you encourage others to empathize with your plight rather than focus on your mistake.

One of the more aggressive uses of this tactic is to label someone else as the bully to preemptively shift blame. By going to HR and declaring that they are the bully, you paint them as the bad actor while positioning yourself as the victim. This move can be effective in tarnishing their reputation and making them seem like the aggressor, even if you were the one who instigated the conflict. While it is possible for the accused to undo this attack, it is incredibly challenging once the victim narrative has taken hold.

It's important to recognize that playing the victim is a high-risk strategy that rarely works in high-ranking positions and is far more effective at lower levels within an organization. At higher ranks, where leadership and decisiveness are expected, the victim strategy can be seen as a sign of weakness or an inability to handle pressure. Managers who rise to the top often view themselves as strong and resilient, and they are less likely to sympathize with those who cast themselves as victims. In fact, many may actively discriminate against those who play the victim card, seeing them as manipulative or lacking the capability to manage challenges effectively.

To deploy this tactic correctly, it is often more strategic to set someone else at a lower level up as the victim. By highlighting a subordinate's supposed mistreatment or unfair treatment, you can manipulate the narrative to make yourself appear more empathetic and supportive, while simultaneously diverting any negative attention away from yourself. This approach keeps the victim narrative at a lower level, where it is less likely to backfire on you directly, and instead positions you as the champion of fairness and support.

That said, playing the victim can still be effective in environments where empathy and support are highly valued. By positioning yourself as a victim, you elicit protective instincts from colleagues or superiors, making them more likely to overlook your errors or even offer additional support. "I'm doing my best, but it's hard when things keep piling up," you might say, subtly implying that any mistakes are more a result of your difficult situation than your competence. This not only deflects criticism but can also lead to additional resources or a reduction in workload, further benefiting you.

The tactic can also be used to deflect blame in situations where you might otherwise be held accountable. For example, if you've been caught spreading misinformation or undermining a colleague, you could turn the tables by claiming you were misunderstood or mistreated: "I only said those things because I felt so isolated and unsupported; I never intended to cause harm." By framing your actions as a desperate response to a perceived slight or hardship, you minimize the focus on your wrongdoing and redirect it toward understanding your supposed suffering.

Playing the victim is not without its risks. If overused or applied too blatantly, this tactic can backfire, leading others to see you as manipulative, self-pitying, or incapable of handling pressure. There's a fine line between eliciting sympathy and appearing weak or incompetent, and crossing it can damage your credibility or make others wary of engaging with you.

Ultimately, playing the victim is about controlling the narrative and shifting the focus away from your faults and toward the supposed hardships you've endured. It's a way to turn criticism into support, blame into sympathy, and obstacles into opportunities. It's a risky tool that, when used sparingly and in the right environment, can help navigate the complex social dynamics of the workplace. However, it's a strategy fraught with potential pitfalls and should be approached with caution particularly at higher levels of an organization where its effectiveness is greatly diminished.

Fake Empathy: Winning Trust

Fake empathy is a cunning tactic where one feigns concern or understanding for another's feelings to gain trust, manipulate emotions, or achieve a specific outcome. Unlike genuine empathy, which involves sincere concern and understanding, fake empathy is a calculated move designed to create a false sense of connection or to manipulate someone into lowering their guard. In the corporate landscape, this tactic is particularly effective in building alliances, defusing tension, and manipulating colleagues into acting in ways that benefit you. It is closely linked to virtue signaling a method of broadcasting your values to appear morally superior. This is a highly effective strategy that corporate sociopaths often overlook, missing out on a powerful tool to influence others.

The essence of fake empathy lies in its ability to make the target feel understood and supported, even when the empathy being offered is entirely superficial. Imagine you've been asked to take on an additional workload by a colleague who is overwhelmed. Instead of outright refusing, you might respond with, "I completely understand how you feel juggling multiple projects, it's so stressful. I wish I could help more, but I'm just swamped with my own deadlines right now." By acknowledging their feelings and expressing a desire to help, you appear empathetic while simultaneously absolving yourself of any obligation to assist. The colleague feels heard and understood, and you avoid taking on extra work without seeming uncooperative.

Fake empathy softens blows. Instead of directly criticizing, say, "You've worked hard, but the results just don't hit the mark. I'm here to help you get there. This approach frames the criticism within a context of support and understanding, making it more palatable and less likely to provoke a defensive reaction.

Another powerful use of fake empathy is in negotiations or conflict resolution. When a disagreement arises, showing a faux understanding of the other party's perspective can create a false sense of compromise or progress. "I see where you're coming from, and I really respect your viewpoint," you might say, even if you have no intention of actually considering their position. By feigning empathy, you can lower the other party's defenses, making them more open to accepting your terms or proposals.

Fake empathy is also effective in building alliances and rapport within teams. By strategically using empathetic language and gestures such as nodding, mirroring body language, or expressing agreement with another's feelings you can create the illusion of camaraderie and trust. "I completely agree with what you're saying; I've felt the same way," can quickly endear you to others, even if you privately disagree or have different intentions. This perceived connection can be leveraged later when you need support, favors, or votes of confidence.

The danger of fake empathy is that if it's detected, it can lead to a severe loss of trust and credibility. People generally value sincerity and authenticity, and if colleagues or superiors start to sense that your empathy is performative rather than genuine, it can backfire. This could result in damaged relationships, loss of support, and increased wariness around you. The effectiveness of fake empathy also depends on how far someone is on the sociopathic scale. If you have some degree of genuine empathy, faking more is relatively easy. However, if you lack empathy entirely, you may struggle with the concept and execution altogether, making it more challenging to fake convincingly.

The trick to successful fake empathy is to be subtle and consistent. It's not about overdoing it or making grand gestures that could come across as insincere. Instead, focus on small, believable expressions of understanding that align with your goals. Use phrases like, "I get that this must be difficult," or "I can see how this situation would be frustrating," to create a veneer of empathy without committing to any real emotional investment.

Ultimately, fake empathy is about exploiting the natural human desire for connection and understanding. It's about creating the illusion that you care deeply about someone's feelings or challenges when, in reality, you're focused solely on your own objectives. Fake empathy is a tool to manipulate trust, build influence, and navigate complex social dynamics all while keeping their true intentions carefully hidden.

Exaggeration and Overpromising: Selling Dreams

Exaggeration and overpromising are tactics that involve making grand, often unrealistic promises or statements to gain support, compliance, or admiration. This strategy is about creating a compelling vision or outcome that others are eager to believe in, even if achieving it is highly improbable or impossible. In the corporate world, exaggeration and overpromising can be used to inspire a team, secure a deal, or gain favor, all while keeping the focus on dazzling possibilities rather than practical realities.

At the heart of exaggeration and overpromising is the art of persuasion. By presenting an overly optimistic scenario or outcome, you tap into people's desires for success, recognition, and advancement. Imagine you're leading a project that has already faced numerous setbacks. Instead of acknowledging the difficulties, you might say, "If we can pull this off, we'll double our market share in just six months!" This bold claim diverts attention from the current challenges and creates a sense of urgency and excitement, encouraging the team to push forward despite the odds. The promise of a significant reward makes people more willing to overlook the current obstacles and invest their time and energy into the project.

Overpromising is also a powerful tool in negotiations or client interactions. When trying to close a deal, you might make lofty commitments: "We can guarantee a 50% increase in efficiency within the first quarter," or "Our solution will completely eliminate your current issues." These exaggerated claims can be very persuasive, especially to clients or stakeholders eager for quick wins and impressive results. Even if the promises are unlikely to be fulfilled, the immediate impact of your confidence and vision can be enough to seal the deal.

Exaggeration can also be used to inflate one's own accomplishments or capabilities, thereby enhancing their perceived value within an organization. For instance, when discussing a previous project, you might state, "I led the team to a record-breaking performance," when in reality, the results were merely above average. By inflating your achievements, you create an aura of competence and success that can be leveraged for promotions, raises, or increased influence.

The effectiveness of exaggeration and overpromising hinges on timing and audience. In high-stakes environments where decisions need to be made quickly, bold promises can be compelling. People want to believe in solutions and leaders that can deliver extraordinary results. But there's a significant risk, if the exaggerated claims are not realized, it can lead to a severe loss of credibility and trust. When the promised results fail to materialize, those who were swayed by the initial overpromising may feel misled or deceived.

To avoid being left holding a time bomb, it's crucial to ensure you're either out of the situation before the fallout or protected by a contract that limits your liability. This approach is common in sales environments, where overpromising can often seal deals, but failure to deliver can lead to significant backlash. The key is to distance yourself from the consequences or ensure there are safeguards in place that protect you when the inevitable disappointment arises.

To mitigate this risk, a savvy manipulator often pairs overpromising with a contingency plan. "While I'm confident we can achieve these results, we may need to adjust depending on market conditions," you might add. This allows you to maintain the appeal of the grand promise while providing an escape route if things don't pan out as claimed. Another approach is to focus on the potential benefits without specifying timelines or exact figures, allowing room for interpretation. "There's a huge opportunity here to significantly boost our presence," is a safer statement than committing to specific numbers or dates.

The key to effective exaggeration and overpromising is to strike a balance between inspiring and plausible. You want to paint a picture that's bright enough to motivate but not so fantastical that it's immediately dismissed as unrealistic. It's about dangling a carrot that seems just out of reach, encouraging others to stretch themselves further while keeping you in a position of influence and authority.

Exaggeration and overpromising are about leveraging hope and ambition creating a narrative of success that others want to believe in. It's a way to galvanize support, secure deals, and climb the corporate ladder, all while keeping the fine print conveniently vague. Remember, the goal is to get ahead, not to deliver on every promise. It's about making sure that by the time the promises are due, you're either long gone or well-protected.

Triangulation: Pulling Strings

Triangulation is a psychological manipulation tactic where one person manipulates two others against each other to control the dynamics and maintain power. In a corporate setting, triangulation involves creating conflicts, misunderstandings, or competition between colleagues or teams, thereby positioning yourself as the central figure who controls the flow of information and mediation. This tactic is a core principle of divide and conquer, which will be discussed in more detail later in the book. It's about leveraging discord to ensure that others remain distracted, divided, and dependent on you for resolution or clarity.

The essence of triangulation lies in its ability to create confusion and conflict between parties, all while you remain seemingly above the fray. Imagine a situation where you pass along selective pieces of information to two colleagues, each tailored to provoke a reaction. To one, you might say, "I heard Jane thinks your approach to the project is too simplistic." To the other, you whisper, "Mark doesn't seem to value your input as much as he should." By planting these seeds of doubt and mistrust, you create tension between Jane and Mark, making them more likely to view each other with suspicion rather than collaborate effectively. Meanwhile, you position yourself as the one they can trust, the only one who understands the full picture.

Triangulation is particularly effective in environments where communication is already strained or where there's a natural competition for resources, recognition, or power. By feeding into these existing tensions, you amplify them, making it more likely that conflicts will arise. The more divided your colleagues become, the easier it is for you to manipulate the situation to your advantage. They become so focused on their disputes with each other that they fail to notice how you are subtly guiding the narrative or influencing the outcome.

This tactic can also be used to consolidate your power by creating a dependency on you as the mediator or peacekeeper. After sowing discord between two parties, you might step in with a solution or offer to mediate, presenting yourself as the voice of reason and calm. "I think there's been a misunderstanding between you two let me help clear things up," you might offer, all while knowing that you created the misunderstanding in the first place. By positioning yourself as the only one who can resolve the conflict, you make yourself indispensable and reinforce your position of control.

Triangulation isn't limited to just creating conflicts; it can also involve fostering competition between two parties to drive them to perform better. For instance, if you're managing two teams, you might subtly hint that one team is outperforming the other, even if it's not true. "Team A has already completed their portion of the project. Are you sure you can keep up?" This tactic can spur both teams to push harder, each trying to outdo the other, while you sit back and reap the benefits of their increased productivity. The competition keeps them focused on each other rather than on your manipulation.

To execute triangulation effectively, subtlety and timing are crucial. The manipulation must be deft, with just enough information shared to create doubt or competition, but not so much that it becomes clear you're the one pulling the strings. The key is to maintain an outward appearance of fairness and support, all while quietly nudging others into conflict or rivalry.

In the end, triangulation is about playing people against each other to keep them off balance and ensure they remain dependent on you. It's a way to control the social dynamics within a team or organization, maintaining your position of power by ensuring that no one else becomes strong enough to challenge it. Triangulation is a way to stay one step ahead, manipulating relationships to create a landscape where they are always at the center, directing the game.

Creating Scarcity: Manufacturing Urgency

Creating scarcity is a manipulation tactic that involves making a situation, resource, or opportunity appear rare or limited to generate a sense of urgency and pressure. By crafting an environment where people believe there is a shortage or a limited time to act, you can influence their decisions and behaviors, often pushing them to act in ways that serve your interests. In the corporate world, creating scarcity is a powerful psychological tool to manipulate negotiations, drive project timelines, or push through policies and decisions without adequate scrutiny.

The core principle behind creating scarcity is simple: people tend to value and desire things more when they believe those things are scarce. This taps into a basic human instinct of fearing loss more than valuing gain. Imagine you're leading a project and need additional resources or support from upper management. You might present the situation as more dire than it is, saying, "We have a very narrow window to capitalize on this market opportunity. If we don't act now, we'll miss our chance." By creating the perception that time or resources are scarce, you push decision-makers to act quickly, often without fully evaluating all the options or potential risks.

This tactic is particularly effective in competitive environments where there is already a fear of missing out (FOMO) or falling behind. By positioning your project, proposal, or product as a rare opportunity, you heighten the sense of urgency among your colleagues or clients. "We only have limited slots available for this pilot program," you might say, even if you're eager to recruit as many participants as possible. The implication that not everyone can participate creates a rush to be included, driving quick decisions and reducing the likelihood of objections or thorough scrutiny.

Creating scarcity is also useful in negotiation scenarios. If you're negotiating a contract or a deal, you might hint that the offer is available for a limited time or that other parties are interested. "I can't promise this price next week; we're getting a lot of interest from other clients," you might say, even if no such interest exists. This creates pressure on the other party to make a quick decision, often leading to concessions or agreements that favor you.

Another effective use of creating scarcity is within team dynamics or resource allocation. Suppose you have a limited budget or set of resources and want to prioritize your project or department. By framing the situation as one where resources are tight, you can persuade others to cut back on their demands or to prioritize your needs. "We're running on a tight budget this quarter, and we need to be very selective about where we allocate resources," you might declare, pushing others to step back or scale down their requests while you secure what you need.

To use this tactic effectively, timing and consistency are key. Scarcity must be introduced at the right moment when people are already leaning toward a decision or when hesitation could mean a lost opportunity. Consistency in messaging is also important; the narrative around scarcity must be maintained across different channels and conversations to reinforce the urgency and pressure.

Creating scarcity is about leveraging psychology to create a sense of urgency and need. It's a way to manipulate the dynamics of decision-making, ensuring that others act quickly and often in your favor. By making situations, resources, or opportunities appear rare or fleeting, you can drive people to decisions they might not otherwise make, all while keeping the pressure on and the advantage firmly in your corner.

Summary

The techniques covered in this chapter reveal just how much of corporate success is built not just on visible achievements but on the unseen strategies that influence outcomes behind the scenes. Understanding these methods whether it's feigning ignorance, cherry-picking data, or creating false consensus provides a window into the realpolitik of the workplace, where perceptions can be managed and power is often a game of shadows.

Mastering these tactics demands more than manipulation it calls for sharp timing and discernment. The corporate arena is a minefield, where every move triggers consequences. The art lies in knowing when to strike and when to hold back. Missteps are costly, and overuse can expose you, leading to a swift fall from grace.

While these strategies can certainly help you navigate the intricate web of corporate politics, they also come with risks. Misjudge a situation, and you could find yourself caught in your own web. It's a reminder that the corporate landscape is as much about avoiding traps as it is about setting them.

As you move forward, think critically about the dynamics at play in your environment. Recognize when others are pulling strings behind the scenes, and consider how best to respond. Being aware of these tactics doesn't mean you have to use them, but it does mean you'll be less likely to fall prey to them. The ultimate advantage lies not just in knowing how to manipulate the game, but in knowing when to walk away or rewrite the rules altogether.

Keep these lessons in mind as you continue your journey through the corporate world. Every environment has its own set of rules, and those who succeed are the ones who understand both the written and unwritten codes of conduct. The power isn't just in playing the game, it's in knowing the full breadth of moves available to you and choosing the ones that align best with your goals.

Chapter 4
Undermining and Psychological Warfare

Success isn't just about strategy and hard work. It's the unspoken power plays that shape every office. Undermining and psychological warfare are the invisible forces that slowly chip away at people's confidence, keeping them off balance while you rise to the top. Dramatic takedowns are fun, but real power lies in slow, subtle, sustained pressure.

This chapter dives into the art of undermining and psychological warfare. Never leave fingerprints. We're talking about microaggressions that make people question their very being, gaslighting that distorts reality, and undermining until there is nowhere solid to stand. Master these tactics, and you'll stay ahead. Ignore them, and you've scuppered your career.

Microaggressions: A Thousand Cuts

Microaggressions are slow acting poison. They're not just insults disguised as polite conversation; they're precision tools to dismantle confidence, layer by layer. Like invisible paper cuts, harmless at first, but bleed enough and you'll make them question their very place in this world.

Imagine you're in a team meeting, and Susan from Marketing shares an idea. You nod, then casually add, "That's interesting, Susan. But have you thought about it from a cultural context?" Now Susan's left wondering if her input even holds weight. It's subtle, almost innocent, and most importantly, it slides right under HR's radar.

My grandmother was terrible at this. One Christmas dinner, she leaned over the table and, in a loud stage whisper, said to my sister, "Wouldn't you be happier if you lost a little weight?" A jibe wrapped in 'concern,' nearly impossible to defend against, especially in polite company. The English, particularly the middle class, have turned microaggressions into a national sport. Comments about education, wealth, success, and love lives are dished out like discounted Waitrose canapés.

A way to counter microaggressions is to look the person straight in the eye and calmly ask, "Are you saying this to be helpful or hurtful?" Microaggressions only work in the shadows. Shine a light on them, and they instantly wither away. Sunlight is the best disinfectant.

Systematic well-placed microaggressions keep your rivals unsure of themselves, trapped in their place. It's not about what you say; it's about how you make them feel. If they feel small, insecure, uncertain, you are on the right path.

Subtle Undermining: Eroding Confidence

Why go for the jugular when a gentle scratch will do? Subtle undermining is the slow, calculated erosion of someone's confidence, a tactic that requires consistency, finesse, and the patience to play the long game. Never one big blow; it's about a thousand little ones, each one perfectly timed to keep your target off balance.

John is a rising star in your department, a bit too talented for your liking. He presents a proposal at the weekly meeting, and you ever the helpful colleague chimes in with, "That's a bold strategy, John. But what will we do if the client doesn't agree?" You've planted the seed of doubt. The room now sees John's proposal not as a working plan but a potential disaster waiting to unfold. Even John is left wondering if his boldness is actually recklessness.

Subtle undermining works best when it appears supportive. Frame your comments as thoughtful concerns or as playing devil's advocate. "I'm just trying to think of all the angles here" or "I just want to make sure we're all covered." The key is to sound like you're on their side while quietly chiseling away their confidence.

Another classic move is the soft whisper campaign. "I've heard some people are a bit concerned about Sarah's ability to lead. Not me, of course, but you know how people talk." You've now successfully raised doubts about Sarah's leadership style without directly attacking her. The beauty of this tactic is that it keeps your hands clean. After all, you're just passing along what you've "heard."

You can also try sly comparisons. "That was a great presentation, almost as good as Mark's from last week. He really did set a high bar!" What you've done here is simple but effective: you've implied they're not the best without directly stating it. Said in front of their peers or better yet underlings you leave the person powerless.

Subtle undermining is control over cruelty. It leaves people unable to operate properly. It's impossible to lead when you're unsure of the ground you stand on.

Invalidating Emotions: Crushing Self-Worth

The aim is to make them doubt their own emotions, to lose trust in their feelings. Downplay their frustrations or excitement until they're left confused. A person that second-guesses their emotions is easy to control.

Lisa, your teammate, just got slammed with a nasty email from a client, and she's visibly upset. Perfect opportunity. As she vents, you lean back, smile slightly, and say, "Oh, come on, Lisa. It's not that big of a deal. Clients get like this all the time. You need to toughen up." And just like that, you've done more than dismiss her feelings you've suggested she's weak for having them in the first place.

The art of invalidating emotions is subtlety. It's not about outright denying someone's experience; it's about reframing it in a way that minimizes their feelings. "You're overreacting again" or "You're just too sensitive" are classics. But for the more sophisticated player, try, "I'm sure you're feeling that way, but is it really worth all this energy?" You've subtly told them that their emotions aren't just wrong, they're a waste of time.

You can also try empathetic invalidation. "I understand you're upset, but everyone feels this way sometimes. You just need to get over it." This move combines a veneer of empathy with a core of dismissal, leaving your target feeling not only misunderstood but also isolated. They're left wondering if maybe they are the problem after all.

And don't underestimate the power of comparison. "I remember when I was in your shoes, I handled it a bit differently." Translation: "Your feelings are not only invalid, your response is inferior." This tactic is particularly effective in group settings, where the subtle undermining of someone's emotional response can ripple outward, making them appear less competent and more emotionally unstable.

Why go to all this trouble, you ask? Simple it sows doubt. Emotions are incredibly powerful diagnostic tools. If you're feeling anger toward someone, it's a clue that they may be feeling anger towards you, even if they aren't showing it. Our emotions act as a mirror, reflecting the other person's feelings. If you can get someone to a point where they're questioning their own emotions, you've not only destabilized them emotionally but also weakened their ability to read others' emotions.

The trick to invalidating emotions is to make it seem like you're offering guidance or tough love. "I'm just trying to help you see the bigger picture here" or "I'm only saying this because I care." It's this kind of language that seems supportive on the surface but leaves them questioning long after the conversation has ended.

Gaslighting: Rewriting Reality

Gaslighting, a term coined by British playwright Patrick Hamilton, is a tactic so subtle yet powerful it makes the target question their perceptions and, eventually, their sanity. In the war of minds, it's the slow, prolonged strategies that win the game. Gaslighting is the act of convincing someone that they are going mad. If you want to truly dominate, make them doubt everything they thought they knew.

Imagine this: You and Sarah have a private conversation where you casually mention that the team might be losing confidence in her. A week later, when she brings it up, you respond with, "I never said that. Are you sure you're not misremembering?" Or worse, you throw in, "Were you drinking last night?" or "Did you take your medication?" Now Sarah's trapped in a spiral of confusion, second-guessing herself. Did it happen? Didn't it? If you can't trust your own memory, it's impossible to defend yourself in the bigger game.

Gaslighting is the art of making someone question their own memory. Deny, deflect, distort and make yourself the only source of truth. "I gave you the notes," you say, as they sit there with a meeting pack missing the notes. Have you ever tried proving something never existed? Nearly impossible.

Pin their legitimate concerns on emotional instability. "You're just being overly sensitive," "You're imagining things again," or a personal favorite, "Are you being paranoid… again?" These phrases don't just dismiss their feelings, they plant seeds of doubt about their mental state. If they're always "overreacting," maybe their judgment isn't as reliable as they think. Convince them they're the problem, and now you are free to do whatever you want.

Rewriting history is an art. "Remember we agreed on that deadline? We talked about it in the kitchen and you had coffee and told me about your weekend." By mixing in truth with the lie, the gaslighting becomes harder to detect. The false "we agreed on the deadline" is buried under a pile of true statements like "you told me about your weekend," making your version sound more credible.

Gaslighting's success lies in gradually eroding someone's trust in themselves. It's not a one-off tactic; it's a slow, continuous process. Push just enough to make them question things, but not so hard that they walk away. In this delicate dance, make sure you are the lead.

Guilt-Tripping: Altering Motivation

Guilt-tripping is another subtle yet powerful tool. It's all about making someone feel responsible, ashamed, or guilty for something they may or may not control. The aim? Increase their shame and self-doubt all while keeping your hands clean and your intentions seemingly noble.

You're in a meeting, and you need a report from Alex, who's already buried in work. Instead of directly asking or offering help, you sigh dramatically and say, "I guess I'll be staying late again to cover this. I know everyone has a lot on their plates, especially with all the personal time people have been taking lately." Now, Alex feels the weight. Was that directed at them? Are they falling short? Suddenly, they're rushing to finish the report.

The trick with guilt-tripping is dressing it up as concern or self-sacrifice. "I just don't want the team to suffer because of a few missed deadlines. I know you're doing your best, but I worry how it reflects on all of us." On the surface, it's dripping with empathy. But underneath, it's morphing their internal motivation to your whim.

Another classic technique is combining the silent treatment with a well-timed remark. You become distant, stop responding to emails. When someone asks, you casually drop, "Oh, I've just been reflecting on how some people aren't as committed to the team's success. But it's fine, I'm sure it's not intentional." The doubt is planted. Who isn't pulling their weight? Gossip will spread, and suddenly, everyone's scrambling to prove their commitment.

Bringing up the past also works. "Remember when I stayed late to help with your project? I just thought we were in this together." By invoking a past favor, you're not just reminding them of your 'kindness' you're subtly calling in the favor, demanding repayment right now.

Why use guilt-tripping? It creates a psychological debt, a sense of obligation they feel compelled to repay. And because it's all wrapped up in goodwill or concern, they can't confront it without looking ungrateful. It's a way to get what you want while appearing to have their best interests at heart.

The brilliance of guilt-tripping is that you get to be both the victim and the puppet master. You're just the selfless team player, doing the best you can to hold everything together. And if others feel bad? Well, maybe they should. As Jiminy Cricket said, "Always let your conscience be your guide."

Seeding Distrust: Growing Division

Seeding distrust is planting a whisper and watching it grow into a forest of suspicion. It turns relationships fragile, alliances into shifting sands. When no one feels safe, control becomes easy. In a high-stress environment, trust is everything so if you are on the attack, your job is to obliterate it.

During a casual coffee break, you lean over to a colleague and murmur, "I overheard Tom and Maria talking about your project yesterday. I didn't catch everything, but it sounded like they weren't going to support it." That's all it takes a vague, ambiguous comment to plant a seed of doubt. Now, your colleague is left wondering: What concerns? Why didn't Tom and Maria come to them directly? Do they have ulterior motives? Their trust in their teammates erodes, and they're left feeling isolated and insecure.

The key to seeding distrust is subtlety. You're not outright accusing anyone of anything you're simply hinting, suggesting, or implying. "Do you think the donations are down when John counts it?" You're not saying it's a fact; you're just putting it out there, letting it simmer in the back of their minds. It's the ambiguity that does the real damage.

Another effective tactic is to play both sides also covered in triangulation. You confide in Jane that Mark has been speaking negatively about her behind her back, and then you tell Mark that Jane has been questioning his decisions. You've now created a feedback loop of distrust where both parties are on edge, wary of each other, and too busy guarding their own backs to notice that you're the one pulling the strings.

Selective truth-telling is also highly effective. Share half-truths or conveniently leave out key details. "I heard there might be some restructuring soon, but I'm not supposed to say anything. You didn't hear it from me." Now your colleagues are caught in a state of uncertainty, wondering what's being kept from them. The paranoia spreads, and soon, everyone's looking over their shoulders, wondering who's in the know and who's being kept in the dark.

Why seed distrust? Because a divided team is a conquered team. When people are busy doubting each other, they can't unite against you. They're off-balance, distracted, and more concerned with protecting themselves than advancing their own goals or challenging yours. Distrust creates the perfect environment for your influence to grow unchecked.

The brilliance of seeding distrust is that no one can point a finger at you because you haven't done anything overtly wrong. You've simply "shared a concern" or "passed along some information." You come off as the helpful, concerned colleague while the seeds you've planted grow into deep-rooted division.

Spreading Rumors: Whisper Campaigns

Reputation is everything. Every schoolgirl knows this trick. Spreading rumors is a devastatingly effective tool damaging or even destroying someone's standing without ever being in the same room. A well-placed rumor is like a virus; it spreads quickly, infecting everyone it touches, weaving a web of doubt that's nearly impossible to untangle.

Take Karen from Accounting, for instance. She's gaining a bit too much influence, good at her job, well-liked, and her ideas are catching on. But instead of confronting her head-on, you start a whisper. "I heard Karen's been looking for jobs elsewhere. You know how it goes, people get distracted when they've got one foot out the door." Now, everyone's wondering: Is Karen really committed? Can we trust her input? Her solid reputation starts to wobble all from a few well-timed words.

Again, you have to keep it subtle. "You know Karen from Accounts? I heard she eats babies" won't work. You never say anything overtly damaging; you just suggest, hint, or question. "I'm not saying it's true, but I've heard some things about Mike's expense reports. I'm sure it's nothing, but maybe it's worth keeping an eye on it." You're not accusing him, you're planting a seed. And as they say, where there's smoke, there's fire. People's natural tendency to gossip and speculate does the rest.

Another move is the double-edged compliment. "Jenna is really ambitious, isn't she? Almost too ambitious, if you know what I mean." You've just taken a positive trait and turned it into a potential red flag, leaving everyone to wonder if Jenna's drive might be a threat to their own positions. It's a clever twist if she fails, she's no longer a threat. If she succeeds, it's because she's "too ambitious."

Then there's the "concerned confidant" routine. You pull a trusted coworker aside and say, "I shouldn't be telling you this, but I'm really worried about Rob. I heard he's been struggling with some personal issues, and it's starting to affect his work." Framed as concern, you come off as caring while also planting doubt about Rob's reliability. And because it's framed as a secret, it feels even more credible and urgent. If you really want to see it spread, use the phrase "don't tell anyone" you may as well print it on a billboard.

Rumors can ruin reputations, sow discord, and create chaos all without direct confrontation. And if you're ever called out, it's easy to backtrack. "Oh, I didn't mean anything by it, that's just something I heard." Meanwhile, the damage is already done.

The effectiveness of rumors lies in their ability to take on a life of their own. Once you set them loose, they're self-sustaining. Gossip is currency. People love to talk, and a juicy piece of gossip spreads like nothing else. Before long, what started as a whisper becomes a full-blown narrative, complete with "facts" and "proof," all of which are impossible to trace back to you.

Isolation Tactics: Out of the Loop

Isolation tactics are all about exclusion, cutting someone out of key meetings, conversations, and social gatherings to make them feel like an outsider, even within their own team. It's a subtle but effective way to erode their influence, undermine their confidence, and keep them always a step behind. In the corporate world, knowledge is power, and the less they know, the weaker they become.

Imagine this: You're organizing a project meeting and "accidentally" forget to invite Dave, the one who's been making waves with his ideas. When Dave confronts you, you feign surprise. "Oh, I thought I added you to the email! Must've been an oversight. Sorry about that!" Meanwhile, Dave is left out of the loop, struggling to catch up while everyone else has moved on. The message? Dave isn't as essential as he thinks.

Isolation can be as simple as withholding information. "Oh, didn't you know? We decided on the new plan during lunch. You weren't there? That's a shame." Now, they're scrambling to catch up, constantly feeling like they're on the outside looking in. It creates that ever-present sense of exclusion, a nagging feeling that they're not really part of the team.

Then there's the social snub. After a meeting, everyone heads out for drinks, but Sarah's left in the dark. "Oh, we thought you were busy," you say with a smile later. The result? Sarah feels left out, her social capital dwindles, and she becomes hesitant to speak up or take initiative. She's left wondering what else she's missing, and that doubt slowly chips away at her confidence.

Selective communication is another tactic. Key information is shared during informal one-on-one chats or small gatherings where the person you want to exclude isn't present. "We talked about it at lunch, didn't you hear?" By the time they're brought up to speed, it's too late for them to contribute meaningfully. They're always a step behind, constantly playing catch-up.

Isolation tactics weaken someone's influence without ever needing direct confrontation. When someone's excluded, they start to feel irrelevant, their confidence dips, and they become less effective. Over time, they'll speak up less, challenge less, and eventually, they start to fade into the background, no longer a threat to your position. They become a shadow, quietly sidelined from the team's decision-making process.

Mocking or Ridiculing: Public Humiliation

Mocking or ridiculing is a powerful tactic for those looking to publicly undermine their target. It's about weaponizing attention and humor. Done effectively, it doesn't just hurt feelings; it shatters them, destroying their respect and authority.

Got a know-it-all on your team? Prep a series of impossible questions. During the meeting, fire them off. Watch as their façade crumbles with each "I don't know," leaving them exposed and flailing. It's a public takedown that leaves them embarrassed, while you sit back, cool and collected.

The beauty of mockery lies in its plausible deniability. "Come on, it was just a joke! Don't take it so seriously," you say if someone calls you out. But the damage is already done. The target feels humiliated, their confidence is shaken, and everyone else in the room has just a little less respect for them. It's not about what's said; it's about how it makes them feel small, exposed, and powerless.

Humiliation isn't about hiding behind jokes, it's a deliberate power play. The point isn't to pretend it's harmless; it's to make it clear you're weak, and I'm strong. Public humiliation, especially when your target is already outside their comfort zone, is a way to display strength at their expense. During a presentation, a pitch, or when they're leading a new project, that's when they're most vulnerable. That's when a well-placed jab can land the hardest.

I remember working closely with one of the world's largest consulting firms. I'll leave them unnamed, given their fondness for lawsuits. They had a brutal management fast track where eager graduates competed against each other for a coveted role. The system was cutthroat. Groups of 12 would enter the program, and every month, they'd all have to give a presentation. The catch? If you had the weakest presentation, you lost your job. As I said, vicious.

I remember watching one of these presentations, given by a young woman who had her slide deck up on the projector. About five minutes in, an inappropriate picture of her sitting on the knee of one of her bosses flashed up on the screen. It was unclear who tampered with her slides, but whoever did it executed it flawlessly. The damage was done. She never recovered and left the corporate world.

Humiliation works because it plays on one of our deepest fears: public embarrassment. Nobody wants to be the fool, especially in front of colleagues. When executed properly, this tool is literally a career ender.

Undermining Competence: Discrediting

Undermining someone's competence is about making people think they can't do their job. Never outright say someone is incapable; instead, it's about planting seeds regarding their abilities, judgment, and qualifications. Make them appear less competent than they actually are, all while maintaining your own façade of support and concern.

Consider this scenario: Emma, your colleague, has just presented a comprehensive plan to improve team productivity. You nod thoughtfully and then say, "Interesting approach, Emma. But don't you think it's a bit... ambitious, given your experience?" Two words ambitious and experienced you've subtly implied that Emma might be biting off more than she can chew. The room starts to wonder: Is Emma really up to the task? You've cast a shadow over her competence without making a direct accusation.

The key to undermining competence is to disguise your criticism in a camouflage of helpfulness. "I'm just worried that you might be overextending yourself with this project. Maybe it's better to focus on something more within your scope?" It sounds like you're being supportive, but you're actually suggesting that they're not capable of handling complex tasks. It's a slow, corrosive tactic that eats away at their confidence and their standing in the team.

Another classic maneuver is the strategic doubt. "Are you sure you've got all the data for this report? I thought I saw a few gaps. Just a heads-up before you present to the higher-ups." Now, you've not only questioned their attention to detail but also made them second-guess their work. Even if their report is flawless, the doubt lingers, affecting how others perceive their competence.

Undermining competence can also be achieved by setting someone up to fail. Assign them tasks outside their expertise and then express surprise when they struggle. "I thought you'd have this under control. I guess I overestimated your capabilities." You're not only framing them as incompetent but also positioning yourself as someone who tried to give them a chance. It's a win-win for you and a lose-lose for them.

Why undermine someone's competence? Because a person who doubts their own abilities is much easier to control and manipulate. If they don't trust their judgment, they'll be less likely to challenge yours. And if others start to see them as less competent, their influence and authority will wane, leaving more room for you to step in and shine.

Like all mind games, you have to keep it subtle. You're not overtly attacking them, you're simply raising "concerns" or offering "constructive criticism." It's the kind of behavior that's hard to pin down as malicious, yet the impact is significant. Over time, it creates an atmosphere of doubt around the person's abilities, leading others to question their suitability for high-stakes projects or leadership roles.

Undermining Authority: Chipping Away

Undermining authority is all about subtly chipping away at a leader's credibility and control. It's a calculated tactic designed to weaken their standing without overtly challenging them. This isn't about direct confrontation; it's about creating a slow drip of doubt that eventually erodes their power. The goal is to make others question the leader's decisions, judgment, and, ultimately, their right to lead.

Ben has a question for his boss, but before he gets there, you step in with the answer. Now, in Ben's mind, he doesn't need to go to his boss, he'll come to you. With that one move, you've quietly chipped away at his boss's authority. Do this with customers, suppliers, other teams, and the rest of Ben's colleagues, and soon, his boss's management authority is gone entirely. In this example, you are replacing Ben's boss.

Another effective strategy is to act as the 'voice of reason' whenever a leader makes a bold or controversial decision. "I understand what you're saying, but have you considered how this might affect team morale?" or

"I just want to make sure we're not moving too fast here. We've seen what happens when we rush things." These statements seem supportive on the surface, but they subtly imply that the leader is impulsive or out of touch with the team's needs.

Undermining authority can also be achieved through strategic alignment with others on the team. You quietly build a coalition of like-minded colleagues who share your concerns. "A few of us were talking, and we think it might be worth revisiting that decision. What do you think?" Now, you've created the impression that there's a groundswell of opinion against the leader's choices, further weakening their position.

Authority is the officially sanctioned version of dominance. Dominance is an animalistic hierarchy hardwired into our brains. You can trigger dominance simply by altering how you present yourself, change the way you dress, lower the tone of your voice, and adjust your body language. Looking like, dressing like, moving like, and talking like the boss will subconsciously trigger people to see you as the leader. It's a subtle but effective way to undermine someone's authority.

Remember, you're not openly challenging the leader; you're just being there, raising concerns, asking questions, and fostering discussion. It's a tactic that can't easily be called out as malicious, yet it sows seeds of doubt that can grow into full-blown skepticism about the leader's competence and judgment.

Forced Compliance: Submission

Forced compliance is all about applying just the right amount of pressure to get someone to do what you want, even if it goes against their better judgment or will. The goal is to make them feel they have no other choice but to agree with you or follow your lead. This isn't about overt threats or brute force; it's about creating a scenario where the only "reasonable" option is the one you've laid out.

Imagine you're managing a project, and you need Susan to take on extra tasks that aren't technically her responsibility. Instead of asking her outright, you frame it in a way that makes refusal seem impossible. "Susan, we're really counting on you to handle these additional reports. I really appreciate your support on this." Now, Susan is caught in a bind. Refusing would make her look uncooperative, and agreeing means taking on more work than she signed up for.

The key to forced compliance is to create a false dichotomy. Make it seem like there are only two options: the one you want and a clearly undesirable alternative. "We could go with your approach, John, but it would delay the project by at least a week. I'm sure you don't want to be responsible for that." You're not just presenting a choice; you're setting up a scenario where the only logical choice is the one you've decided on.

Another tactic is to appeal to a higher authority or the "greater good." "We're all in this together, and sometimes that means making tough choices. I know this isn't ideal, but it's what's best for the company." By invoking the greater good, you're positioning yourself as the one who is willing to make the hard decisions while subtly pressuring others to fall in line, lest they seem selfish or shortsighted.

Forced compliance can also involve leveraging social proof. "Everyone else has agreed to stay late to meet the deadline. I'm sure you will too, right?" This tactic plays on the fear of standing out or being the odd one out. No one wants to be the only dissenting voice, especially when it seems like everyone else is already on board. By creating the illusion of consensus, you're pushing them toward compliance.

You're not issuing direct orders or making threats; you're simply guiding people toward the conclusion you want them to reach. Create false choices, appeal to the greater good, and leverage social proof to your advantage. Make them believe that the only path forward is the one you've paved.

Work-Life Balance: Disrupting Sleep

Disrupting someone's sleep or work-life balance is an incredibly effective way to wear them down. This isn't about launching a direct attack; it's about creating constant pressure that slowly grinds them down. By strategically assigning tasks or setting up situations that encroach on their personal time, you can erode their energy, focus, and overall well-being, making them less effective and more compliant.

I had a friend who worked with a well-known publicly traded electronics firm on a major restructuring. A key part of the plan hinged on a massive outsourcing deal. The firm insisted that the announcement had to be made on Monday afternoon, which meant the contract had to be signed by Monday morning.

All weekend, the firm kept rejecting, changing, and tweaking details. Lawyers on both sides worked non-stop, pushing through four days of 18-hour shifts. By the time they finally reached an agreement, minutes before the deadline, the firm pulled a ruthless move. They swapped out the contract for one with much more favorable financial terms for themselves. The consulting firm's legal team, completely exhausted, didn't catch the switch and signed the deal.

The lawyers should have known better this is a classic strategy, and the electronics firm had a reputation for these kinds of tactics. Exhaust the opposition with endless revisions and last-minute changes, then slip in the terms that suit you when they're too tired to notice. The consulting firm fell right into the trap, despite all the red flags.

This tactic works just as well on individuals as it does on large corporations. Exhaust them, disrupt their sleep, and watch the cracks form. When their personal life starts falling apart, you'll know they're primed for your next move. If you know someone is already sleep-deprived and off balance, schedule a meeting for 5 p.m. on a Friday. Their mind won't be on the meeting; they'll just want to get home before things blow up with their significant other.

So, keep the pressure on. Disrupt their sleep, invade their personal time, and let burnout do the rest. A well-rested opponent is a dangerous one. Better to keep them tired, stressed, and always on the back foot, while you stay sharp and in control.

Intimidation: Fear

Intimidation is a straightforward yet effective tactic designed to create an atmosphere of fear and compliance. It's about making it clear, either overtly or subtly, that crossing you comes with consequences. This isn't just about yelling or making threats; it's about using your presence, your words, and your actions to instill a sense of unease and caution in others. The goal? To make them think twice before challenging you or stepping out of line.

You walk into a meeting with a cold, unyielding demeanor. You don't have to say much, just a few pointed remarks about how disappointed you were with the team's performance on the last project, followed by a long, uncomfortable silence. The message is clear: you expect better, and you're not afraid to show your displeasure. Everyone is on edge, afraid of being singled out next. The fear is palpable, and it's working in your favor.

Intimidation can be as subtle as a lingering stare or as overt as a raised voice. "I thought we agreed that this report would be flawless. Am I missing something, or did someone drop the ball here?" Even if you don't mention names, the implied threat is there. Someone messed up, and you're not happy about it. The ambiguity makes everyone feel the pressure, keeping them on their toes and more likely to comply with your demands to avoid being the next target.

Another effective intimidation tactic is the strategic use of personal space and body language. Stand just a bit too close when speaking to someone, lean in during conversations, or use a firm, unyielding tone. It's not about physical threats, it's about using your presence to create a sense of unease.

You're subtly reminding them of your dominance, making them feel small, insignificant, and wary of provoking you.

Intimidation also works well when paired with unpredictability. Be mercurial one moment, you're calm and collected; the next, you're snapping at someone for a minor mistake. This keeps everyone on edge, unsure of how to behave or what to expect from you. It's a classic tactic of psychological control: when people don't know what will set you off, they'll bend over backward to stay in your good graces, even if it means compromising their own interests.

Fear is a powerful motivator. A team that fears you is less likely to challenge your authority or resist your decisions. They're more likely to comply, even if they don't agree, because the cost of dissent feels too high. Fear keeps them in line, keeps them quiet, and keeps you firmly in control.

Summary

Psychological warfare is a game of patience and precision. It's not about grand gestures or obvious power plays. It's about staying just under the radar, applying pressure where it counts, and letting the effects unfold over time. Microaggressions, gaslighting, and undermining don't need to be loud to be effective, they just need to be consistent.

By now, you know how to quietly dismantle someone's confidence and keep them distracted with self-doubt. The key isn't to destroy them in one blow, but to let them unravel slowly, all while you maintain your steady climb. The beauty of these tactics is that they're nearly impossible to call out, leaving you in control while everyone else scrambles to figure out why they're falling behind.

In the end, success isn't just about winning; it's about making sure the competition never gets close enough to challenge you. Keep playing the long game, and let your rivals wear themselves down.

Chapter 5

Divide and Conquer Strategies

Teamwork is great at least in theory. Teams can produce great results, but they can also be difficult to control. When a team works well together, they support each other, and that can be a hurdle for those who want power. In this chapter, we'll dive into another Sun Tzu, Art of War classic: Divide and Conquer. Why compete with a well-functioning team when it's much easier to turn them against themselves? By the time you've mastered these tactics, no one will trust each other and they'll all look to you as the only one who knows what's really going on.

Selective Sharing of Information: Misdirection

Information is currency, and the skill lies in knowing when and how to spend it. Selective sharing isn't about hoarding secrets; it's about sculpting perception. It's the difference between spreading individual rumors and telling a well-thought-out story. Control who knows what, and suddenly, the game shifts in your favor.

Imagine this: you're a manager hiring for a position. Two candidates are applying. One you want to see in the role, the other, not so much. What do you do? You selectively share the job criteria with your preferred candidate, making sure they're armed with exactly what they need. If you're really playing the game, you drop a bit of misinformation to the other one enough to send them down the wrong path. Then, with a show of good will, you step back, citing a conflict of interest and remove yourself from the selection process. Your candidate sails through, having been fed the answers. The other stumbles, tripped up by the wrong cues.

Selective sharing isn't just about feeding information; it's about understanding how it will be used. Some people collect information, hoarding it, not acting on it. I've never trusted these people. Why collect what you would not use? Then there are the impulsive ones who take information and act immediately, without thinking. They are common. And finally, you've got the strategic players, the ones who sit on information and wait. The higher up the ladder you go, the more likely you are to find these types. They're patient, calculating, and dangerous in their own way.

When someone shares information with you, you need to ask yourself: What's true? What's false? And, what's missing? Once you've got the facts, what's their motive? Why are they telling you this now? And why did they choose this method; face-to-face, email, public, private etc? Often the how and why tell you more than the information itself.

Unlike other forms of manipulation, selective sharing demands a carefully crafted plan. This isn't something you can wing. You need to think it through, mapping out both individual and group objectives. Take your time. Plant the seeds of your narrative slowly and deliberately.

Inconsistent Communication: Keep Them Guessing

Inconsistent communication is all about sending mixed signals. Tell one team member the presentation should focus on data, and tell another it's all about storytelling. Better yet, tell the whole team both, just at different times and watch how they interpret it. One minute, the priority is speed; the next, it's all about quality. Today, collaboration is key; tomorrow, it's all about individual contribution. Keep shifting the narrative just enough to keep everyone on their toes, constantly second-guessing themselves and each other.

There's beauty in chaos. When people are confused, they become more dependent on the one person they think holds the answers. And that person should be you. You become the eye of the storm, the calm amidst the confusion, the only one who seems to have a firm grasp on what's going on.

But don't just throw out contradictions. Each inconsistency should be delivered with intent. Be strategic. Who benefits from the confusion? Who loses? Use that to your advantage. A little frustration here, a hint of doubt there, and suddenly, people aren't sure who to trust anymore.

An advantage of contradictions is, if done right you are never wrong. If you tell the team, "It must be bigger," and later say, "It must be smaller," when the client finally chimes in, you're covered. Forget the direction you got wrong, highlight the one you got right.

Remember to deflect: it's never your fault if people didn't understand. Maybe they just weren't paying attention. Maybe they're not as bright as they think they are. After all, it's impossible to move forward effectively if the direction keeps changing.

On a side note: this is a recurring problem in software development. In 25 years, I've never encountered a customer (internal or external) who knew exactly what they wanted at the start of the project. This drives developers mad, for all the reasons mentioned above. The solution I found is to make part of the project scope "the customer doesn't know what they want." When explicitly said, developers seem to get it. Ensure all code is written in small, discrete components that can be easily moved and modified as the customer changes their mind. Do not build large blocks of code that need to be rewritten when the scope changes. I admit this is harder to execute outside of IT, but it is still an effective strategy for dealing with inconsistent communication.

Playing Devil's Advocate: Stirring the Pot

The origins of the term "devil's advocate" come from the Catholic Church. When someone was proposed for sainthood, the Church would appoint a skeptic, often an atheist or someone with no religious affiliation to argue against the candidate's canonization. This person, known as the "devil's advocate," would scrutinize the proposed saint's story, looking for any flaws or reasons they should not be declared a saint.

In the workplace, using this strategy isn't just about being the contrarian in the room. It's about creating just enough friction to keep everyone on edge, second-guessing themselves, and most importantly each other. Playing devil's advocate is less about having a different opinion and more about ensuring that no one feels too comfortable.

When someone floats an idea, your job is to poke holes in it, to find the weak spot and show it to the world. Not to improve the idea, mind you, but to subtly suggest that perhaps the person proposing it hasn't thought it all the way through. When done right, you're not just questioning the idea; you're questioning their competence.

You're not outright attacking anyone; you're just raising "valid concerns." Your tone is always one of thoughtful skepticism: "I'm just playing devil's advocate here, but have we considered…?" It's disarming because it positions you as someone who's simply looking out for the team, ensuring all angles are covered.

Over time, this tactic works wonders on team dynamics. Colleagues become wary of sharing ideas openly, knowing they're likely to be met with a well-placed jab from you. Some might even start to feel a bit paranoid, wondering if they're being set up to fail. That's exactly what you want in an environment where no one feels safe.

Mix the methods and add in inconsistency. Play devil's advocate against one person's idea, then support someone else's. Let the confusion and resentment simmer. Before long, people will be more focused on protecting themselves from your next attack than on actually collaborating. When the team is divided, you can mold them however you want.

Withholding Credit: Silence as a Weapon

You know what's easier than doing something? Not doing something. You'd be surprised at how effortlessly you can sow discord by simply failing to acknowledge someone's contributions. Recognition is a powerful currency, and by controlling its flow, you can determine who gets rich and who gets poorer.

Let's say a team member, Dave, comes up with a brilliant idea during a meeting. You smile, nod, even throw in a few affirmations. But when it comes time to recap the meeting's highlights, suddenly, that brilliant idea gets attributed to "the team" or, better yet, to a more favored colleague. Just like that, Dave's balloon of accomplishment deflates. He's left questioning whether his work is truly valued or if it was even noticed at all.

You're not blatantly ignoring someone's effort that would be too obvious, too easy to call out. No, you're simply failing to be specific. You're letting praise float around like a cloud with no clear destination. This ambiguity does more damage than any outright slight ever could. It's like a tiny splinter annoying, hard to remove, and driving them nuts over time.

You create an environment where everyone starts watching their back. They're no longer just worried about doing their job; they're worried about getting credit for it. Paranoia sets in. People start keeping records of their contributions, sending "friendly" reminder emails, cc'ing half the office just to make sure their work is noticed. Suddenly, a simple task becomes a chess match, with every move calculated to ensure personal recognition.

Withholding credit often leads to credit theft. One person will take credit for someone else's work. A culture of credit theft can become hard to control. If this happens to you, use a public humiliation technique. Rapid-fire detailed questions about the idea. If they didn't come up with it, they're unlikely to be able to answer them.

It's not just about making individuals feel undervalued, it's about pitting them against each other. By selectively acknowledging contributions, you can foster jealousy and resentment. You praise Sarah for a team project but "forget" to mention that James did the heavy lifting. Now, James isn't just frustrated with you; he's frustrated with Sarah, too. He might start to think she's taking credit for his work, whether she is or not. And Sarah? She might start to feel a bit guilty or, worse, superior. Either way, you've successfully planted a seed of discord.

And if you're called out on it? You play the innocent card. "Oh, I thought everyone knew it was a team effort!" Or, "I'm so sorry, it slipped my mind, but of course, we all know how much work you put in!" A few placating words, a smile, and you're off the hook. Meanwhile, the damage is done. People are left feeling just a little bit less secure, a little more competitive.

Selective Promotion of Ideas: Picking Favorites

Selectively promoting certain ideas while quietly ignoring others. This isn't about being fair or balanced; this is about playing favorites with a purpose. You're not just choosing the best ideas, you're choosing the ones that best serve your agenda, the ones that keep your chosen few feeling special while leaving the rest simmering with resentment.

You're in a meeting, and ideas are flying around the table. You nod approvingly when Karen, your unofficial ally, suggests a course of action that's half-baked at best. You praise it as "innovative" and "forward-thinking," giving it just enough airtime to make it seem like the next big thing. Meanwhile, when Doug, who's not exactly on your favorite list, pitches a well-thought-out plan, you offer a polite smile, a lukewarm "we'll consider it," and quickly move the conversation along.

What you've just done is more than a little sleight of hand. You've planted the idea that some contributions are more valuable than others, not because of their merit but because of their source. And in doing so, you've created a hierarchy, a pecking order where only the chosen few feel valued, while the rest start to question their worth and, more importantly, each other's.

The beauty of selective promotion is in its ripple effect. The favored employees, basking in the glow of your approval, will start to see themselves as superior, more in tune with the company's needs. They'll become more confident, more vocal, and let's face it a bit more arrogant. Meanwhile, the others will start to feel sidelined, underappreciated, and, eventually, resentful. That resentment doesn't just disappear; it festers, it grows, and soon enough, it turns colleagues into rivals.

Do it right and you're never the bad guy. You're just "encouraging open dialogue," "championing innovation," or "trying to move things forward." If anyone calls you out for favoritism, you've got a ready-made defense: "I'm just trying to highlight the ideas that have the most potential. Everyone's input is valuable, but we can't pursue every idea at once." A quick pivot, and suddenly, the person raising the concern looks like the one with the problem.

Selective promotion of ideas isn't just about picking winners and losers, it's about controlling the narrative. You decide which ideas get traction and which fade into the background. You create an environment where people are less focused on collaboration and more on vying for your approval. And in that scramble for favor, alliances break down, trust erodes, and you emerge as the one person everyone needs on their side.

Favoritism: Cultivating Jealousy

Some might say it's a dangerous game; I'd call it a calculated strategy fostering division and jealousy. Playing favorites isn't just about being nice to a few chosen ones; it's about creating a clear divide between those who are "in" and those who are left out. And if you're left out, you'd better fight to get back in.

Let's say you have a team of ambitious, eager individuals all vying for recognition, promotions, or just a pat on the back. Perfect. Start by identifying your chosen ones who, for whatever reason, you decide will be the beneficiaries of your approval. Maybe it's because they're useful, pliable, the boss's son, or just clueless enough not to see the game being played. Whatever the reason, they're about to become your new best friends.

Now, start showering them with subtle signs of favoritism. Nothing too overt, no need to be obvious. A few extra words of praise in meetings, a drink on you, a special project assignment, or maybe an invitation to a lunch "meeting" that somehow doesn't include everyone else. These small gestures are like drops of water on a stone slowly, steadily wearing down the morale of those left out.

What happens next is a predictable spiral of jealousy and division. Those not in your inner circle begin to notice the special treatment, the inside jokes, the extra opportunities. Naturally, they begin to resent it. They won't just resent you, they'll resent your favorites as well. Why does Tom always get the good assignments? Why is Lisa constantly being asked for her input while I'm left to do the grunt work?

Before long, you've got a divided team on your hands, one half smug in their newfound status, the other half seething with jealousy. In that simmering cauldron of emotions, teamwork begins to erode. Communication breaks down. People start looking out for themselves, more worried about getting into your good graces than actually doing their jobs.

If someone dares to call out your favoritism, you can always counter with a sweet, "I treat everyone fairly based on their performance," or, "I value each of you, but I have to reward those who go above and beyond." Just like that, you've turned the tables, making it seem like anyone raising a concern is just bitter or lazy.

But don't stop there. Use the jealousy and resentment you've cultivated to your advantage. Want to keep someone in line? Dangle the carrot of favoritism just out of reach. Want to divide and conquer? Drop a few subtle hints about how "disappointed" you are in someone's recent work, then watch as they scramble to get back into your good books. In a world where being favored is everything, people will do just about anything to stay on the right side of the line.

Favoritism isn't just about being nice to a few, it's about creating a division where everyone is fighting for your attention, your approval, your favor. It's about ensuring that, while they're all busy tearing each other down, you're the one who remains untouched, unchallenged, and firmly in control.

Encouraging Backchanneling: Secret Conversations

Now that you've got the team nicely divided, it's time to push things a step further with another one of my favorites: backchanneling. We're not talking about whispering in hallways or sending covert texts during meetings. No, this is about creating a culture where secretive, behind-the-scenes communication becomes the norm. The kind of environment where no one knows exactly what's being said, but everyone assumes the worst. The beauty of backchanneling is that it feeds into people's natural paranoia, leaving them constantly questioning who's really pulling the strings and what's being decided without them.

Backchanneling creates layers of communication. There's what's said openly in meetings, and then there's the real conversation happening behind closed doors, on private calls, or in discreet messages. You want to blur the lines between the two, to the point where no one is ever quite sure if what they hear publicly is the whole story.

Encourage different versions of the truth to different people. Say something to one group in confidence, then casually mention a slightly different take to another. Before you know it, you've got factions forming, each convinced they're the ones who have the "real" scoop. They start to distrust the official channels of communication after all, if you're willing to share off-the-record details with them, who's to say you're not doing the same with everyone else?

This tactic creates distrust and paranoia. People become more focused on their private conversations and less on their actual work. They start second-guessing each other, wondering who's been privy to what information, who's in the loop, and who's out of it. The result? A fractured team, each faction looking out for its own interests, always wondering what's being said behind closed doors.

If someone confronts you about backchanneling? Simple. You play the concerned leader: "I encourage open communication! I'm surprised to hear there's been backchanneling. Maybe we need to work on being more transparent as a team." You've just spun their concern right back at them, casting yourself as the champion of openness while subtly implying that the issue lies with them, not you.

Backchanneling isn't a communication strategy, it's a control tactic. By encouraging secret conversations, you keep everyone slightly off-balance, always guessing, always unsure. They're too busy wondering what's being said about them to focus on the big picture. And in that fog of uncertainty, you hold the reins. You decide what's known, what's not, and who knows what. The person who controls the flow of information holds all the power.

Undermining Relationships: Seeds of Doubt

Undermining relationships isn't about tearing people apart through hostility, it's about planting tiny seeds of doubt. Start small. A well-placed comment, a raised eyebrow, a sigh at just the right moment these are your tools. Say, for instance, you're in a meeting with two colleagues, Laura and Steve, who usually work well together. After the meeting, you casually pull Laura aside. "Hey, I noticed Steve seemed a bit off today. Did you catch that too? Maybe he's feeling overwhelmed with all the work you've been doing together?" Just like that, you've introduced a tiny seed of doubt.

Or better yet, frame your comments as if you're looking out for their best interests. "I know you trust Sarah, but I heard she's been a bit critical of your project to some higher-ups. Just thought you should know. But maybe it's nothing, she's probably just stressed." This way, you position yourself as a friend, someone who's just trying to help, while simultaneously injecting a little poison into their relationship.

You're not outright accusing anyone of anything. You're just "mentioning" things, just "noticing" things. People naturally trust their own judgment. Once the doubt is there, they start looking for evidence to support it. Every delayed email response, every awkward hallway interaction becomes "proof" of a hidden agenda. As they start to distance themselves, to protect themselves, the relationship weakens.

Before long, people who once collaborated smoothly are second-guessing each other, holding back, no longer sharing openly. They become more guarded, more isolated. And that's exactly what you want: a team of individuals, not a unified front. Because individuals are easier to manipulate, easier to control.

In the event of confrontation, play innocent. "I'm so sorry if I caused any misunderstanding! I was just trying to keep everyone in the loop. Maybe I shouldn't have said anything. Sometimes I care too much about making sure we're all on the same page." You've just deflected any blame while subtly reinforcing your role as the well-meaning confidante.

In the end, a fractured team is a distracted team, and a distracted team is easier to control. Keep planting those seeds of doubt, keep watching them grow, and soon enough, you'll have exactly what you want.

Instigating Minor Conflicts: Disputes to Distractions

Having laid the groundwork with gossip and backchanneling, it's time to spice things up by instigating minor conflicts. Don't start a full-blown war, at least not at first. The goal is to stir up just enough tension to keep everyone slightly on edge, distracted, and focused on petty squabbles rather than the bigger picture. Think of it as setting small fires all over the battlefield, forcing your opponents to constantly put them out while you advance your position.

Start with a subtle nudge. Maybe you "accidentally" let slip to Jane that Paul feels she's been slacking off lately. "I'm sure he didn't mean anything by it, but I thought you should know. I'd hate for there to be any bad blood between you two." It's a seemingly innocent remark, but watch how Jane's demeanor changes the next time she's around Paul. Now she's on the defensive, maybe even a bit confrontational. The tension starts to build.

Or try this: bring up a point in a meeting that you know will get a reaction. "I was thinking about Peter's approach to the project, but someone mentioned it might be a bit too… ambitious for our current resources. Thoughts?" Suddenly, Peter's on the back foot, defending his work while everyone else chimes in with their opinions. You've just created a mini-debate, all without ever stating your own position. It keeps everyone distracted, focused on the wrong issues.

The trick with instigating minor conflicts is to keep things low-level. You don't want an outright explosion. You want simmering discontent, those little sparks of irritation that flare up just enough to cause distraction but not so much that they overshadow everything else. It's about managing the temperature, keeping the pot just hot enough to boil over when you need it to.

These small conflicts tend to escalate on their own. Once people are wound up, they'll start seeing slights and challenges where none exist. A missed email here, a curt response there, and suddenly, colleagues are seeing enemies where they once saw friends. All the while, you're the calm in the center of the storm, the one person everyone turns to for clarity that, conveniently, only you can provide.

Should anyone call you out for stirring the pot, you can easily play the part of the well-meaning mediator. "I just wanted to make sure everyone's on the same page. We're all adults here, right? Just trying to encourage healthy debate." And just like that, you've deflected any blame while still keeping your hands firmly on the controls.

Minor conflicts serve as excellent smoke screens. They keep everyone so busy managing their bruised egos and petty grievances that they don't see the larger maneuvers happening right under their noses. By the time they realize what's really going on, it's already too late. You've shifted the battlefield in your favor, moved the pieces where you want them, and positioned yourself as the only one who seems to have any control over the chaos.

Playing People Against Each Other: Divide and Conquer

Now that you've got a steady undercurrent of minor conflicts bubbling away, it's time to master one of the most effective tactics: playing people against each other. To execute this effectively, you need to be slow, steady, and strategic. Start by identifying the natural fault lines within the team. Are there two ambitious colleagues who often clash over credit? Is there a group that's a bit too cozy, maybe even a little cliquish? These are your opportunities. Focus on widening those cracks, turning minor disagreements into major divides.

The key here is to subtly encourage competition and conflict without making it seem like you're instigating. Take two colleagues, Alice and Bob, who have differing opinions on how a project should be handled. Privately, express support for Alice's idea to Bob, but with a twist: "Alice has some good points, but she does tend to be a bit overbearing, don't you think? It's important that you make sure your perspective is heard." Then, go to Alice and say, "Bob's idea is interesting, but he doesn't quite see the big picture like you do. Maybe you should help guide him."

What happens next is completely predictable. Bob, feeling a surge of determination (and a hint of resentment), becomes more vocal, more defensive. Alice, confident in your support, becomes more assertive, maybe even condescending. The result? A clash of egos, each one convinced they're in the right, both of them oblivious to the fact that they're being played.

Play the long game. Encourage small, seemingly benign competitions: "Let's see who can come up with the most cost-effective solution," or "Maybe we should have a little contest to see whose idea the client likes best." These friendly competitions might start off harmless, but with a little encouragement, they soon become all-out wars. And as they do, loyalties shift, trust erodes, and you're right there in the middle, quietly fanning the flames.

The beauty of this tactic is in its self-sustaining nature. Once people are pitted against each other, they'll do most of the work for you. Resentment is a powerful ally. They'll undermine each other's efforts, spread their own little rumors, and generally create a toxic environment where cooperation becomes a distant memory. And in this fractured, competitive landscape, one person remains above the fray: you.

Just a quick side note on resentment. If I had to pick one psychological issue plaguing the modern world, it would be resentment. Resentment from jealousy and social interactions is the root cause of so many problems. I read a meta-study that combined several papers on how to treat people struggling with resentment. The most common treatment currently used by psychologists is CBT, or cognitive behavioral therapy. In a gross oversimplification, CBT involves recognizing when you're feeling resentful and distracting yourself with another thought. But according to this meta-study, CBT didn't even make the top five most effective treatments. The most effective was "gratitude" training teaching people to be grateful and the second was, surprisingly, voodoo. So, if you're looking for a business opportunity, start selling voodoo dolls.

Playing people against each other isn't about chaos for its own sake, it's about control. It's about ensuring that the people around you are too busy fighting their own battles to ever unite against you. It's about making sure that, no matter what happens, you're always the one holding the strings, orchestrating the drama, and keeping everyone dancing to your tune. Because in a world where everyone is at each other's throats, the one person who can navigate the chaos the one person who everyone turns to for direction is you.

Creating Factions: Building a Loyal Army

Now that you've successfully sown seeds of doubt and set colleagues against one another, it's time to concrete the factions. Your own loyal army within the company, a select group that sees you as their leader, their champion. The goal is simply to divide the workplace into distinct camps, each loyal to you in their own way, and each wary of the others.

Creating factions is more than just encouraging competition or playing people against each other. It's about establishing clear, almost tribal, lines within the team. Your mission is to craft small, exclusive groups that owe their existence to you and are therefore eager to serve and defend your interests. To do this effectively, you'll need to identify your loyalists, the ones who are already inclined to follow your lead, and those who are dissatisfied enough with the current state of affairs to consider switching allegiances.

Start by giving your chosen few special attention. Organize private meetings under the guise of "strategy sessions" or "brainstorming sessions." Make them feel included, like they're part of an inner circle. Share just enough information to make them feel valued and in the know maybe even drop a few hints about upper management decisions or confidential plans. The idea is to make them feel special, different from the rest.

Meanwhile, subtly alienate those who are outside your chosen circle. Exclude them from important meetings or key email threads. Downplay their contributions in public forums while elevating your chosen faction members. When they express concerns or ideas, offer lukewarm responses at best. The aim is to make the outsiders feel marginalized, less important, and, most importantly, less connected.

As your factions start to form, fan the flames of rivalry. Suggest that one group's success depends on outperforming another. Use language that encourages a sense of competition: "I'm really counting on you guys to lead the charge here. It'd be great to see you outperform the other team on this project." Or, "Let's show them what a real team effort looks like." This stirs up a competitive spirit, but more importantly, it reinforces the divide between "us" and "them."

But the real power of factions lies in how you use them. With multiple groups vying for your favor, you become the kingmaker, the person who decides which faction rises and which falls. This puts you in a position of unparalleled power. Each group will strive to win your approval, following your lead and executing your strategy without question, because their success and their very existence depends on it.

Creating factions isn't just about forming groups, it's about building alliances that ensure your power and influence are unchallenged. It's about creating an environment where everyone is so focused on their own little kingdom that they never see the bigger picture. And in that divided landscape, you stand alone at the top, orchestrating the moves, playing each side against the other, ensuring that no one faction ever becomes strong enough to challenge your authority. Because in a world where everyone is loyal to you, you are the unquestioned ruler.

Double-Booking Tasks: Conflicting Agendas

Now that you have your factions in place, it's time to stir the pot even more with a simple yet effective tactic: double-booking tasks. Engineer direct conflicts between your newly formed factions. The goal here is to set them on a collision course, forcing them to compete for dominance, resources, and, most importantly, your favor.

Double-booking tasks is straightforward, assigning the same project or task to multiple people or groups without letting them know they're not the only ones working on it. Perhaps both Jane's and Tom's teams are given the same "critical" report to prepare for the same client presentation. Make sure each team believes they're the only ones responsible for the deliverable, and watch the fireworks.

What happens next is predictable. Each team dives into the task, investing time, effort, and maybe even a bit of their pride. As the deadline looms closer, they start to sense that something's amiss. Maybe a few questions pop up about overlapping work or who's in charge of which part. But by the time they realize they've been double-booked, it's too late the tensions have already started to rise.

Teams will likely approach you to resolve the confusion, and this is where your masterful manipulation shines. Express surprise, maybe even a little disappointment: "Oh, I must have misunderstood. I thought both teams were working together. But since you're already deep into it, why don't we make this a little healthy competition? Let's see who can deliver the best results." This approach turns the conflict into a race, further escalating the tension and rivalry.

The key here is to encourage each group to see the other not as collaborators, but as competitors. Make it clear without saying it outright that the winning team will earn more of your favor. Drop hints like, "I'm really looking forward to seeing who comes out on top with the most innovative solution," or, "This will really show me who's capable of leading future high-stakes projects."

Years ago, I witnessed an interesting approach to internal competition. The senior leadership team divided company functions like marketing and HR into separate, competing units. Each function was split across different internal businesses, and projects were tendered out, forcing these internal departments to compete for the work. If a department underperformed, it was dismantled, and new leadership and staff were hired to replace it. Surprisingly, despite the high-pressure environment, the speed and quality of output improved significantly. I expected people to despise working this way, but from the conversations I had, many actually preferred it.

By setting your factions against each other through conflicting tasks, you maintain control over the narrative and ensure that no group ever becomes complacent or too comfortable. They're too busy battling each other to see that the real game is happening behind the scenes, orchestrated by you.

Setting Contradictory Goals: Internal Strife

Having successfully double-booked tasks to create direct conflict, you can extend the strategy by setting contradictory goals. This tactic is beyond simple confusion; it's about pitting entire teams against each other by giving them conflicting objectives that ensure they can't possibly all succeed. The result? A landscape of constant internal strife, where everyone is too busy battling each other to challenge your authority.

Assign different teams or individuals objectives that are mutually exclusive or incompatible. For example, tell one team their priority is to cut costs on a project while instructing another that their focus should be on innovation, regardless of the expense. Or, ask one group to maximize customer satisfaction while telling another to increase sales volume. These objectives inherently conflict one team's success with another's failure.

As the teams begin working toward their goals, the tension quickly builds. The cost-cutters will accuse the innovators of being reckless with the budget. The customer satisfaction group will clash with the sales-driven team over tactics that might alienate clients. Each group becomes entrenched in their mission, convinced that they're the ones following the "correct" directive, while the others are seen as obstacles or even adversaries.

This conflicting dynamic is exactly what you want. It forces teams into a defensive posture, always looking over their shoulders, always ready to point fingers at why things aren't going as planned. And the more they focus on each other as the problem, the less they're likely to notice who set them on this collision course in the first place.

When the inevitable conflict comes to a head, you play the role of the peacemaker, the rational leader who "wants to understand all sides." Call a meeting to "resolve" the differences, letting each team air their grievances. This meeting, of course, will turn into a blame game, with each side defending their approach while subtly (or not so subtly) undermining the other. While they're busy bickering, you're assessing the situation, figuring out who's most loyal, who's most easily manipulated, and who might need to be put in their place.

Your response is critical. Express disappointment at the lack of "team cohesion" and emphasize the need for everyone to "align their goals better." This vague directive leaves the door wide open for future manipulation. If the goals aren't perfectly clear, you can always reinterpret them later to suit your needs. And if anyone dares question the wisdom of setting contradictory goals in the first place? Deflect. "I wanted to challenge the team to think outside the box."

The brilliance of this tactic lies in its ability to keep everyone on edge, never fully comfortable or secure. They're constantly worried that the rules might shift at any moment. In this fragmented and distracted environment, you hold all the power. When everyone's goals are in conflict, you're the only one who knows the real objective, the only one with the full plan.

Encourage Competition for Resources: Compete!

With the stage set for conflicting goals and double-booked tasks, it's time to throw another wrench into the works: encouraging competition for resources. This strategy is about more than just fostering a competitive spirit, it's about creating a sense of scarcity that forces your teams to fight among themselves for every scrap. The objective here is to make them believe that the pie is too small for everyone to have a slice, pushing them to compete for your favor and whatever limited resources you choose to dole out.

Start by subtly hinting at budget cuts or resource constraints, even if none exist. Mention in passing that "we have to be mindful of our expenses" or that "resources are going to be tight this quarter." Let this notion of scarcity settle into the team's consciousness. When people believe resources are limited, their natural instinct is to hoard what they can and ensure their team or project isn't left out in the cold.

Then, begin to allocate resources unevenly. Provide one team with ample budget while giving another just enough to get by. Praise one department for "making do with less," while subtly chiding another for "over-relying on resources." Encouraging the idea that resourcefulness is code for "doing more with less" and is a valued trait in your eyes. This drives teams to prove themselves in your favor, to compete not just for success but for survival. They'll become more aggressive, more cutthroat, and less willing to collaborate, all because they're now trapped in a zero-sum game of your own making.

Watch as the competition intensifies. Team A is now resentful of Team B for getting the lion's share of funding, while Team B feels justified in their superior position. You might even hear whispers of sabotage like "misplaced" files or uncooperative behavior actions driven by the fear of falling behind in the resource race. Every department starts to operate like a silo, fiercely protecting their domain, their budget, and their assets. The more they see each other as threats, the more they see you as the only ally who can provide what they need.

Resources aren't limited to just budget or equipment they include people. Why do you think we call it human resources? If you're competing with another team, identify their top performers and poach them. Ideally, you want to bring them over to your side, but if you can't get them to jump ship, you can always entice them to look for opportunities elsewhere. In many areas of business, team performance often follows a Pareto distribution, with 20% of the people doing 80% of the work. If you can steal that top 20%, you've crippled their productivity.

If someone questions the fairness of resource allocation, you have your response ready: "I allocate resources based on where I see the most potential for impact. If you feel your team needs more, show me why. Prove it." This not only puts the onus back on them but also subtly reinforces the idea that they must compete to prove their worth. And if the complaints become too vocal or public, remind everyone of the "current economic climate" or "the need for tighter belts," reinforcing the narrative of scarcity.

Encouraging competition for resources isn't just a tactic; it's a long-term strategy that keeps everyone on edge, always looking for ways to outdo each other. It breeds an environment of mistrust, where collaboration becomes secondary to self-preservation. And in such a fragmented, self-centered culture, the true winner is always you. Because when everyone else is fighting for the crumbs, you're the one who's already eaten the whole pie.

Summary

In this chapter, you've learned how to fracture teams without getting your hands dirty. Selective sharing of information lets you control the narrative, ensuring confusion reigns. Inconsistent communication keeps everyone second-guessing themselves and each other. Playing devil's advocate? Stirs up doubt and undermines confidence. By withholding credit, seeding resentment, and selectively promoting ideas, you create rivalries where none existed before. Once the team is divided, they are easier to control.

Chapter 6

Exploiting Systems and Structures

In the intricate web of corporate life, systems and structures are often seen as the pillars that hold everything together meant to ensure fairness, consistency, and order. But for those with a keen eye and a sharper mind, these systems aren't just there to maintain the status quo. They are opportunities. Bureaucracy, hierarchy, rules, and relationships all present weaknesses ripe for exploitation. In this chapter, we'll dive deep into how these seemingly rigid structures can be bent, twisted, and manipulated to your advantage. By learning how to leverage these systems, you'll discover that corporate power isn't about following the rules, it's about mastering them.

Leveraging Bureaucracy: Exploiting Rules

Bureaucracy, by its very nature, is a tool of control and consistency. It's not a necessary evil; it's the technique favored by middle management to stop undesirable behaviors. Bureaucracy often appears as a reaction to a problem. As the old saying goes, "Those who don't understand create processes." Bureaucracy is not restricted to the domain of corporate sociopaths, but the manipulation of other people's bureaucratic processes definitely is. Red tape holds the world together.

Bureaucracy falls into five main categories. Each type of bureaucracy has its own weaknesses and manipulation techniques.

First, there's hierarchy. Every company loves a corporate structure: a clear visual diagram to dangled promotions and advancement to keep the grunts motivated. Bypassing immediate supervisors and going straight to top management is a classic undermining of a hierarchy. Another tactic is to fabricate your own structure. Especially as a consultant or external member, you can change people's perceptions by name-dropping. "I was just chatting with the CEO, and he mentioned a desire for this project." Humans love hierarchy; it's built into us on an evolutionary level. Depending on who you read, hierarchies can be shown to exist at least 100 million years ago, with some arguing they date back as far as 750 million years ago. Bear in mind, humans have only been around for 200,000 years. Either way, our built-in desire to create and follow hierarchies doesn't just predate humans; it predates primates and likely even land animals.

The next category is rules. Bureaucracies live and die by their rules, and for good reason: they create the illusion of fairness and consistency. But rules are only as strong as the people enforcing them. Selectively applying them is the subtle art of control. Deliberately misinterpreting them is another tactic. Enforce the rules to the letter for some while turning a blind eye for others.

Division of labor: In theory, it's about spreading the workload, but in reality, it's one of the most commonly manipulated. An issue I have come across many times in my career was with IT help desk workers. The KPIs were simple, recording how many tickets each agent closed over the day. Help desk agents tended to choose the simple, quick-to-resolve tasks like resetting a password. As a result, they had more completed tickets over a day. I also witnessed a particularly nasty manager single out one team member and assign them every difficult task. Their stats went from over 100 tickets resolved a day to less than 2. This person was ultimately sacked due to their numbers.

Standardization of procedures is always fun. These procedures are supposed to streamline operations, but when manipulated, they become a convenient excuse for slowing things down or pushing your own agenda. Misinterpreting guidelines also known as passive resistance can be enough to delay tasks, create bottlenecks, and even kill entire projects. Good procedures are incredibly difficult to write. Managers who focus on writing procedures are often blind to their knowledge gaps.

Finally, relationships or the lack thereof. Bureaucracies pride themselves on objectivity and fairness, but the smart players know that personal connections still matter. Emotional appeals or quietly leveraging relationships with decision-makers can turn an impersonal system into one that works just for you. One of the important roles of senior management is overruling a policy or procedure.

Corporate bureaucracy is a huge topic, but the fundamental idea is that each process and procedure is designed to maintain order. If you can manipulate a system that is designed to maintain order you have the ability to push the organization in any direction you want. It's a judo concept using the opponent's strength against them.

Creating Red Tape: Introducing Procedures

In the same way that bureaucracies are there to control behavior, red tape is there to slow or even stop it. Creating red tape is about more than just following the rules; it's about manufacturing them. When you sense a decision coming that doesn't quite align with your interests, it's time to get creative. Propose a new procedure, an additional layer of review, a mandatory compliance check whatever it takes to grind the decision-making process to a halt. If you are really good, you get someone else to propose the process.

Let's say there's a big project on the horizon, one that threatens to shift the spotlight away from you. Instead of wasting energy trying to discredit it, simply propose a new "review committee" to assess its feasibility. Of course, this committee should be composed of individuals who either have no stake in the project or, better yet, are hopelessly indecisive. Suddenly, that project is mired in months of analysis paralysis, and the heat is off you.

The trick here is triangulation and subtlety. You don't want to be seen as obstructive. Try to get someone else to play the role of excessively cautious do-gooder. Get them to suggest that it's in the company's best interest to add a few more checks and balances. Maybe introduce a new approval layer that requires sign-off from several senior executives. Not only does this slow things down, but it also creates a perfect storm of conflicting interests and opinions. If you convince a third party to take the lead, you can even be seen as the good person fighting the bureaucracy.

Take a page out of the government playbook. Have you ever noticed how decisions get lost in committee? Borrow that tactic. Whenever someone presents a new idea, respond with, "This is worth exploring further. We should form a task force to evaluate the potential impacts and provide a comprehensive report." Task force is a fancy name for a black hole where good ideas go to die.

Red tape isn't just about stopping progress; it's about redirecting energy. When your colleagues are bogged down with extra paperwork, navigating through an endless series of approval gates, or stuck in a cycle of reviews and revisions, they're not challenging you. They're not moving forward with their agendas. They're exactly where you want them to be, treading water while you steer the ship.

And if anyone dares to question why you're making things so complicated, just flash that winning smile and remind them that you're "ensuring quality and compliance" or "protecting the company's interests." Most people are too polite or too afraid to challenge the guise of corporate responsibility.

In the end, your goal is to create a culture where nothing moves quickly unless it's to your advantage. The obvious counter to red tape is to ignore it. You can always fall back on Rear Admiral Grace Hopper's quote: "It's easier to ask for forgiveness than for permission." You just turned rule-breaking into taking initiative.

Gatekeeping Information: Access Denied

Information is power. It's not just an old cliché; it's the rule of life. Another way of looking at it is: it's not just about having all the information. It's about making sure no one else does. The less they know, the more you control. And in this game, knowledge isn't just a weapon, it's a resource.

Gatekeeping is a classic maneuver for a reason. You're not just a manager or a director; you're the keeper of secrets, the guardian of knowledge. You know who knows what, and more importantly, who doesn't know what. Think of yourself as the bottleneck through which all critical information flows or better yet, gets stuck.

Got some crucial data on that new project? Maybe a game-changing insight into the market? Don't just hand it over on a silver platter. Instead, dole it out in dribs and drabs, making each piece feel like a gift. And for those not on your good side? Well, they can just keep waiting.

Let's say there's an important client pitch coming up, and your team needs some specific numbers to seal the deal. Do you send out a clear, concise report to everyone involved? Absolutely not. Instead, mention in passing to a select few that you "might have some insights" and let them come to you, cap in hand, asking for the details. Now they owe you, and you've just reinforced your position as the indispensable cog in the machine.

And if anyone tries to bypass you? Time to invoke the sacred art of the "data protection policy." Start dropping phrases like "sensitive information" and "need-to-know basis." Make it sound like you're protecting the company, when really, you're just safeguarding your power base. The more people feel they need you to access key information, the more indispensable you become.

Here's the secret sauce: people fear what they don't understand, and in a corporate setting, that fear is your best friend. By controlling who knows what and when you keep everyone off-balance. They'll be too busy scrambling for scraps of information to realize they're being manipulated.

Take Jane, our ever-resourceful heroine. She didn't just keep her cards close to her chest; she kept them in a locked safe. She didn't "forget" to include key data in the meeting minutes by accident; she did it because that information was her ace in the hole. When people came knocking, she could dole it out piece by piece, ensuring they always had to come back for more. She became the gatekeeper, the guardian of the sacred scrolls, the one who could make or break a project with a single withheld document.

Being the gatekeeper isn't about being petty. It's about being strategic. You're not just holding back information to be difficult; you're doing it to maintain the upper hand. The less predictable you are, the more people will bend to your will, just in case they need you tomorrow.

And what about those who try to pry information out of you? Simple: always have an excuse ready. "Oh, I thought you already knew that." Or, "I was under the impression this had been communicated." Feign surprise, maybe even a little offense. Make them feel like they're the ones who dropped the ball. It's not just about withholding information; it's about controlling the narrative around that information.

So, remember: be the gatekeeper. Hold the keys. Control the flow of information, and you control the flow of power. And in this world, power is everything.

Leveraging Organizational Silence: Silence is Platinum

I always felt people undervalued the saying "silence is golden." Maybe the saying should be "silence is platinum or diamond." The quieter you become, the more you can hear. When everyone else is fumbling for words, listen and plot your next move. Silence is the differentiator between the corporate sociopath and the narcissist. Don't be a victim of your ego. Stay quiet, listen, and observe.

There is beauty in letting silence fill the room. Picture this: a tense meeting where everyone is scrambling to fill the gaps in conversation, desperate to avoid the awkward pause. You, however, embrace it. While others rush to speak, trying to make sense of what's happening, you sit back and let the silence linger just a little too long. It's in these moments that people reveal their insecurities, their uncertainties, their true intentions.

But organizational silence isn't just about what's said in the boardroom it's about what isn't said. In an environment where communication is carefully controlled, you can use silence to your advantage. When rumors start to swirl or when decisions seem to be made without input, keep quiet. Let the silence create an air of mystery, a fog that shrouds the truth. The less people know, the more they speculate. Speculation is the enemy of clarity and the friend of manipulation.

When there's a lack of communication, people tend to fill in the blanks with their own narratives. Use this uncertainty to plant seeds of doubt, redirect attention, or quietly consolidate your own position. No announcements, no memos, just a quiet, steady accumulation of power while everyone else is lost in the fog.

When a decision comes down from above that isn't well-received, say nothing. Just observe. Let the frustration simmer and grow. The more discontent there is, the easier it becomes to position yourself as the voice of reason, the one who "understands" the chaos. You can then subtly guide the narrative, whispering solutions or even fanning the flames, depending on what suits your agenda best.

Remember, in a culture of silence, fear is your ally. The fear of saying the wrong thing, the fear of asking the wrong questions, the fear of speaking up. When people are afraid, they tend to stay quiet, and when they stay quiet, you remain in control. Create an environment where speaking up feels like stepping on a landmine, and you'll find that most people will opt for silence, giving you free rein to maneuver.

But there's a subtlety to this strategy. You're not advocating for a complete blackout of communication that would be too obvious. Instead, advocate for "focused" communication. Push for meetings that are "streamlined," updates that are "concise." Present it as efficiency. But in reality, it's just a way to control the narrative. The less information that's available, the less likely anyone can piece together what's really happening and the less likely they are to challenge your authority.

Think of yourself as the director of a play where the less said, the more people interpret with their own story. You can still control the script, the pauses, the cadence. Each quiet moment is an opportunity to wield influence, to let others reveal more than they intend, to guide the story without ever saying a word.

Exploiting Loopholes: Gaps in Policies

Rules are rarely black and white, and even when they try to be, embrace the gray. Treat rules as guidelines. While others see policies and regulations as constraints, you see them as opportunities for unwritten invitations to bend the rules, stretch the definitions, and find that sweet spot where anything goes.

Loopholes are the little cracks in the foundation of corporate governance. They exist because no policy is perfect, no regulation airtight. They're the result of sloppy drafting, lazy thinking, or simply the impossibility of predicting every possible scenario. Your job is to find those cracks, those little escape hatches that let you slip through undetected while everyone else is stuck on the straight and narrow.

Think of loopholes as Easter eggs hidden within the dense, dry text of corporate policy manuals. Got a new performance metric that doesn't quite fit your style? Scan the fine print. There's always a clause, an exception, a technicality you can exploit to flip the script in your favor. And if anyone challenges you, just shrug and point to the rules. "Hey, I'm just following the guidelines," you say with an innocent smile. After all, you're not breaking the rules, you're interpreting them.

Consider the case of our friend Alex. Faced with a new company policy that capped departmental spending, Alex didn't panic. Instead, he noticed a little oversight in the wording: the policy didn't specify what counted as departmental spending. So, he cleverly shifted a few costs around, reclassifying them under a different budget line. The result? He stayed within his spending limits on paper while continuing to allocate resources as he saw fit. And when questioned, he simply pointed to the policy. He wasn't bending the rules just thinking outside the box.

This is the art of the loophole: never settle for the surface interpretation of a rule. Dig deeper. Find the ambiguity, the contradictions, the gray areas that can be molded to suit your needs. Remember, most policies are written to cover general cases, not specific scenarios. Your job is to find the scenarios that fall outside the general, to maneuver in the spaces where the rules don't quite apply.

Don't just think about the present, anticipate the future. When new policies are introduced, look for the gaps they create. Often, in the rush to solve one problem, management creates several new ones, each with its own set of exploitable loopholes.

Exploiting loopholes isn't just a reactive strategy, it's a proactive one. It's about constantly scanning the horizon for new opportunities, always ready to pounce on the latest oversight. It allows you to operate with a veneer of legitimacy. You're not a rebel breaking the rules; you're a savvy operator navigating them.

When someone eventually catches on and they will, your defense is: "If it wasn't allowed, why didn't they write it into the policy?" Throw the blame back on the rule-makers. Make it seem like their oversight, their fault. You're just playing the game by the rules they created or failed to create.

In this world, success isn't about adhering to the rules; it's about understanding them better than anyone else. It's about knowing not just what's written, but what's left unsaid, what's implied but not enforced. So go ahead, exploit the loopholes. Because in a world bound by red tape, the ones who know how to untangle it are the ones who come out on top.

Weaponizing Policies: Using Rules Selectively

Policies, they're the bricks in the walls of corporate governance, the guidelines meant to keep everyone on the straight and narrow. Policies aren't about fairness they're about control. And in the right hands, a policy isn't just a guideline; it's a weapon. A finely honed tool for keeping your allies safe and your enemies exactly where they belong under your thumb.

Weaponizing company policies is a delicate dance. The trick is to enforce the rules, but selectively. The goal is not to eliminate infractions altogether. What fun would that be? Instead, you want to wield these rules like a surgeon's scalpel, cutting away at those who threaten your position while leaving your loyal followers untouched.

Start by familiarizing yourself with the rulebook. Know it inside out better than the HR department if possible. Understand every clause, every penalty, every loophole (we've already covered how useful those can be). The more you know, the more you can control how they're applied. Remember, policies are rarely enforced uniformly. There's always room for discretion.

Imagine this scenario: a rival is getting a bit too comfortable, maybe even threatening your empire. It's time to dust off the old rulebook and find that obscure policy they've been breaking. Maybe it's something as trivial as a misreported expense or an overlooked compliance form. Whatever it is, make it sound like a grave offense. "We must uphold the highest standards," you'll say with a straight face. And just like that, their petty infraction becomes a cardinal sin.

Meanwhile, your closest ally is doing the exact same thing. But for them? A gentle reminder, a quiet word. "Just fix this before anyone notices," you whisper. The message is clear: you protect your own. This dual approach keeps your friends loyal, who wouldn't want to be shielded from the full weight of the corporate hammer? And your enemies? They learn that crossing you comes with consequences.

Take the story of Martin. A mid-level manager who knew the power of selective enforcement. When a team member he didn't like started gaining too much influence, Martin didn't confront him directly. Instead, he dug through the company handbook until he found an outdated policy about email usage. Was it ever enforced? Rarely. But Martin made sure to enforce it now, pointing out the "serious breach of protocol" to higher-ups. The result? A formal warning for the upstart and a lesson learned by everyone else.

Weaponizing policies isn't just about taking down adversaries it's also about protecting your inner circle. Policies can be bent, interpreted creatively, or ignored altogether when it suits your needs. If your ally misses a deadline or fudges some numbers, no problem. It was a "clerical error," a "miscommunication," something that doesn't need to be blown out of proportion. This isn't favoritism; it's just good management. Or at least, that's the story you'll sell.

So, go ahead. Arm yourself with the company rulebook and wield it with precision. Use it to keep the ranks in line, to cut down rivals, and to build an army of loyal followers. The rules aren't there to be followed, they're there to be enforced. Selectively. Strategically. And always to your advantage.

Manipulating Reporting Lines: Control the Flow

It's not just what you know, but who you know... and what they know. Manipulating reporting lines is a game as old as hierarchies themselves. Monkeys have been seen doing it, keeping food sources secret. Birds have been observed falsely chirping to signal immediate danger. If it works for animals, it'll work for you. Keep sensitive information close, divert unwanted attention, and throw in false information to keep everyone guessing.

The art of manipulating reporting lines is in controlling the flow of information both up and down the hierarchy. Be aware of natural flows. Praise travels up and blame travels down. When sending a story up the river, phrase it in a positive light. When down a negative. Fighting against the current isn't easy or necessary.

Take control of the narrative by positioning yourself as the sole gatekeeper. Reports go through you, decisions go through you, even casual conversations somehow find their way through you. You want to be the one who decides what gets passed up to the bosses and what stays conveniently buried. And if anyone tries to circumvent you, well, that's a violation of protocol, isn't it? Best to remind them of the chain of command.

You are a filter system. Anything beneficial to your position or detrimental to your rivals gets amplified, highlighted, and strategically escalated. Everything else? Downplayed, delayed, or outright dismissed. Need to explain away a missed target or a failed project? Blame it on "miscommunication" from below. Did something go spectacularly well that you had little to do with? Spin it so that it seems like it was all your guidance that made it happen.

Consider the case of Eleanor, a seasoned pro at manipulating reporting lines. She wasn't just a middle manager; she was the bridge everyone had to cross to get to senior leadership. By carefully managing what her team reported upwards, she painted a picture of competence and control. Meanwhile, she carefully throttled the flow of information downwards, ensuring her team only had half the story. The result? She looked like a strategic mastermind, while her team remained in the dark, unsure why they were always scrambling to catch up.

The more layers there are between you and the top brass, the harder it is for anything to stick to you. Create enough distance, enough layers of plausible deniability, and suddenly, you're untouchable. After all, you're just following the process, right? If something gets messed up, it's because of the breakdown in communication somewhere along the chain, not because of anything you did.

And what about those pesky colleagues who might try to report around you? Time to play the loyalty card. "All communication should go through the proper channels," you'll say, implying that anyone who breaks rank isn't a team player. Or, better yet, make them seem like a loose cannon. "We can't have everyone just going rogue, sending reports up without proper vetting. That's how mistakes happen." Never mind that it's not the mistakes you're worried about, it's the scrutiny.

The more levels you insert between you and accountability, the more protected you are. Use the hierarchy to obscure, deflect, and delay. Ensure that anything that could tarnish your spotless record gets lost in the maze of reporting lines, while anything that could shine a light on your brilliance finds a clear, unobstructed path to the top.

Gaming Performance Metrics: Performance Indicators

Perception is everything. Forget about the reality of your performance; what truly matters is how it looks on paper. Enter performance metrics the numbers that supposedly speak for themselves. Numbers lie and if they don't, it's your job to make them. Gaming performance metrics isn't about working harder; it's not even working smarter; It's telling a story about how smart and how hard working you are.

Metrics are the corporate world's version of a scoreboard, and everyone's watching. But unlike in sports, you get to set the rules. You decide which stats matter and which ones can be conveniently ignored. The first step? Know the metrics that matter to the powers that be. Is it sales numbers?

Client satisfaction? Project completion rates? Whatever it is, make sure you're the star of the show.

You can also redefine metrics. Let's say your performance is being measured by the number of new clients brought in. Don't just chase every potential lead instead, focus on the low-hanging fruit. The easier the win, the better it looks on your end-of-year report. Meanwhile, let your competitors chase after the difficult clients. When they inevitably fall short, you're the one who looks competent.

And here's a classic trick: when metrics are vague, exploit the ambiguity. If your target is "increased client engagement," what does that really mean? A well-timed email blast to your client list can be spun as "a targeted engagement strategy." If someone challenges you, point to the uptick in responses, even if half of them are out-of-office replies. Numbers are numbers, right?

Take David, the crafty executive who knew how to play the metric game better than anyone? His secret weapon was redefining success. When tasked with reducing costs, he didn't slash budgets outright that would draw too much attention. Instead, he reclassified expenses, moving them from one department to another, all while boasting about his "innovative cost-cutting strategies." To the untrained eye, it looked like he was achieving more with less. In reality, he was just shuffling the deck, making it look like he held all the aces.

Why not manipulate the metrics to undermine your rivals? Let's say you're in a position to influence how performance is measured. Maybe you've got the ear of HR or a friendly relationship with the finance team. Subtly push for metrics that play to your strengths and exploit your rivals' weaknesses. If you're great at turning quick profits but they excel at long-term strategy, push for quarterly earnings to take center stage.

There's always the fallback strategy: when the numbers don't go your way, blame the data. "These figures don't capture the full picture," you might say, hinting at some unseen variable or external factor. Better yet, suggest that the metrics themselves are outdated or flawed.

It was never about what you've actually done; it's always been what you can prove. Make the numbers work for you. Inflate, deflate, twist, and turn them until they tell the story you want to be told. Truth isn't what happened, it's what people believe happened.

Tokenism: Virtue Signaling

Tokenism is the corporate equivalent of a magician's sleight of hand, a clever distraction that makes people think something significant is happening when, in reality, everything stays exactly the same. It's all about appearances. In a world increasingly obsessed with diversity, inclusivity, and change, tokenism is your best bet to appear progressive without actually, you know, progressing.

The goal here is simple: give just enough to keep the critics at bay while ensuring that no real shifts in power or culture occur. It's a balancing act, and when done right, it allows you to maintain control while seeming to embrace change. How? By sprinkling in a little diversity here, a nod to inclusivity there all carefully calculated to create the illusion of transformation.

Consider this scenario: the company is getting heat for its lack of diversity in leadership. Do you overhaul the system? Restructure the hierarchy? Of course not. Instead, you appoint a single individual who checks all the right boxes but poses no real threat to the existing order. You make a big show of it: send out a company-wide email, host a virtual town hall, maybe even arrange a feature in the company newsletter. "Look at us," you say without saying it, "we're changing."

The beauty of tokenism is that it's a cheap trick. It costs almost nothing but pays dividends in goodwill and public perception. You get to pat yourself on the back for being forward-thinking while keeping the status quo firmly intact. It's a win-win.

But tokenism isn't just about people; it's about policies too. When whispers start about outdated practices or lack of innovation, roll out a shiny new initiative. Maybe a "Diversity and Inclusion" committee or a "Green Office" campaign. Keep it vague, keep it broad, and most importantly, keep it underfunded. You want the appearance of action without the burden of actual results.

Take our friend Lisa, a master of tokenism. When her company faced criticism for not having enough women in leadership, she proposed a mentorship program. It sounded great on paper with lots of buzzwords like "empowerment" and "leadership pipeline." But here's the catch: the program had no budget, no clear goals, and no real support from the top. It was all smoke and mirrors. Yet, Lisa got credit for being proactive and progressive, all while making sure no real change occurred.

Every now and then, someone will push back, demanding actual change. Don't panic. Double down on your tokenism. Introduce a pilot program, suggest a lengthy "research phase," or propose a task force to "explore the complexities" of the issue. The goal is to create just enough bureaucracy to stall any real action while making it seem like you're fully committed to the cause.

And remember, when you're accused of tokenism, act offended. "We're doing the best we can," you'll say, shaking your head in feigned exasperation. Suggest that real change takes time, and that these initiatives are "just the beginning." It's all about deflecting criticism while keeping your agenda on track.

Tokenism is all about optics. It's about knowing that in a world that values perception, the appearance of change can often be more important than change itself. So, sprinkle a few tokens here and there. Make a gesture, give a speech, start a committee. Keep the critics busy while you continue doing exactly what you were doing before.

Hijacking Meetings: Dominating and Derailing

Meetings are often the battlefields of power dynamics, a stage where dominance and hierarchy play out in real time. Like any battlefield, they're ripe for exploitation. Hijacking a meeting isn't just about dominating the conversation; it's about steering the narrative, silencing your opponents, and pushing your agenda forward, all while making it look like a productive discussion.

The first rule of hijacking a meeting: come prepared. Not with facts or data those are secondary. Come armed with tactics. Know who's likely to speak up and who's likely to stay quiet. Anticipate objections and have your counterarguments ready. But more importantly, know the weak spots of your opponents. If someone dares to challenge you, you need to be ready to exploit their hesitations and mistakes.

One of the most effective ways to hijack a meeting is to dominate the floor right from the start. Speak first, and speak confidently. Set the tone of the meeting. Present your perspective as if it's the only sensible one. Frame your agenda in terms of the company's goals and values. Make it difficult for anyone to oppose you without seeming like they're against the company's best interests. The goal is to establish yourself as the authority, the one with the clearest vision and the most compelling plan.

And if someone tries to derail you? Time to pivot. Redirect the conversation back to your strengths. Use phrases like, "That's a good point, but what we really need to focus on is..." or, "I hear what you're saying, but let's not lose sight of our main objective here." It's all about control. The more you control the flow of the conversation, the less room there is for dissent.

Sometimes, though, subtlety is key. Let's say a rival has brought a proposal to the table that you'd rather not see succeed. Instead of outright opposing it which could look defensive or self-serving adopt a more strategic approach. Praise the proposal's intent, then systematically dismantle it with questions. "I like where you're going with this, but have you considered…?" or "This sounds promising, but I'm concerned about the potential risks. Can you provide more detail?" Keep them on the defensive. The more they have to explain, the less confident they'll seem, and the more doubt you'll plant in the minds of others.

Take a cue from Roger, the master of meeting manipulation. When confronted with a proposal he didn't like, Roger never outright rejected it. Instead, he would flood the discussion with questions, technicalities, and procedural concerns. "We need more data," he'd say. Or, "This might require legal review." By the end of the meeting, what started as a straightforward proposal would be mired in uncertainty, with everyone convinced it needed more time, more analysis, more everything except approval. Roger's proposals, on the other hand, always seemed to sail through unopposed.

Another advanced tactic? The sidebar. This is where you subtly shift the focus of the meeting to a side issue preferably one that highlights your expertise or someone else's incompetence. It's a diversion tactic. While everyone is distracted, you can quietly push your agenda forward. And when the meeting inevitably runs out of time? "Well, we didn't get everything, but we made some great progress today." Mission accomplished.

Let's not forget the power of silence. Not every hijacking requires words. Sometimes, the best way to derail an opponent is to say nothing at all. Let their ideas hang in the air, unchallenged, unsupported. The longer the silence stretches, the more uncomfortable they'll become. It's a classic power move, forcing them to either over-explain themselves into a corner or awkwardly wrap up and sit down.

Circumventing Decision-Making Processes: Proper Channels

Rules and protocols every company has them, and most people follow them like sheep. Real power isn't about playing by the rules; it's about knowing when to ignore them altogether. Circumventing decision-making processes is the art of sidestepping bureaucracy, cutting through red tape, and getting things done your way. It's not about anarchy; it's about efficiency at least, that's what you'll tell everyone.

The first step is to recognize the gaps in the decision-making process. Every organization has them: those little cracks between departments, those ambiguities in policies, those moments of indecision where nobody quite knows who's in charge. The more complex the organization, the more opportunities there are to bypass the usual channels and take matters into your own hands.

Let's say there's a project you want to push through quickly, something that might ruffle a few feathers or step on a few toes. You could wait for the endless rounds of approval, the tedious back-and-forths between departments, the endless meetings that lead to more meetings. Or, you could just... not. Why bother when you can go straight to the source? Pick up the phone, send a quick email, make a decision on the fly. Act now, apologize later if anyone even notices.

Consider the case of Susan, the queen of circumvention. She didn't waste time waiting for committee approvals or cross-departmental sign-offs. When she saw an opportunity, she took it. A quick text to her buddy in procurement, a casual lunch with a sympathetic executive, and before anyone knew it, her project was already halfway done. When the inevitable questions came, Susan simply smiled and said, "Oh, I thought we had consensus on this. I must have misunderstood, let's discuss it at the next meeting." By then, of course, it was too late. The ball was already rolling, and stopping it would take more effort than anyone was willing to expend.

The key to circumventing decision-making processes is to act decisively and create a sense of inevitability. Make it seem like your decision was the natural, obvious choice, the path of least resistance. Most people are conflict-averse; they'd rather go along with a decision that's already in motion than push back and cause a scene. Leverage that inertia. The more momentum you create, the harder it will be for anyone to stop you.

But remember: subtlety is crucial. Don't flaunt your disregard for protocol; cloak it in the guise of expediency. "I was just trying to keep things moving," you'll say, or "I thought this was what everyone wanted." Play the role of the overzealous doer, the one who cuts through the nonsense to get results. Frame your actions as a commitment to efficiency, a dedication to getting things done. Who could argue with that?

And when someone does try to call you out for bypassing the proper channels? Deflect, deflect, deflect. Blame the process itself. "I wasn't aware there was a formal procedure for this," you might say, even if you were. Or better yet, point out how the existing process is outdated or ineffective. "I thought it was time for a change," you'll suggest. Turn the tables, make it seem like you're the one pushing for progress, while everyone else is stuck in the past.

Get things done on your terms, without the tedious oversight of committees, the meddling of rivals, or the interference of higher-ups. You become known as the person who makes things happen, who doesn't get bogged down in the minutiae.

Exploiting Power Dynamics: Manipulate and Intimidate

Power dynamics are the invisible strings that control the puppet show of corporate life. Knowing how to pull those strings or better yet, how to cut them is what separates the puppeteers from the puppets. Exploiting power dynamics isn't just about knowing where you stand; it's about understanding where everyone else does and making sure they stay there or move to where you need them.

At its core, exploiting power dynamics is about leverage. It's about using your position, your connections, and your influence to get what you want, whether that's securing a promotion, shutting down a rival, or simply making sure everyone knows who's really in charge. You're not bullying; you're "leading." You're not manipulating; you're "managing." It's all in the spin.

The first step is to establish your dominance subtly but firmly. Don't outright declare your power that's too obvious, too crass. Instead, make it felt. Use your position to subtly remind others of your influence. Drop casual mentions of your close ties with upper management, or hint at your sway over key decisions. The goal is to create a sense of uncertainty and an unspoken understanding that crossing you might not be the best career move.

Take Ben, a mid-level manager with outsized influence. Ben never shouted, never threatened. He didn't need to. Everyone knew he had the CEO's ear, and he made sure to drop enough hints to keep it top of mind. "I was chatting with Karen (the CEO) over lunch," he'd say, then pause, letting the name hang in the air like a loaded gun. Nobody wanted to end up on the wrong side of Ben, not when he could so casually slip their name into his next "chat."

The strategic favor; do a favor for someone, but make sure it's one they can't easily repay. Lend your support on a high-visibility project, pull a few strings to get their budget approved, or offer a glowing recommendation to the higher-ups. Now they're indebted to you, and that debt is power. When the time comes and you cash in, they'll have no choice but to comply.

But what about those who resist? The ones who won't play ball or worse try to undermine you? Time to switch tactics. Intimidation doesn't always have to be loud or overt. It can be as simple as a well-timed silence in a meeting, a pointed look when they speak up, or a casual "suggestion" that they might not want to take on that new project after all. Make them second-guess themselves, make them hesitate, make them fear the unseen consequences of their actions.

Or take the direct approach. Invite them for a "friendly" one-on-one. Keep your tone light, your smile pleasant, but make sure your words have weight. "I've been hearing some interesting things about your recent work," you might say, letting the ambiguity hang heavy. "Just wanted to make sure everything is okay." The message is clear: you're watching, and you're not afraid to step in if things aren't "okay."

And then there's the nuclear option: public humiliation. This one's for when you really need to make an example. Wait for a public forum, a team meeting, a departmental briefing. Let them stumble, let them falter, and then strike. Question their data, challenge their assumptions, poke holes in their logic. Make it clear to everyone that stepping out of line has consequences. It's risky, but sometimes a well-placed public humiliation is all it takes to keep the rest in line.

The key to exploiting power dynamics is balance. You want to keep people off balance, guessing, unsure of where they stand with you. When they don't know how much power you hold or how you might use it they'll tread carefully. And that's exactly where you want them: cautious and compliant.

Exploiting HR Processes: Removing Threats

HR isn't just the department that handles paperwork and mediates disputes, it's a weapon, a tool to be wielded. When used correctly, HR processes can be your personal strike force, enabling you to remove threats, silence dissent, and protect your position all under the guise of "following company policy."

The key to exploiting HR is understanding how to manipulate their processes to serve your needs. It starts with building a good rapport with the HR team. You want them to see you as an ally, someone who understands the importance of rules, compliance, and maintaining a "positive work environment." Offer to help with new policy rollouts, attend HR seminars, volunteer for the ethics committee anything that builds your credibility as a team player and a policy advocate.

Once you've established your bona fides, it's time to use them. Identify your targets, those who pose a threat to your power or those who simply annoy you. Then, start collecting evidence. HR loves documentation, so you'll need to gather a trail of minor infractions. Nothing too dramatic, just a series of "concerns" that, taken together, paint a picture of a problematic employee. A late arrival here, a missed deadline there, maybe a vaguely inappropriate comment in a meeting. Each on its own is nothing, but together? They're the start of a case.

Carla, is pro at wielding HR. When a rival started making moves to undermine her, Carla didn't confront them directly. Instead, she began "noticing" their behavior. A casual complaint to HR about "unprofessional conduct" here, a concern about "poor performance" there. Nothing concrete just enough to get them on HR's radar. By the time her rival realized what was happening, the wheels were already in motion. A formal investigation, a probationary period, a quiet exit all while Carla's hands remained clean.

You're not targeting anyone; you're just following procedure, raising concerns, and ensuring compliance. And if the target tries to fight back? They're not fighting you; they're fighting the system.

If you're feeling particularly strategic, use HR policies not just to remove threats but to protect your allies. Ensure that your inner circle is well-versed in company policy. Let them know the rules that matter and, more importantly, how to bend them without breaking. Should they find themselves in hot water, step in as the wise mentor. "Let me help you navigate this," you'll say, guiding them through the maze of HR processes. They'll see you as a protector, a valuable ally and they'll owe you.

Most organizations accept "anonymous" tips. HR departments love them, as they allow them to appear proactive without actually having to gather their own information. So why not use this to your advantage? Send in a few tips yourself anonymous, of course about your target's behavior. Just a few well-placed hints about "issues" that HR might want to keep an eye on. The goal isn't to get them fired immediately; it's to create a cloud of suspicion, a lingering doubt that makes them a liability rather than an asset.

This isn't about causing chaos. It's about control. HR processes are the rules of engagement. By selectively enforcing policies, you maintain order on your terms, ensuring that your position remains secure while your rivals are caught in the crosshairs of "policy enforcement."

Summary

At the core of every company lies a set of structures designed to bring order hierarchies, rules, standardized procedures, and the division of labor. Yet, as we've explored in this chapter, these same structures can be powerful tools of control. Whether it's bypassing hierarchy to create crises that benefit your position, selectively applying rules to control outcomes, or withholding information to create dependency, the corporate battlefield rewards those who can skillfully exploit the system. The art of corporate manipulation lies in mastering these processes, bend them to your will, but try not to break them.

Chapter 7

Social Engineering and Surveillance

As I have said many times, knowledge is power, and the ability to gather that knowledge through social engineering and surveillance is the path to power. This chapter dives into the art of exploiting human weaknesses and technological oversights, using tactics that range from the subtle charm of building false friendships to the more audacious techniques of impersonation and phishing. The key to social engineering is simple: why force your way in when you can be invited? Whether it's by creating a fake persona on social media or eavesdropping on conversations in a coffee shop, this chapter will guide you through the art of using trust, curiosity, and a touch of deception to get exactly what you need.

Social Media Profiling: Stalking Made Respectable

You don't need a trench coat and dark alley to be a stalker. You just need a decent internet connection and the ability to click and scroll. Social media is a modern-day goldmine for manipulators no need to dig through trash when people willingly put their dirt online, pictures of breakfast, dog birthdays, political rants, and oversharing about that "amazing" new job. Each post is a breadcrumb leading you straight to their vulnerabilities.

People love to talk about themselves. They'll share their favorite coffee shop, the name of their childhood pet (hello, password hint), and even post about their recent frustrations at work. Every tweet, every status update is a puzzle piece. Put them together, and you've got yourself a pretty clear picture of your target's likes, dislikes, insecurities, and, most importantly, what strings you can pull.

But you're not just scrolling for fun here; you're on a mission. Your goal? To find that one soft spot to poke whether it's their obsession with being seen as intellectual or a need for validation every time they post a gym selfie. Maybe they're posting about a recent breakup, looking for sympathy. Perfect. Offer a friendly ear, slide into those DMs, and before they know it, they're spilling secrets they didn't even know they had.

Always look at their connections. Social media isn't just about what they share; it's about what their friends share too. Someone tagged at a bar last Friday? There is a good chance they were there too. Scanning through their friends' posts can give you even more leverage. It's all about building a comprehensive profile, knowing your target better than they know themselves.

You don't need to be a hacker to infiltrate someone's life; most people have already left the door open. You just need to learn to read between the lines. The more you know about your target, the easier it is to craft that manipulation strategy. Whether it's pretending to share their interests or creating a fake persona that seems tailor-made for them, the groundwork is laid out for you on their profile page.

Next time someone tells you social media is for connecting people, remember: it's also for exploiting them. As they share their latest brunch, you're figuring out your next move.

Building Rapport: Faux Friendship

You've gathered all the intel from social media, and now you're armed with enough information to write a small biography. Sadly, knowledge by itself isn't enough. To manipulate someone effectively, you've got to make them like you, trust you. This is where building a rapport comes in. You one stage now gives the audience what they want.

Start simple. Shared interests are the easiest bait. If they're into yoga, you're suddenly on a wellness kick. If they love a certain band, you're now their biggest fan. You'd be amazed at how quickly someone opens up when they think they've found a kindred spirit. With time comes trust. The goal isn't just to be liked; it's to be trusted. Trust is the currency of manipulation.

Take it slow, like always subtlety is key. You're not some hyperactive puppy bounding up to them. You're a chameleon, transforming and blending. Make them think this connection is organic, like you two were destined to cross paths. Smile at the right moments, nod in agreement, toss in a well-placed compliment. People love hearing how great they are, especially when it seems like you've 'just noticed.'

Slowly get personal, not too personal, but enough to move past shared interests. Share a little about yourself (fake or real, doesn't matter). The more they think they know you, the safer they feel revealing their own stories, and those stories flow when they think they're in a judgment-free zone. Let them talk. People love to talk about themselves. It's their favorite subject. And you? You don't just listen, confirm their biases, validate their feelings, encourage them to dig the hole deeper.

As the rapport grows, you'll start to notice them letting their guard down. That's when you start to slip in your real agenda casually, like it's no big deal. Drop hints about needing help or advice. Make them feel important, like their opinion really matters. Flattery isn't just about boosting egos; it's about lowering defenses.

Don't rush it. Building rapport isn't a sprint; it's a marathon, patience is key. You're playing the long game here. The deeper the rapport, the harder it is for them to believe you could ever have a hidden motive. You're not just some acquaintance, you're their confidant.

Pretexting: Plausible Lies

If social media profiling and rapport-building is the warm-up, pretexting is where you start to break a sweat. This is the art of creating a convincing backstory, a carefully crafted lie designed to pry open the vault of someone's guarded information. If you've done the first two steps right this will be easy.

Pretexting is all about crafting a believable scenario that compels your target to help you. Don't just ask them outright. You're giving them a reason to trust you, a reason to believe that sharing this information is not only safe but necessary. It's a performance, and you're the actor who brought a member of the audience on stage. They haven't read the script. It's your job to guide them through the performance.

Let's say you're after some sensitive data a password, perhaps, or an insider tip. You don't just waltz in asking for it. Instead, you create a situation where they feel compelled to hand it over. Maybe you're the 'IT specialist' from corporate, calling to inform them of a 'security breach' that requires immediate action. You drop in a few key details you've picked up like the name of their supervisor or a recent project they're working on to establish credibility. Once they're hooked on the idea that you're legitimate, they'll be handing over that password faster than you can say "security protocol."

The trick is to keep it simple but believable. Your scenario needs to be plausible, grounded in enough reality that they don't start questioning things. Overcomplicate it, and you risk tipping your hand. Keep it clean, keep it direct, and always, always be prepared to improvise. Sometimes, they'll throw you a curveball, a question you didn't anticipate, a detail you didn't know. Stay calm. Smile through the phone if you have to. Act like you expected the question all along. The more confidence you exude, the more likely they are to buy your story.

It's not just about what you say; it's how you say it. Your tone, your inflections, your pauses these are the tools of your trade. Sound too rehearsed, and they'll smell a rat. Sound too casual and they might not take you seriously. Find that sweet spot where authority meets familiarity.

Think of it as the voice of a trusted, but slightly impatient, expert. They don't know it, but they want to believe you.

Impersonation: Wearing the Mask

If pretexting is the art of crafting a believable story, then impersonation is its bolder, more audacious father. This is where you don't just create a scenario you step into a role. You become someone else entirely, borrowing their identity, their authority, their reputation, all to get what you want. In the game, sometimes the quickest route to the top is simply to not be you.

Impersonation is about confidence. It's not enough to wear the mask; you've got to make them believe it's your real face. Whether you're pretending to be an HR executive, a delivery driver, or even someone's old college buddy, you need to sell it with every fiber of your being. Slip up, and the whole charade falls apart. But nail it, and you'll find doors opening, secrets spilling, and information flowing like a broken dam.

The first rule of impersonation: do your homework. You can't just pick a persona out of a hat. You need to know the ins and outs of whoever you're pretending to be. Learn their quirks, their catchphrases, their mannerisms. Maybe the person you're impersonating always has a cup of coffee in hand or starts every conversation with a peculiar phrase. Small details, sure, but details that lend authenticity to your act. Remember, people believe what feels familiar, what fits the pattern they've come to expect.

Let's talk about voice. Your voice isn't just random sounds; it's a signal. It tells the target who you are or, rather, who you want them to think you are. A corporate executive doesn't speak like a college intern. A seasoned IT manager has a different cadence than a sales rep. Listen to how your target's contacts speak, their tone, their speed, their choice of words. Mimic it until it feels like second nature. And when you finally pick up that phone or send that email, you need to sound like that character.

Impersonation isn't just about sounding right; it's about access. Physical or digital, you're aiming to get somewhere or something that's off-limits. Maybe you're tailgating your way into a restricted area, flashing a fake badge with all the confidence of someone who's done it a hundred times before. Or perhaps you're on a call with customer service, sounding exactly like the account holder, down to that slight sigh they always make. The more precise your impersonation, the smoother the access.

What about the target's suspicions? There's always the risk they'll catch a whiff of something off, a nagging feeling that something's not quite right. This is where you deploy a little psychological judo: redirect, reassure, and, if necessary, play the victim. "I'm sorry, is my line breaking up? Damn these phones!" Distract them with an apology, a quick joke, a flustered excuse. Anything to keep them from looking too closely at the man behind the mask.

In the end, impersonation is about blending in. You're not just playing a part; you're living it, if only for a few minutes. And in those minutes, you can achieve what hours of questioning, pleading, or even outright threats might never accomplish. Because in the realm of deception, sometimes it's not who you are, but who they think you are, that counts.

Phishing: Net not Spear

Phishing is the digital world's answer to casting a wide net, but instead of pulling in fish, you're hoping to snag someone's secrets. It's a game of digital deception, where the bait could be anything from a fake email from their bank to a bogus password reset request from their IT department. The goal? Trick someone into giving up their sensitive information, and they won't even realize they've been caught until it's too late.

At its core, phishing is simple: you create a message that looks legit, plays to the target's expectations, and convinces them to hand over the goods. Timing is everything. Send a fake tax notice around tax season, or a phony Amazon alert during the holiday shopping frenzy. People are creatures of habit, after all. They see something that fits their current situation, and they instinctively react. Your job is to make sure their instincts lead them straight into your trap.

People are getting better at spotting phishing attempts. You have to make it look good. Spot-on logos, perfect grammar, and a tone that matches the sender. Miss a detail, and the jig's up. Attention to detail is what separates the amateurs from the pros. Throw in a sense of urgency "Your account has been compromised!" "Immediate action required!" and you've got a ticking clock that will push your target to act before thinking. Panic is a powerful motivator, and most people will click that link or download that attachment just to make the bad feeling go away.

Where phishing is casting the net wide, spear phishing is taking precise aim at a single, carefully chosen target. Think of it as the difference between firing a shotgun into a crowd and using a sniper rifle. Phishing might hit anyone, spear phishing is hit or miss.

This isn't a generic scam email you're sending out to the masses. This is a tailored attack, crafted with care and precision. You've done your homework. You know your target's habits, their fears, even their boss's name. You craft a message so perfect, so specific, that even the most cautious recipient will lower their guard. A generic "Your account has been compromised" won't fool a tech-savvy manager, but an email from the "CEO" referencing a recent company event? That's a different story. Attach a document infected with malware, and watch as they take the bait.

Spear phishing isn't about flashy alarms or scare tactics. It's about blending into their routine, making your message feel like just another part of their day. And you don't have to stick to email; LinkedIn, social media, even text messages can all be effective channels. The more familiar the medium, the less likely they'll question it.

Timing is just as critical in spear phishing as it is in regular phishing. Use current events or internal company news to your advantage. The more relevant your message, the quicker they'll react. But remember, the closer your shot, the higher the stakes. If you miss, you risk alerting not just your target, but their entire organization. That's why when it comes to spear phishing, precision is key. One clean strike, in and out, no loose ends.

In the end, whether you're casting a wide net or taking aim at a single target, it's all about deception. Phishing relies on volume, while spear phishing bets on precision. But with the right bait, everyone's a potential catch.

Baiting: Lure of the Unattainable

Baiting is one of the oldest tricks in the book, a classic move. It's all about creating a temptation that's just too juicy to resist. Dangle something desirable in front of your target and watch as they walk right into your trap. Whether it's a free gadget, an exclusive offer, or a mysterious USB drive labeled "Confidential," baiting leverages the most primal of human instincts: the desire to get something for nothing.

The key to a successful baiting operation is understanding what your target wants, what will make their eyes light up, what will trigger that all-too-human impulse to reach out and grab. And remember, it's not always about monetary value. Sometimes, the best bait is something that appeals to vanity, curiosity, or even a sense of urgency.

Let's say you're trying to gain access to a company's internal network. You could go through the front door, dealing with passwords and security systems, but why bother when you can take a shortcut? Leave a few strategically placed USB drives around the office labeled "Year-End Bonuses" or "Confidential Layoff List." Trust me, someone will plug it in, eager to see what juicy details might be inside. And just like that, you're in. The Trojan horse of the digital age, a baited hook, camouflaged as irresistible temptation.

Baiting isn't just about digital traps, though. It's equally effective in the physical world. Maybe you're trying to get someone to show up at a particular place at a particular time. Send them a personalized invitation to an "exclusive" event, something that makes them feel special, like they're getting insider access. Throw in a few free drinks, a swag bag, or a chance to hobnob with industry bigwigs. Next thing you know, they're right where you want them, blissfully unaware of what's really going on.

It's not just about what you offer; it's about how you present it. The bait has to look perfect, just the right mix of attainable and just out of reach. Too easy, and they'll smell a rat. Too difficult, and they might not bother. You're threading a needle here, crafting a temptation so compelling that the target can't help but bite.

The best bait often has an expiration date. Create a sense of urgency "Only 10 left!" or "Offer expires in 24 hours!" That ticking clock compels people to act quickly, without thinking things through. And that's when they make mistakes. The tighter the window, the more likely they are to leap without looking.

Baiting isn't without risks. If the target gets wise to your game, they could turn the tables, using your own bait against you. That's why you always need a backup plan and an escape route for when things don't go as planned. Remember, the more tempting the bait, the more suspicious the target might become. The best bait is the kind that feels like it was meant for them, a reward for being in the right place at the right time.

In the end, baiting is a test of patience and psychology. You're setting the stage, crafting the perfect lure, and waiting for just the right moment to reel them in. It's a delicate balance of anticipation and execution. When it works, there's nothing quite as satisfying as watching someone walk right into a trap they never saw coming.

Reverse Social Engineering: Problems to Solutions

If baiting is all about luring the target in, reverse social engineering takes it a step further by creating a problem just so you can be the one to solve it. Think of it as playing both the arsonist and the firefighter: you set the fire, then swoop in to save the day, earning trust, gratitude, and, most importantly, access.

People naturally trust those who offer help. If you are the one offering the solution, you're not just a helpful hand, you're a savior. And who would ever suspect the savior of starting the fire in the first place?

First, you create a problem: a virus on their computer, a corrupted file, a mysteriously malfunctioning device. The trick is to make it seem random, like bad luck or a glitch. But in reality, you've orchestrated the whole thing. It's got to be just disruptive enough to cause panic, but not so catastrophic that they can't use their usual channels to solve it. You want them to be just desperate enough to turn to you, the ever-helpful "expert" who conveniently shows up at the right moment.

For example, say you're targeting a small company. You introduce a minor bug into their network, something that slows things down or causes random errors. Not enough to shut down operations, but enough to annoy. Then, you casually reach out, offering your "services" as a freelance IT consultant who's just heard about their troubles through the grapevine. "I've seen this kind of issue before," you say confidently. "I can fix it in no time." Grateful and out of options, they let you in. And once you're in, you're free to poke around, plant your malware, or extract the data you need.

Another variation? Go physical. Create a 'problem' in a secure area like jamming a door or messing with a security camera. Then, pose as the maintenance guy, ready to fix the issue. With a clipboard in hand and a confident nod, most people won't think twice about letting you in. While you're "fixing" the problem, you're gathering intel, mapping out the territory, or slipping a USB into an unattended computer.

The success of reverse social engineering hinges on three things: timing, subtlety, and credibility. Timing is everything you need to show up just as the problem becomes apparent. Too early, and you look suspicious. Too late, and they might have already called for backup. Subtlety is key, too. The problem you create can't scream "sabotage"; it needs to feel like a natural occurrence. And credibility? That's your ace in the hole. Whether you're posing as a tech expert, a security consultant, or a good Samaritan, you need to sell it with everything you've got.

You don't always have to solve the problem immediately. Sometimes, stringing them along, making them increasingly dependent on you, can yield even better results. You become their go-to person, their "trusted" resource. And with every problem you "fix," their guard drops a little more.

Reverse social engineering is about control. You create chaos, you provide calm, and in doing so, you position yourself as indispensable.

The Honey Trap: The Sweetest Deception

In the vast arsenal of manipulation tactics, the honey trap is one of the oldest and simplest. Why hack into someone's email or dig through their trash when you can get them to give you their secrets willingly, all in the name of love or at least lust? Honey trapping is about playing to the most primal of human desires, using romance, flirtation, or outright seduction as the bait to extract information, gain access, or simply control a target.

The essence of honey trapping lies in creating a connection or the illusion of one. You're more than a role; you're a fantasy, something irresistible. You're the charming new colleague who takes a special interest, the attractive stranger at the bar who just happens to share a love for obscure Russian literature, or the online persona who seems to be everything they've ever looked for. The key is to be exactly what they need at that moment, to fill that void.

Honey trapping isn't about genuine emotion; there's a risk you might fall for your target. This is why many intelligence agencies avoid the strategy. Remember, you're playing a part. Compliment them just enough to make them blush, share just enough about yourself (real or fabricated) to build a sense of intimacy, and then, when the moment is right, slip in a well-placed question or request. People are more likely to share sensitive information when they think it's in the context of a trusted relationship or when they're simply too flattered, or flustered, to think straight.

Let's say you're targeting a mid-level executive with access to sensitive corporate plans. You don't just stroll up and ask for the information directly. Instead, you engage them in conversation, slowly building rapport. Maybe you drop a few hints about your own "disillusionment" with your job, fishing for a reaction. Over time, as the conversations become more personal, you start nudging them towards discussing their work frustrations, slowly coaxing out details they wouldn't normally share. Before they know it, they're telling you about the upcoming merger or the new product line because, well, they "trust" you.

If a little harmless flirting doesn't do the trick? Turn up the heat. You'd be surprised what people will reveal under the soft glow of candlelight, or after a few well-timed glasses of wine. The more they're invested in the fantasy, the more eager they'll be to keep it alive even if it means sharing things they shouldn't. If things get serious? Well, that's just more leverage for you.

I'm willing to bet many of my readers are straight men, and many of their targets will be straight men too. That doesn't mean the honey trap won't work. Attraction can be a strange thing. It's entirely possible to flirt and get a positive reaction from someone who has no interest in sharing a bed with you. In my experience, straight men are often more susceptible to a bromance than to a pretty woman. When an attractive woman approaches a man, especially one in a position of power his defenses tend to go up.

Of course, honey trapping isn't without risks. You're playing with real emotions, yours and theirs. Get too involved, and you risk losing your own objectivity. Let them get too close, and they might start asking questions you're not ready to answer. Then there's the danger of discovery. If they find out they've been played, the fallout can be explosive. That's why it's crucial to maintain control at all times. Keep your story straight, your emotions in check, and always have an exit strategy.

But when it works, honey trapping is like nothing else. There's a certain thrill in seeing someone let down their guard, in watching them share their secrets, all because they've been seduced by a carefully crafted illusion. In this game, there's no sweeter victory than one earned through the art of seduction.

Eavesdropping: Secrets Overheard

Eavesdropping is another one of the oldest tricks in the book so old, in fact, that it often goes unnoticed in our high-tech world. A well-placed ear can yield just as much, if not more, than any email hack or phishing scam. It's low-tech, but it's effective. And the best part? The people you're listening to won't even know they've been compromised.

Eavesdropping is about being in the right place at the right time or better yet, creating that right place and time. Don't hide behind the door or in a closet. Instead, casually position yourself within earshot, blending into the background like a piece of corporate furniture. Maybe you're the unassuming janitor quietly emptying the trash, or the colleague who's "forgotten" their phone charger and just happens to be nearby when the juicy details are spilled.

The trick is to know where and when people talk freely. Break rooms, elevators, smoke breaks, late-night office cleaning rounds these are prime times for overheard whispers. People are creatures of habit. They talk about the same things, in the same places, over and over again. All you have to do is figure out their routines and position yourself accordingly.

Eavesdropping doesn't have to be just passively listening. Sometimes, you need to nudge the conversation in the right direction. A well-timed comment or an innocuous question can set the stage for a revelation. "I heard the marketing team is working on something big...," you might muse aloud, and suddenly, they're confirming your suspicions or, better yet, elaborating with details they probably shouldn't be sharing. All because you created the space for the conversation to happen.

Never underestimate the power of eavesdropping in public spaces. Coffee shops, restaurants, even airport lounges are treasure troves of corporate gossip. Honestly, it's what drives half the banking sector. Executives love to show off, love to talk loudly about their latest deal or merger, believing that no one around them cares or understands. But you care. You understand more than they'll ever know. Keep your ear to the ground literally and you'll be amazed at what slips through the cracks.

There's also the digital side of eavesdropping. Surveillance cameras, unsecured conference lines, even baby monitors can become inadvertent tools of corporate espionage. With a little technical savvy, you can tap into these feeds and listen in on private conversations without ever being physically present. Just remember to keep your tracks covered; nothing ends a good eavesdropping operation faster than getting caught in the act.

Eavesdropping has its pitfalls. You're relying on overheard snippets, partial conversations, and it can be easy to misinterpret what you hear. A rumor picked up from the break room might turn out to be nothing more than office gossip. That's why it's crucial to corroborate the information you hear with other sources, check it against what you already know, and always be on the lookout for misdirection and red herrings.

Eavesdropping just works. There's a special kind of satisfaction that comes from learning a secret not through trickery or coercion, but simply by being smart enough to listen when others are careless enough to talk. In the end, it's about letting others do the work for you while you sit back and enjoy the show. Because sometimes, the best secrets aren't the ones that are kept, they're the ones that are shared, often without the sharer even realizing.

Shoulder Surfing: Take a Peek

Sometimes, the easiest way to get someone's secrets is to just look over their shoulder. Shoulder surfing is as straightforward as it gets: you're simply observing someone's private information as they enter it, unaware of your presence. It's a classic maneuver, and while it might seem almost too simple to include in this book, its simplicity is precisely what makes it so effective.

Shoulder surfing thrives in environments where people feel secure. Busy coffee shops, airport lounges, open office spaces, anywhere people are likely to pull out their laptops or tap away on their phones. The more crowded the space, the less likely they are to notice someone discreetly peering over their shoulder. Believe me, people are far less cautious than they should be. They'll type out passwords, bank account numbers, even sensitive emails without a second thought.

The trick to shoulder surfing is blending in. You don't want to look like you're spying; you want to look like you're just another person in the background, lost in your own thoughts or glued to your own screen. Maybe you're sitting at the table next to them, casually scrolling through your phone. Or perhaps you're standing behind them in line, pretending to check your watch while your eyes discreetly flick to their screen. The key is to act naturally like you're supposed to be there, like whatever's on their screen isn't the least bit interesting to you.

Timing is everything. You want to catch them at just the right moment when they're logging in, filling out forms, or reading confidential emails. Too early, and you'll get nothing. Too late, and you've missed your window. Watch for those tell-tale signs: the way they lean in slightly, the concentrated look on their face, the quick glances around to see if anyone's watching. That's when you know they're entering something important.

It's not just about getting passwords or financial information. Shoulder surfing can yield all sorts of valuable intel email addresses, client lists, internal memos, you name it. People handle a lot of sensitive information in public spaces, mistakenly believing that because they can't see anyone watching, no one is. Your job is to be that unseen observer, picking up what they're laying down.

The closer you get, the greater the chance of getting caught. People don't like their personal space invaded, and if they catch even a hint that you're creeping, they'll shut down fast. That's why you need to be smooth, subtle, and always ready with a cover story. Maybe you were just looking for the nearest exit. Or you're lost and thought they might help. Never let them see you sweat.

If you really want to up your game? Consider using technology to aid in your shoulder surfing exploits. A discreetly placed camera with a high-quality zoom can let you record screens from a distance, eliminating the need to physically get close altogether.

Shoulder surfing is taking advantage of a momentary lapse in judgment a second where someone lets their guard down, believing they're safe. Sometimes the simplest methods yield the best results.

Dumpster Diving: One Man's Trash

In a world obsessed with digital security, it's surprising how often secrets are thrown away. Dumpster diving is rooting through discarded materials to uncover sensitive information that was carelessly thrown away. It's not glamorous, and it's definitely not for the faint of heart, but it's a time-tested method that can yield surprising results. After all, people throw away a lot more than just garbage.

Confidential memos, customer lists, meeting notes, even passwords scribbled on sticky notes if it's been printed out and tossed away, it's fair game. Companies can spend millions on cybersecurity, but all it takes is one lazy employee or one overly confident exec to toss a piece of paper they shouldn't have, and suddenly, you've got your hands on a goldmine of data.

The key to successful dumpster diving is knowing where to look. Not all trash is created equal. You want to hit up the dumpsters behind office buildings, especially around accounting, legal, or HR departments are all places where sensitive documents are more likely to be discarded. And don't just dive headfirst; take a moment to scope out the lay of the land. Is the area well-lit? Are there security cameras? Do regular trash pickups happen in the dead of night, or can you stroll by during the day and casually peek in? Timing and reconnaissance are critical.

And let's be clear: you don't necessarily have to dive into the dumpster itself. Sometimes, the best finds are right on top. Shredded documents? Even better, most people don't bother shredding everything, or they do a half-assed job of it. A little patience, a little puzzle-solving, and suddenly you've got yourself a reconstructed document that no one else thought was worth the time to destroy properly.

It's not just paper, either. Old hard drives, USB sticks, discarded laptops, anything that might still have some juice left in it. People upgrade their tech all the time and don't always wipe their devices properly before tossing them, in that oversight lies opportunity. A quick trip to the dumpster, and you've got yourself a hard drive full of old files, all just waiting to be explored.

You've got to be ready to get your hands dirty, both literally and figuratively. You've got to be mindful of the law depending on where you are, diving into someone's trash might be perfectly legal or it could get you arrested for trespassing. Always do your homework and know the local regulations before you jump in. It's one thing to get caught snooping; it's another to get caught trespassing with a fistful of sensitive documents.

Cover your tracks. If you've found something good, don't just take it and run. Leave the rest of the trash undisturbed, make it look like no one's been there. If you're too obvious, they'll start locking dumpsters, investing in shredders, and tightening up security measures. You want to leave things just as you found them, so you can come back again and again.

Dumpster diving is finding value where others see none. It's about turning someone else's carelessness into your opportunity. You would be amazed what people throw away.

Tailgating: Slipstreaming Access

Not every infiltration requires a forged ID or a fancy disguise. Sometimes, all it takes is a little confidence and perfect timing. Tailgating also known as "piggybacking" is the art of slipping into a restricted area by closely following an authorized person. It's like drafting behind a semi-truck on the highway; you let someone else do all the heavy lifting while you ride in their wake, unnoticed and unhindered.

Tailgating relies on one of the most fundamental aspects of human nature: politeness. Most people don't like to challenge others or make a scene. You've probably seen it yourself: someone holds the door open for the person behind them, assuming they belong there. Or an employee waves someone through a secure door, too preoccupied with their phone or their coffee to check for a badge. That's your moment to strike.

No need for complicated backstories or elaborate ruses. You don't need to pose as an HVAC repairman or a corporate bigwig. You just need to look like you belong head held high, eyes forward, maybe a casual nod or a smile. Blend in with the flow of people, and before anyone realizes they don't recognize you, you're already through.

Timing is everything. You need to pick the right person to follow, someone who looks like they're in a rush or someone with their hands full. The more distracted they are, the better. An employee juggling their laptop, a coffee, and a badge is far less likely to notice a stranger slipping in behind them than someone who's fully alert and on guard. If you're really lucky? You might find an employee who's already in the habit of holding doors for others the perfect mark in the tailgating game.

Once inside, you've got to keep your cool. Act like you've got every right to be there, and most people will assume you do. Start walking with purpose, as if you know exactly where you're going. Don't linger in the lobby or look lost. The moment you start hesitating, you raise suspicion. Confidence is your best disguise.

But be ready for the unexpected. Maybe someone does challenge you, asks who you are or why you're there. Have a quick story ready, maybe you're new, you're there for an interview, or you're just the IT guy coming to check the servers. The more generic and plausible your excuse, the less likely they are to dig deeper. Remember, the goal is to get in and get out with what you need don't overstay your welcome.

You're relying on the assumption that people won't want to be rude or confrontational, and most of the time, that's true. But there's always that one security-conscious employee who wants to play hero, or the overly observant receptionist who doesn't remember signing you in. That's why it's crucial to always have an exit plan. Know the layout, identify the exits, and if things start to go south, be ready to bail.

Tailgating is all about exploiting human nature, their instincts, their politeness, their willingness to assume the best. It's a low-tech, high-reward strategy that can get you past barriers that would stop more sophisticated attacks dead in their tracks. So next time you're looking for a way in, consider the simplest option: just follow someone else who's already got the keys.

Data Mining: Diamonds in the Rough

Data mining is the process of sifting through vast amounts of information to find patterns, anomalies, or hidden insights that can be exploited for gain. It's not about hacking into servers or breaking through firewalls; it's about digging deep into what's already available, finding the nuggets of gold buried in the mountains of digital dirt.

Data mining might not have the flash and drama of a social engineering scheme or a high-stakes hack, but don't let that fool you. It's a powerhouse tactic. Companies collect data on everything from customer habits, employee behaviors, sales trends, market shifts. Often, they're sitting on a mountain of valuable information without even realizing it. That's where you come in.

Most of the time, you're not breaking any rules; you're just using publicly available information in ways the average person wouldn't think to. Maybe you're scouring LinkedIn for employee names and roles, cross-referencing with social media to build detailed profiles. Or perhaps you're digging through publicly available reports, financial statements, and press releases to piece together a company's strategy or spot a weakness in their armor.

A customer service rep mentions a "glitch" in a tweet. An IT technician grumbles on Facebook about "long hours fixing server issues." A middle manager lets slip on LinkedIn about "exciting new changes coming soon." On their own, these bits of data might seem harmless, even mundane. But when you start to piece them together, you can build a picture that shows you where the weak points are, where the doors are cracked open, and where you can slip in undetected.

Data is the most undervalued resource in the world. There are massive companies whose entire business models revolve around data mining. In the social media world, if you're not paying for the product, you are the product. Yet, even these data giants are still missing a lot. I predict that in the next 20 years, with advances in processing power and AI, data mining will become unrecognizable compared to what it is today.

It's not just about external data. If you've already managed to infiltrate a company, even at a low level, the real treasure trove is often internal data, emails, chat logs, and internal documents. Mining this data can reveal a lot: who's disgruntled, who's up for promotion, who's about to jump ship. Every scrap of information helps build a profile that can be exploited, whether for blackmail, manipulation, or just good old-fashioned espionage.

The sheer volume of data available can be overwhelming. You need to know what you're looking for, or you risk drowning in a sea of irrelevant information. Not all data is good data, some of it is misleading, outdated, or just plain wrong. The trick is to sift through the noise, find the signal, and focus on what really matters.

A lot of data is publicly available, but that doesn't mean it's meant to be used against someone. You're walking a fine line between what's legal and what's ethical, the line is always shifting. Keep your wits about you, stay adaptable, and always have a justification ready, even if it's just for yourself.

Summary

Take your time and play the long game. From social media profiling, where people willingly broadcast their vulnerabilities, to pretexting and impersonation, where a well-crafted lie can pry open even the most guarded vaults, this chapter has shown how manipulators can weave their way into the lives of others. Whether it's through phishing scams or the more intimate approach of honey trapping, the goal is always the same: exploit trust and gather information. By mastering these tactics, you can turn every interaction into an opportunity to uncover secrets, bend decisions, and outmaneuver your corporate opponents. As always, knowledge is power.

Chapter 8

Cult of Personality and Charismatic Manipulation

It's not about having the best ideas, it's about making people think you do. In this chapter, we're not just talking leadership, we're talking worship. Crafting a persona goes beyond confidence or presence; it's about manipulating perception. Done right, it won't matter if you don't have all the answers they'll still follow.

This chapter will teach you how to dominate the room, promote yourself without seeming desperate, and speak in a way that hooks people. You'll learn how to use charm to lower defenses and manipulate emotions to cement yourself as someone they can't afford to ignore.

Creating a Visionary Persona: Follow the Leader

We're all insecure. Am I smart enough? Do people like me? This is why we follow visionary leaders. We hope their brilliance will rub off on us. Visionaries aren't born, they're made. Don't wait for the world to put you on a pedestal, build it yourself. Being a "visionary leader" means convincing everyone you know more than you do.

Picture this: the boardroom lights dim, the PowerPoint flickers to life, and there you are, standing at the head of the table like an all-knowing corporate messiah. What are you selling? Not just a product, not just a plan no, you're selling a future, a way of thinking. One so bold, so inspiring, that everyone in the room forgets to question the fine print. Because, in their eyes, you're not just another executive you're the one with the answers, the one who sees what no one else can.

You don't need to have all the answers no one ever does. The goal is to make them think you do. Creating a visionary persona is about cultivating an aura of certainty. Speak with conviction, even when you're not entirely sure. Lean into that paradox: the more uncertain things become, the more certain you must appear. Take time to think about answers privately so that when everyone else is scrambling for a solution, you deliver a rehearsed speech. Perception is reality, and if they believe you're the visionary leader, then you are.

Remember flair, visionaries don't just walk into a room; they command it. Dress the part, be confident, talk about 'big ideas' the kind that sound revolutionary, even if they're short on specifics. Get your cadences right. Look at American preachers or presidential speeches. Drop a buzzword or two 'disruption,' 'innovation,' 'synergy' or even make one up; you're prophesying. The sound, the rhythm, the performance matters more than the content.

Don't worry about the details. If people like you and want to follow you, they'll fill in the blanks. What matters is creating the sense that you've got a grand, unshakable vision. People only remember the ones you get right. Once they buy into it, they'll follow you anywhere.

Self-Promotion: I'm the Best

Take a leaf out of the corporate narcissist's handbook. In the U.S., self-promotion is woven into the culture. Narcissists thrive there because talking yourself up is expected, not frowned upon. In the UK, it's a game of subtlety; self-promotion works, but don't be seen as arrogant. Pretending to be a narcissist is far more powerful than actually being one. Real narcissists have a weakness: they put ego above all else, making them self-destructive. Imitation works better unlike corporate sociopaths, where the real ones dominate, genuine narcissists burn themselves out.

Start subtle. Drop hints about that last project you single-handedly saved. Casually mention the long nights you spent while others were catching up on their Netflix queue. You're not bragging; you're just ensuring people know the facts. Craft your own narrative, because if you don't, someone else will, and they won't paint you in the best light.

Self-promotion doesn't just work on others; it works on you too. If you keep telling yourself you're going to be successful, you will be. If you tell yourself you're confident, you are. "Whether you think you can, or you think you can't you're right." Henry Ford. Tell yourself every day in the mirror: I'm amazing, and I am successful. You'll see the difference in months.

Share your success, but make it seem effortless. You didn't win that deal because you're brilliant (though you did) it was just the right time and place. Fake humility goes a long way. You're letting others bask in your glow, everyone knows who the real star is.

The best kind of self-promotion? Getting others to do it for you. A strategically dropped hint, a nudge in the right ear, and soon enough, people are talking you up without you lifting a finger. Build a reputation that spreads organically, and by the time it's done, you're the go-to person for everything important.

Charismatic Speaking: I had a Dream

When we like someone, we follow them. Words don't just convey ideas, they spark emotions, and once you've tapped into someone's feelings, they'll follow you without question. Charismatic speaking isn't about delivering facts and logic; those are secondary. Your job is to inspire, persuade, and make people feel something. When you've hooked their emotions, their minds will trail behind, whether they realize it or not.

Start with your voice. People trust a voice that sounds confident, even if you have no idea where you're going. Great public speakers know this. Churchill's repetitive cadence "We shall fight on the beaches, we shall fight on the landing grounds, we shall fight in the fields" is a perfect example. It's about rhythm and pattern, repeating phrases to create a sense of inevitability and strength. Or take floating opposites: "lower taxes and raise living standards." It's simple, but it sticks. Science backs it up people retain ideas better when there's a rhythm, a structure they can latch onto.

Have fun with cultural clichés. Drop one, and people know exactly what you mean without further explanation. "If you open a can of worms, you'll let the cat out of the bag, and before long, you'll be up the creek." Cultural clichés show your audience that you are one of them. You speak their language. People recognize the patterns, and that familiarity builds trust.

The message itself? Keep it big, avoid details, bold, and just vague enough that everyone can project their own hopes and fears onto it. You're not talking about a minor increase in quarterly earnings, you're talking about "reshaping the future" or "unlocking potential." People won't remember specific figures; they'll remember the feeling of excitement you left them with.

While you've got them caught up in your grand vision, you're slipping in exactly what you want them to do without them ever noticing. Whether it's getting their buy-in on your project or pushing for that promotion, make it seem like it's their idea. You make them want to follow you.

Tell a story, use a metaphor, anything that makes you seem relatable, and if it's not relatable make it inspirational. "I was racing my yacht last week...", "The trick to breeding horses...". Personal stories stick far longer than facts and figures. People want to feel like they know you, that you're not some untouchable figure preaching from above. It doesn't even have to be true, just something that makes you seem human. What matters is how it makes them feel.

They won't remember the exact words, but they'll remember the emotional impact. Once you've got them feeling the way you want, you've got them exactly where you need them ready to follow.

Using Charm and Flattery: Smile and Switch

No matter who you are, everyone loves a compliment. It's not about you, you aren't trying to be likable; it's about making them feel likable. When people feel good around you, they'll follow you anywhere and you won't even need to ask. Charm is disarming. It lowers defenses. When those walls come down, you can walk right in and rearrange the furniture.

Flattery is where it starts. Done right, it doesn't feel like manipulation at all. People love to be complimented, especially when it's wrapped in sincerity or at least something that looks a lot like sincerity. You don't just throw compliments around like confetti, though, you have to tailor them. Make them specific, personal. Tell someone they're a "great employee" and they'll thank you. Tell them they're "the one person who really understands the nuances of the project" and they'll move mountains for you. Why? Because now you've made them feel special, indispensable.

When I was 20, I moved to London and worked in a swanky cocktail bar. Part of the service included having someone stand at the front door to compliment every guest, whether they were male or female it didn't matter. "I like your shirt," "Nice hair," "Awesome shoes." At first, the staff found it challenging, but after a while, it became second nature.

After a few months, I started noticing a pattern. When I, as a man, complimented women, I'd either get a polite smile or be ignored. But when I complimented men, it hit them differently. Straight men rarely receive compliments and are starved for approval. If I told a man I liked his shirt, he'd often break eye contact and look down. After a few drinks, once their confidence had built, they would sometimes come back to thank me. It clearly meant a lot.

This wasn't about flirting or attraction. Straight men live in a world where their emotional need for validation is not only unmet but often denied. "Boys don't cry." It is truly sad what we have done to them. Plutonic compliments will open doors you would never imagine possible.

Use charm to get your foot in the door. Smile, laugh at their jokes, make them feel like they've known you forever. Once you're inside, start laying on the flattery. Build their confidence up just enough that they trust your judgment without question. Stroke their ego while guiding their hand. Before they know it, they're doing exactly what you want thinking it's all their idea.

People rarely question motives when charm is involved. After all, who suspects manipulation from someone who's always so warm, so likable? Charm creates a buffer, a sort of plausible deniability for your actions. When you sprinkle in just enough flattery, you can get away with practically anything.

Performative Empathy: The World is Your Stage

Empathy is the ability to feel someone else's emotions. Performative empathy, is about appearing to feel them, without actually getting bogged down in the mess. It's about using the appearance of concern to get what you want while maintaining the image of someone who's deeply in touch with their team.

Let me show you how powerful this can be. Did you notice what I did earlier? In the previous chapter I wrote, "It is truly sad what we've done to them," referring to straight men. Did that line move you? Did it make you think I'm a kinder, more caring person? Whether you noticed consciously or subconsciously, that line probably shifted how you view me. But did it actually change who I am? Of course not. As I said earlier in the book, look at people's actions, not their words. The real action here? I wrote a handbook for corporate sociopaths. Not exactly consistent with a "soft and fluffy" personality.

When it comes to empathy, the setup is simple. You don't need to feel someone's pain, but you do need to act like you do. A well-timed sigh, a furrowed brow, maybe even a hand on their shoulder all signals that you're in tune with them. You understand them. Whether it's true or not doesn't matter. Empathy is a skill, and like any skill, it can be learned. Practice spotting it in people. A lack of empathy is the hallmark of a sociopath. Imagine what a sociopath who can recognize and fake empathy could achieve. The sky's the limit.

The beauty of showing empathy, fake or otherwise, is that it makes people want to confide in you. They'll share their fears, frustrations, and insecurities, believing you truly feel their pain. Once they've shared those thoughts, they can't take them back. You can then use that information to your advantage, subtly turning it into opportunities to control or manipulate. It's a perfect disguise too. Who would question the motives of someone who just spent an hour listening to their problems with such care?

Performative empathy also buys loyalty. People want to follow someone who seems to care about them. When you throw on that mask of concern, they feel seen, heard, understood even if you're already thinking about your next move while they're pouring out their heart. It costs you nothing. A few nods, a couple of sympathetic murmurs, and boom you've got them hooked.

You can use performative empathy to defuse tension, win allies, or manipulate situations to your advantage. If someone's pushing back on your latest brilliant idea, show them you understand their concerns, then gently guide them toward seeing things your way. They'll think you're a leader who listens, but in reality, you're the one steering the entire conversation.

Too much empathy, and you'll come off as fake, even to the most oblivious. Just enough, though, and they'll keep believing you're the leader who truly understands them.

Heroic Storytelling: Standing Tall

Everyone loves a good story, especially when it's about a hero. What's better than a hero's tale? One where you are the hero. Heroic storytelling is your chance to create a legend around yourself, one that places you front and center as the bold, fearless leader who always triumphs against the odds. It's not just about what you've done, but about how you spin it. A boring success can be reshaped into a thrilling adventure, and a minor win into a monumental achievement.

The best heroic stories have three elements: conflict, perseverance, and victory. You don't just want to tell people you succeeded; you want to take them on a journey. Start with the obstacles you faced bonus points if they were supposedly impossible to overcome. The more you emphasize the adversity, the more impressive your eventual triumph becomes. Did you pull off a major deal that saved the company from going under? Or maybe you had to "step in" at the last moment to rescue a project from a certain disaster? Perfect. Inflate the stakes and make sure everyone knows just how close the situation was to total disaster.

Make sure you paint yourself as the relentless figure who never gave up. Even if the reality was a bit more, shall we say, mundane, the point is to make it sound like you were the only one who could have pulled it off. Use phrases like, "It wasn't easy, but I knew I had to make it work," or "I wasn't going to let the team down, no matter the cost." Now you're not just the hero, you're the selfless hero, the one who shoulders the burden for the greater good.

Finally, the victory. This is where you bask in the glory, but with a calculated humility. Make sure you share the credit just enough to seem gracious, but not so much that anyone forgets who's the real star of the story. "We pulled together as a team, but someone had to make the tough decisions," you might say, reminding them that without you, none of it would've been possible. In the retelling of the story, your legend only grows.

Once people start believing your version of events, they'll begin to repeat it. With every retelling, the details get a little more dramatic, a little more heroic. Soon enough, you won't even need to tell the story yourself; others will be doing it for you. You'll become the leader who can "always be counted on in a crisis," whether or not you actually did much at all.

So, the next time something goes right under your watch, don't just let it pass as a routine success. Craft the story. Embellish where necessary. And most importantly, make sure everyone knows that, in the end, it was your brilliance, courage, and sheer force of will that made it happen.

Mythmaking: Creating the Monster

Every great leader needs a few myths circulating around them stories that go beyond the usual accomplishments and border on the legendary. If you want to cement your place at the top, it's time to let a little mythmaking do the heavy lifting. Don't worry, you don't have to start the rumors yourself. Just drop a few hints, let people run with them, and watch as your reputation grows far beyond anything grounded in reality.

The beauty of mythmaking is that it allows others to inflate your abilities for you. Sure, you may have just closed a standard deal, but give it some time, and the story will evolve into how you saved the entire company singlehandedly. It's like playing a game of corporate telephone, but instead of the message getting garbled, it just gets bigger, grander, more heroic. Once the myth sticks, good luck trying to dislodge it.

When I was 23, I had a flat in central London, just 50 meters from work. I was heading up software development at a creative agency, and I'd built a reputation for being confident, ruthless, and a bit eccentric. Everyone knew I lived close by, but I never invited anyone over. Keeping that air of mystery gave me a certain power.

One day, at a Christmas market, I impulsively bought a genuine reindeer skin. It seemed like a good idea at the time. But when I got it home, it started shedding white hairs everywhere. My clothes, suits, bag, everything was covered in the stuff.

After the holidays, I went back to work, and someone remarked, "I didn't know you had a dog," referring to the hair on my clothes. Without missing a beat, I looked up from my desk and said, "It's a reindeer," then went back to work. And just like that, a myth was born. From that day on, I was known as the guy eccentric enough to keep a pet reindeer in central London.

Never outright deny the stories, but don't fully endorse them either. The power lies in ambiguity. "Oh, that? I was just doing my job," you'll say with a modest shrug, while knowing full well that your 'job' is now being talked about like something out of a Hollywood script. This makes people believe the story even more because you appear too humble to admit the full extent of your greatness. If you're humble, then clearly you must be even more impressive than the rumors suggest.

You'll also want to encourage a bit of mystique. Let people believe you're capable of things that others wouldn't even attempt. Maybe you have some "secret method" that no one else knows about. Maybe you've got an uncanny ability to foresee market trends or "read the room" in negotiations. Whatever it is, don't explain it too much. Just let the myth build itself. The less you say, the more people will fill in the blanks with their own inflated ideas of your brilliance.

Mythmaking also has a defensive aspect. When you've got a larger-than-life image, people hesitate to challenge you. Why question someone who's already been anointed as the untouchable genius? The myth insulates you from scrutiny, because after all, would anyone dare confront the person who's practically a legend? It's like armor you never had to put on; others will wear it for you.

Myths are a long-term investment, once planted, they grow on their own. People love a good story, especially when it involves someone they already admire. Before you know it, your myth becomes a permanent fixture, part of the lore that surrounds your name. Just sit back, let the legend take on a life of its own, and enjoy the benefits of being the person everyone assumes can do no wrong.

Grand Gestures: Light the Beacon

I know the theme of the book has been subtlety but on occasion, subtlety is overrated. When you really want to leave a mark, nothing makes the point like a grand gesture. These are the moments that don't just turn heads; they cement your place in history. The trick isn't in the gesture itself; it's in what it represents. You're not just making a move, you're making a statement, and you want it to echo long after you've left the room.

Grand gestures are about reinforcing your persona as someone who isn't afraid to take bold actions. Maybe it's donating a chunk of your bonus to a cause everyone's talking about. Or perhaps it's dramatically stepping in at the last moment to save a failing project, even though the whole thing could've been handled by your team. It doesn't matter whether the gesture was necessary, what matters is that it looks heroic.

These gestures need to be broadcasted, memorable, and perfectly timed. You want people talking about it, replaying the scene in their heads, and more importantly, telling others about how impressive it was. Think of it as theater: you're not just solving a problem; you're staging an unforgettable moment where you're the undisputed star.

Grand gestures don't have to be costly, sometimes, it's enough to make a symbolic action that signals your power and influence. Maybe it's shutting down a meeting you deem unproductive, or making a last-minute decision that completely changes the direction of a project. The point is to show that you can, that you have the authority to make sweeping decisions, and you're not afraid to use it.

Don't forget to dress these actions up with a touch of humility, though. You want people to see you as the leader who goes above and beyond, but without appearing egotistical. "It was just the right thing to do," you'll say with a modest smile, while knowing full well that everyone is still buzzing about how you pulled off the impossible.

Symbolism is key, too. Even small actions can have a huge impact if they're loaded with meaning. Declaring an open-door policy to your team? It's not just about being accessible, it's about reinforcing the idea that you're approachable, that you're the kind of leader who's always there in a crisis. Giving up your corner office for a more 'down-to-earth' workspace? You're signaling humility and solidarity with the team, even if you're still very much in charge. These symbolic actions resonate, creating the illusion of leadership without you having to say a word.

Grand gestures and symbolic actions aren't about the actual effect they have, they're about the image they create. You're not solving problems; you're sculpting perceptions. And in this game, perception is reality.

Controlling the Narrative: Tell Them What to Say

If you don't control the story, someone else will and that's the last thing you want. Controlling the narrative is about ensuring that no matter what happens, you're always cast in the best possible light. It's not enough to simply succeed; people need to see you succeeding, and more importantly, they need to believe that any setback or misstep was all part of the plan. Think of yourself as the director of a film, carefully editing out the bad takes and presenting only the most flattering version to the audience.

Start with the facts then reshape them. Sure, something might have gone wrong, but the story you tell is one of resilience, quick thinking, and decisive action. The failed project? That was an intentional learning experience, a necessary step toward something even greater. The internal conflict? Merely a test of your leadership skills, which you, of course, passed with flying colors. Always frame the narrative so that no matter what, you emerge looking smart, strategic, and in control.

Timing is everything when it comes to controlling the narrative. You want to get ahead of the story, shaping it before anyone else has the chance. Drop a carefully placed hint about your intentions before something goes public, so that when the news does break, it fits perfectly into the narrative you've already set. This way, everyone's just following your lead, repeating the story you've crafted.

Don't be afraid to revise history a little. People's memories are surprisingly malleable, especially when they've already bought into the idea that you're a brilliant leader. Did that major initiative nearly collapse under your watch? Not according to your version of events. By the time you're done retelling it, the near-miss becomes a stroke of genius, something you foresaw and corrected just in time.

Controlling the narrative also means controlling the voices within it. Make sure your loyal supporters are vocal, spreading the word about your achievements and reinforcing the story you want told. Whether it's through casual conversations, social media posts, or official company communications, these voices should echo the narrative you've crafted. They're your PR team, whether they realize it or not.

Make sure the narrative sticks, even when things aren't going your way. If a crisis hits, don't panic. Spin it. Frame it as part of your long-term vision, a challenge you expected and are already handling with grace. People love a comeback story, especially if you're the one telling it.

Controlling the narrative is about making sure every story that's told about you serves your goals. You're not just the subject of the story, you're the author. And if you write the script well enough, everyone else will follow it without question.

Promoting a Cult of Loyalty: Protect the Leader

Loyalty is valuable, but absolute loyalty, priceless. Building a cult of loyalty means more than just fostering trust or respect; it means creating an environment where loyalty to you is the defining characteristic. It's no longer about doing what's right or even what's best for the group; it's about doing what's best for you, and your followers are more than happy to oblige. The cult of loyalty is a manipulation masterpiece: when everyone's invested in you, dissent becomes treason, and personal ambition gets tied to your success.

The first step in promoting a cult of loyalty is to make it clear that loyalty is the ultimate currency in your world. You reward it publicly, lavishly, and often. The people who back you without question are promoted, praised, and given more influence. The message is obvious: if you want to thrive here, align yourself with me. Success isn't just about performance, it's about allegiance.

At the same time, you create consequences for disloyalty. These don't have to be overt, but they should be unmistakable. A whisper campaign against someone who questioned you, an assignment mysteriously going to someone else, a subtle freezing out from key meetings all quiet reminders that loyalty isn't optional. Once people start seeing what happens when loyalty wavers, they'll be too afraid to step out of line.

The key to making this work is to tie loyalty to identity. People should feel like their sense of self, their place in the organization, even their future, is bound up with being loyal to you. It's not just about what they do; it's about who they are. You can promote this by fostering a "we're in this together" atmosphere. Frame loyalty to you as loyalty to the mission, the vision, the team. Questioning you isn't just insubordination, it's a betrayal of the entire group.

Then comes the cult part: make them feel that loyalty is a two-way street. This isn't a dictatorship (at least, not outwardly) you care about them, and they, in turn, must care about you. Share stories about how you've always stood by your loyal followers, even in tough times. Build a narrative where loyalty isn't just one way; it's reciprocal. In reality, you may not lift a finger for them when things go south, but the illusion is what counts. They'll be convinced that sticking with you through thick and thin is the safest, smartest, and most rewarding path.

When someone does dare to step out of line? Make an example out of them. Publicly, you might seem forgiving and measured, but behind the scenes, ensure that the message is crystal clear: betrayal will not be tolerated. They'll be sidelined, shut down, or quietly phased out. The group will watch and learn. The lesson is simple: loyalty to you is non-negotiable.

A cult of loyalty doesn't just protect you, it empowers you. It turns your followers into guardians of your influence, willing to do anything to maintain their place in your orbit.

Creating Dependency: Aren't You Glad I'm Here

Loyalty is one thing, but true control comes when people feel they need you to survive. Creating dependency is a masterstroke of manipulation, where your followers believe their success, and even their ability to function, is tied directly to you. It's not enough for them to respect or admire you; they need to feel that without your guidance, they'd be lost. Once you've made people dependent on you, they'll do anything to stay in your good graces, and they'll be far less likely to ever question your authority.

The first step in fostering dependency is to present yourself as the indispensable problem-solver. Every major success, every key decision frames it so that it appears to hinge on your involvement. You're the one who swoops in at the last moment to provide the brilliant solution, the one who has the answers no one else can see. You don't just solve the problem; you make sure everyone knows it couldn't have been solved without you. It's not arrogance, it's just a fact. Slowly but surely, people start to internalize the idea that they can't function effectively without your input.

Don't just stop at solving problems. Offer guidance, even when it's not explicitly asked for. Position yourself as the mentor who always knows best, the one with the experience and insight to steer them in the right direction. Your advice, even on small issues, should become something they rely on. At first, it's just small decisions like how to handle a tricky client, what tone to use in an email but over time, they'll start to second-guess themselves without your approval. You've become their crutch, and once that happens, they'll be too afraid to make a move without checking in with you first.

It's also important to subtly undermine their confidence. Nothing too obvious, just small reminders that they're better off with your guidance. A few well-placed comments like, "I'm glad you asked me first this could've gone badly if you hadn't," or "I'm not sure everyone else would've caught that mistake, but I've been through this before," can go a long way. You're not tearing them down directly, you're just reinforcing the idea that they need your expertise to avoid disaster.

Dependency also thrives when you create complexity. Make certain processes or decisions appear more difficult than they actually are, and then position yourself as the one who can navigate those complexities. Whether it's understanding company politics, managing key relationships, or mastering some obscure technical process, you make it seem like only you can truly handle these tasks. The more they believe that these areas are beyond them, the more they'll depend on you to manage them.

Of course, none of this works if they realize they're being manipulated, so be careful not to overplay your hand. Dependency needs to feel organic, like it's a natural outcome of your brilliance and their need for guidance. Once they're dependent on you, they won't even want to challenge you. They'll believe that without you, they'd be adrift professionally, maybe even personally.

When people feel they can't succeed without you, they'll not only stay loyal, but they'll also defend you fiercely. After all, they're not just defending you, they're protecting the foundation of their own success.

Emotional Manipulation: Understanding Drivers

When logic fails, emotions take over. If you want to truly control people, you need to master the art of emotional manipulation. It's not about playing fair, it's about playing to their feelings, their fears, their desires. Get people to feel something, and you can get them to do almost anything. Emotions cloud judgment, override reason, and make people act against their own interests all of which can be used to your advantage.

The first step is to understand what drives the people around you. What are they afraid of? What do they crave? Emotional manipulation works best when it's tailored to the individual. Some people need validation, others fear rejection, and many are desperate for approval. Once you figure out what makes them tick, you can use it to guide their behavior.

Fear is a particularly powerful tool. When people are afraid, they make rash decisions, and fear can be stoked in subtle ways. A casual remark about potential layoffs, a cryptic comment about how "things might be changing soon," or even a simple look of disappointment can set off alarm bells. Fear of losing status, losing favor, or losing security will push people to do whatever it takes to stay on the right side of things.

Guilt is another highly effective emotion. Make people feel like they owe you something, that they've let you down, or that they're not pulling their weight, and they'll bend over backward to make it right. You don't even have to directly accuse them; just a few well-timed sighs, a disappointed look, or a remark like, "I was really counting on you," will do the trick. People hate feeling like they've failed someone they respect, and they'll work even harder to win back your approval.

On the flip side, you can use flattery and praise to emotionally manipulate as well. People crave validation, and when you give it to them, they become emotionally invested in you. Praise them for their hard work, but make it conditional: "You're one of the few people I can really count on," or "I knew you'd come through, others just don't have what it takes." These compliments aren't just about making them feel good; they're about making them feel dependent on your approval. Once they're hooked on that emotional high, they'll do whatever it takes to keep receiving it.

Empathy, or at least the appearance of it, is so important. People want to feel understood, and by feigning concern for their personal struggles, you can create a bond that feels genuine, even if it's purely transactional on your end. Listen to their problems, nod at the right times, maybe even offer a few words of sympathy. By making them feel like you're emotionally invested in their well-being, you can deepen their loyalty and make them more likely to do what you want in return.

Never underestimate the power of gratitude. Make people feel indebted to you emotionally. You helped them out in a tough spot, gave them advice when they needed it most, or simply "believed in them" when no one else did. That emotional debt is hard to repay, and people will go to great lengths to try. They'll stick by you, support you, and defend you all because they feel emotionally tied to you in a way they can't quite explain.

Emotional manipulation is about using people's feelings as leverage. It's subtle, it's powerful, and when done right, it's almost impossible to detect. People won't realize they're being manipulated; they'll just feel compelled to act, convinced that they're following their own hearts when, in fact, you've been pulling the strings all along.

Summary

Leadership isn't about having the best ideas; it's about making people believe you do. In this chapter, you learned how to craft a powerful, visionary persona to manipulate perception and create influence. From self-promotion to charismatic speaking, it covered how to dominate the room and manipulate emotions to get others to follow.

Key strategies included creating an aura of certainty, speaking with confidence even when unsure, and mastering the art of self-promotion without coming off as arrogant. You explored how to get others to sing your praises, use charm and flattery to lower defenses, and employ performative empathy to gain trust and loyalty.

By using heroic storytelling and mythmaking, you discovered how to elevate your persona into something larger-than-life. The chapter also highlighted the importance of controlling the narrative, ensuring that any setback could be reframed as part of your grand plan. Grand gestures, symbolic actions, and fostering dependency were shown as methods to create a strong grip on those around you, ensuring that people not only respected you but felt they needed you for their own success.

Ultimately, the chapter emphasized the power of emotional manipulation. Whether through fear, guilt, or empathy, understanding what drives people emotionally gives you the tools to steer their actions without them realizing they were being controlled.

Chapter 9

Legal and Financial Manipulation

Power isn't just about titles or positions, it's also mastering and manipulating systems. Legal and financial manipulation is where the real influence is exerted, far from public scrutiny and hidden under layers of complexity. This chapter delves into the strategies that allow savvy players to exploit structures designed to ensure fairness. Whether it's dodging taxes, concealing wealth, or rigging contracts, these techniques enable manipulators not just to survive but to thrive. The trick lies in operating within legal frameworks, walking the line between what's permissible and what's forbidden without always crossing it.

Corporate sociopaths view systems not as limitations but as opportunities. Tactics like underreporting income, creating phantom expenses, or engaging in insider trading aren't just ways to boost profits; they're part of a broader strategy to outmaneuver competitors, skirt regulations, and tighten control. Every law or regulation is seen as a hurdle to sidestep, or better yet, exploit. This chapter provides insights into effective methods of financial manipulation, teaching you how to use legal loopholes and strategic deception to your advantage while minimizing risks.

Underreporting Income: Vanishing Profits

One method some business owners use to reduce their tax burden, lower royalties, or downplay their financial success is underreporting income. This involves not disclosing all revenue generated by the business, which can have significant financial benefits, especially in businesses where cash transactions are common.

Imagine running a bar, where sales come through both cash and card payments. Card transactions leave a paper trail, making them difficult to underreport. However, cash transactions present an opportunity. By keeping some of the cash sales off the books, the owner can avoid reporting that income, effectively reducing the sales tax liability potentially saving 20% or more depending on local tax rates. Additionally, avoiding personal income tax on the unreported earnings can nearly double the amount taken home.

This approach can serve multiple purposes beyond just reducing taxes. Underreporting can also create the appearance of lower profitability, which might discourage potential buyers or competitors from showing interest in acquiring your business. When it suits your strategy to delay a sale or stave off attention, manipulating the numbers can buy you time until the situation is more favorable.

However, underreporting income comes with risks. While it may increase overall profit, it can harm you in scenarios where showing higher revenue is more advantageous. For example, if you're looking to sell your business, inflating revenue rather than underreporting it may help increase the valuation. The tactic is the same manipulating perception but used in reverse.

It's important to remember that what's provable matters most. Cash is more difficult to track, but card transactions are auditable and leave a trail. Tax authorities may eventually take a closer look, and ignorance won't be a viable defense in most cases. The risks of getting caught include fines and penalties, and while some business owners may attempt to explain discrepancies as "mistakes" or "oversights," tax agencies generally aren't lenient on intentional misreporting.

Manipulating financial reporting can provide benefits, but it also requires careful consideration of risks and consequences. Always weigh whether the short-term gains are worth the potential long-term costs, especially when the stakes include financial audits and legal scrutiny.

Tax Mitigation: Your Biggest Expense

When it comes to taxes, there's a fine line between being tax-efficient and crossing into illegal territory. While tax evasion is against the law, finding tax-effective solutions within legal frameworks is entirely possible, though it requires caution, as the rules can change frequently, sometimes even retroactively.

The first step in tax efficiency is understanding the various structures available, such as businesses, limited corporations, partnerships, and trusts. Each structure has its pros and cons depending on your situation, and the key is finding what works best for you. Speak to multiple accountants to get varied perspectives. A good accountant won't just say "no" to your idea, they'll offer alternatives that are legal and effective. If a minor tweak can make a plan viable, you've likely found someone worth keeping.

Another consideration is tax jurisdictions. The global economy allows for "tax shopping" finding the best location for your business or personal finances. This isn't practical for everyone; for instance, if you're running a farm, you're tied to a specific physical location. But for IT professionals, accountants, lawyers, and others in services not bound by geography, changing your country of residence or where your company is registered can have a significant impact on your tax liabilities.

For example, at least at the time of writing this book, Estonia offers a digital company option for foreigners, allowing them to register businesses with zero corporate tax. Pair that with a personal tax residency in a country like the UAE, which has zero percent personal income tax, and you can potentially create a very tax-efficient setup. However, let me be clear: I am not an accountant, and this is not tax advice. Always seek guidance from certified professionals, and get multiple opinions, especially if your plan involves any degree of risk.

Risk is a key factor. If you're reducing your tax burden moderately, you're likely to fly under the radar. But if you avoid taxes entirely, you're much more likely to attract scrutiny from authorities. Understanding the risks and positioning yourself accordingly is critical to maintaining a balance between efficiency and legality.

In short, tax planning is about making informed decisions, not about shortcuts. Always get proper tax advice from accredited professionals, and be aware that pushing too far can bring unwanted attention.

Phantom Expenses: Life is Expensive

Phantom expenses refer to another method used to alter financial records, either to reduce taxable profits or to reallocate resources in a way that benefits the business owner. This tactic involves inflating or fabricating costs to change the perception of a company's financial health, potentially shifting money from one area to another. While this approach may sound complex, it's important to understand that the legality and risk vary greatly depending on how it's executed.

In most tax systems, businesses are taxed on their profits, not their revenue. By reporting higher expenses, companies can lower their taxable income. Service fees are a common method used for this, as they're more difficult to track than physical goods. I once encountered a case where someone moved money between companies using service fees, which was completely legal, at least in theory. By exploiting different tax jurisdictions with varying fiscal year start dates, this individual managed to indefinitely postpone paying corporate tax.

He would move the money from company to company, labeling it as "marketing consulting," "tax consulting," or "IT consulting." The key was timing. The money would leave each company before the end of its tax year and be transferred to another company that was just beginning its fiscal year. As a result, the money was never in any company at the close of its tax year, and therefore never had to be reported as profit.

This is where the line between legal and illegal can blur. Having multiple companies and conducting legitimate transactions between them is common practice. However, if those transactions become fictitious or manipulated solely to avoid taxes or mislead stakeholders, you're entering risky territory.

On paper, it looks like your business is spending money on legitimate expenses, consulting fees, services, equipment upgrades. In reality, the money may be going somewhere else, such as into a personal account or another business entity. The aim is to lower taxable profit by increasing reported expenses.

Phantom expenses can be more than just a tax tool; they can also be used strategically in corporate environments to damage competitors or manipulate internal finances. For example, shifting an expense from one budget to another can make one department look worse while keeping overall company finances intact.

It's crucial to remember that inflating expenses to reduce tax liabilities is illegal and is considered tax evasion, which can carry severe consequences. Always consider the risks carefully, and consult with legal and financial professionals before engaging in any financial strategies. Large, obvious phantom expenses are far more likely to attract unwanted attention from auditors or regulators, so if you're operating in any legal gray areas, it's important to ensure you're compliant with all relevant regulations.

Phantom expenses can offer significant advantages, but the stakes are high. Understanding the legal framework and the potential risks is essential in determining whether or not this strategy aligns with your business goals. Always seek professional advice, and keep in mind that pushing the boundaries too far could invite scrutiny.

Insider Trading: First Mover Advantage

Insider trading refers to the illegal act of buying or selling shares of a publicly listed company based on non-public information. In most jurisdictions, strict regulations are in place to prevent this. For example, senior directors of publicly traded companies, as well as their family members and close associates, are often subject to a blackout period typically around three months during which they cannot trade the company's shares. This is designed to prevent them from using confidential information, like an upcoming merger or disappointing earnings, for personal financial gain.

Stock markets are meant to be free and fair, relying on all participants having equal access to information. This is why publicly listed companies are required to release detailed financial reports, sometimes quarterly, that disclose key information such as major projects, revenue, leadership changes, shareholder interests, and potential conflicts. This ensures that all investors are working with the same data when making decisions, whether it's buying or selling shares.

The problem with insider trading becomes apparent when someone has access to privileged information ahead of public disclosure. For example, if you know that a major tech company's latest mobile phone launch has underperformed, and this hasn't yet been announced, you could sell your shares before the public finds out. Once the news is out, and others start selling, the stock price will likely drop. Your ability to act on this information before anyone else gives you an unfair advantage over the rest of the market.

Insider trading is particularly prevalent in certain industries. In places like the City of London, it's not uncommon to overhear investment managers and brokers sharing insider tips over a drink in the local pub. While investment firms may try to present this as having better research or analysis, the reality is often more about sharing confidential information that can influence market decisions.

The challenge for these firms isn't making money; it's getting away with it. Regulators are constantly on the lookout for abnormal profits. If most investment managers are generating returns between 7% and 12% annually and one manager suddenly pulls in an 80% return, it raises eyebrows. The fundamental principle of investing in a well-regulated market is that risk and reward are balanced. In other words, higher-risk investments can bring higher returns, but they can also lead to greater losses. Conversely, lower-risk investments generate lesser returns with lesser losses. If an investment manager is spreading risk across various assets, the risk and therefore the returns should average out.

When selecting an investment manager, it might seem tempting to go with someone who has a history of exceptional returns, but that could be a red flag. A manager who delivers a steady return of 5%–10% above inflation year after year is likely manipulating the system. A few years of unusually high returns, say 50% or more, suggest that they are cheating too much, and their days of operating under the radar are probably numbered.

I once worked in a think tank tasked with finding ways to improve investment returns. While most of the group focused on developing advanced analysis techniques, I submitted a different proposal. I argued that we already knew how to significantly boost returns through insider trading. The real challenge was figuring out how to avoid getting caught. I proposed that the firm invest in an unnecessarily complicated AI system, one so complex that even top computer scientists couldn't fully explain how it worked. Then create a large marketing campaign that touted the never seen before accuracy of this AI, while behind the scenes, traditional insider trading would be used to generate high returns. When regulators eventually flagged the fund for investigation due to its high performance, the firm could point to the AI and claim it was simply outsmarting the market.

Disclaimer: I am not advising you to engage in insider trading, it is illegal simple as that. This is simply an example of how some exploit the system.

Unlike most of this book this is not an area where ethical boundaries are blurred. Even though insider trading is common in certain circles, it remains illegal, and the penalties are severe.

Kickbacks and Bribes: Greasing the Wheels

In many countries, bribes and kickbacks are considered illegal and are tightly regulated by anti-corruption laws. However, in certain regions, these practices may be considered a normal part of doing business. In parts of Africa, Asia, and the Middle East, for example, "facilitation payments" can be expected for getting deals through. The form and subtlety of these transactions vary by culture, and the language used to describe them may differ, but the effect remains similar.

Elsewhere, companies use terms like "commissions" or "finder's fees" to incentivize behavior, which while legal, can create negative outcomes. For instance, commissions contributed to the 2007-2009 global financial crash, especially in industries like mortgages, where sales people were encouraged to give loans to people who couldn't afford to pay them back. This resulted in a worldwide mortgage market collapse. Causing pain and suffering all around the world.

It's also worth remembering that bribery isn't always cash exchanging hands. It can take many forms, lavish gifts, promotions, entertainment, or a well timed favor. The more underpaid or under-resourced a gatekeeper is, the more likely they are to accept these incentives. For example, in countries where police forces are underfunded, officers may be more open to accepting bribes compared to their well-compensated counterparts in wealthier nations.

Business relationships often determine the success of securing a deal. You might be bidding on a government contract or trying to secure a partnership with a key supplier, and "incentivizing" decision-makers could be a tool used to ensure success. While commissions may remain above board, a small, well-timed gift or favor can tip the scales, pushing your bid ahead or helping your paperwork sail through.

Kickbacks are particularly common in industries where decision-makers have concentrated power like construction, defense contracts, pharmaceuticals, and similar sectors. A kickback usually follows after a deal closes, rewarding the individual who facilitated the agreement. This could take the form of a consultancy contract or a bonus that benefits both parties while keeping everything discreet.

Bribes, by contrast, are more upfront. They're used to influence decisions in real time whether it's getting a customs officer to overlook a shipment or encouraging a local official to support your project. Cash isn't always involved; the "payment" could be a lavish trip or tickets to an exclusive event that helps sway the decision-maker in your favor.

Discretion is vital. Anti-corruption laws are strict in many countries, and overt bribes or kickbacks can land you in trouble. The key is making everything look legitimate on the surface, whether by funneling payments through consulting contracts or turning favors into business deals that provide hidden profits. The goal is to avoid raising suspicion, especially when operating in regions with tough anti-bribery regulations.

It's also important to be mindful of excess. Overusing bribes or kickbacks can raise red flags. If deals start looking too good to be true or your gifts become too generous, people may start asking questions. Subtlety and restraint are key. The objective isn't to throw money at every problem but to ensure the right people get just enough to keep the wheels turning in your favor.

In the end, it's essential to know the local legal frameworks and cultural expectations before engaging in activities that could be seen as bribery or kickbacks. Always stay informed and seek legal counsel when necessary to ensure you remain compliant with the law.

Financial Pressure Tactics: Squeezing

Sometimes, charm and incentives won't get the job done. When subtlety fails, financial pressure tactics come into play, strategies designed to push competitors, partners, or even employees into a corner using the power of leverage. It's less about negotiating and more about applying pressure until the other side has no choice but to comply.

Imagine you're in a deal negotiation, and the other party won't budge. You've tried diplomacy, but they're holding firm. This is where leverage comes into play. Perhaps you control resources they need, or maybe you hold the key to their financial stability. Either way, you apply the pressure until they have no choice but to fold.

One common tactic is withholding payments. Say you owe them money, but the terms of the contract allow some flexibility. You stretch out the payment timeline, just enough to cause financial stress. Their cash flow tightens, and they become desperate. By the time you finally release the funds, they'll be in such a bind that they'll agree to whatever terms you put in front of them, grateful just to keep their business afloat.

Another approach is calling in debts earlier than expected. They thought they had time, but you demand immediate repayment. Panic sets in as they scramble to find the funds. With no way to meet your demands, they're now vulnerable to your next move. You can offer "help," but of course, it comes with new conditions, perhaps a larger stake in their business or a revised deal that favors you. Either way, you've taken control of the situation, and they're too weak to resist.

Cutting off credit or financing is another way to tighten the screws. If you know they rely on credit to keep operations going, you pull the plug. Force them to pay upfront, knowing they can't. As their business falters under the pressure, you step in as the solution. By the time they recover, you'll have cemented your position of power.

Financial pressure isn't limited to companies. Individuals can be just as easily cornered. If employees push for higher wages or better conditions, remind them of the realities of layoffs or restructuring. If a partner gets too ambitious, make it clear their future hinges on your continued support, which you can withdraw whenever it suits you. When their job or livelihood is at stake, people tend to fall in line quickly.

The key is to keep these tactics looking like standard business operations. You're not applying undue pressure, you're just "restructuring" or "adjusting terms." It's all part of the game, and by the time they realize what's happened, it's too late. They've agreed to your terms, thinking they had no other option.

Fraudulent Contracts: Fine Print

Contracts are meant to protect both parties, but when you're in control of the terms, they can be weaponized to benefit you while trapping the other side. A well-crafted contract can look perfectly legitimate on the surface, but the hidden clauses and legal jargon can turn it into a financial trap. Lock the other party into terms they don't fully understand, leaving you with a clear advantage.

I knew someone who worked in car sales, and in that world, contracts were often manipulated. He frequently told me about situations where they would forge a customer's signature to finalize deals. There were three main reasons for this: First, the sales process itself was a bureaucratic maze, and missing a single document could delay or cancel a sale. Forging a signature was their quick "fix" for the problem. Second, errors would sometimes occur during the vehicle manufacturing process. For instance, a customer might order a car with leather seats, but due to a mistake at the factory, the car would be delivered without them. Rather than going through the expensive process of retrofitting the seats, the salesperson would alter the sales contract to make it look as though the customer had never requested leather seats in the first place. Finally, in the finance department, salespeople often falsified documents to push through financing deals, motivated by commissions. These types of unethical practices were rampant during the lead-up to the 2008 financial crisis, and given the commission-driven nature of the automotive industry, it wouldn't be surprising if it were the next sector to face a major scandal.

So, if you are buying a car remember to keep copies and check your paperwork. If you don't it could be very costly.

Imagine negotiating a partnership. The other party is eager to sign, skimming through the document without noticing the hidden traps. Perhaps you've included a clause that allows you to change terms at your discretion or penalties for late payments that are impossible to overcome. By the time they realize they're in trouble, it's too late. You hold all the power.

A particularly clever trick is the "ever-changing terms" clause. At first, the contract looks straightforward. However, there's a hidden provision allowing you to revise the agreement after a certain period always in your favor. The other side thinks they've locked in a deal, but six months later, they're hit with new terms they didn't expect. Whether it's an increase in pricing or changes in deliverables, they're stuck complying with your new demands.

Then, there's deliberate ambiguity. By using vague language like "reasonable," "industry standard," or "to the best of our ability," you leave room for interpretation. The other side may push back, but your lawyers will argue that everything is perfectly clear. Ambiguity gives you the flexibility to shift the contract in your favor whenever you need.

Fraudulent contracts aren't just about squeezing someone into a bad deal, they can be a form of legalized extortion. You create impossible terms that you know the other party can't meet, and when they default, you swoop in with "solutions" that strip them of any remaining power. Or, you take them to court, collect damages, and walk away with whatever you can extract.

The beauty of a fraudulent contract is that, on the surface, it's all legal. The other party signed it, and you're simply following the agreed terms. By the time they realize the full extent of the con, you're already miles ahead, counting your winnings while they're left with the fallout.

Hidden Ownership: Owning Without Owning Up

One of the classics in corporate strategy is hidden ownership, the ability to control assets or businesses without revealing who's really in charge. This isn't just about staying under the radar; it's about gaining influence and wealth while avoiding scrutiny. Think of it like Sun Tzu's The Art of War: "All warfare is based on deception." By hiding your ownership, you're denying your rivals key information, keeping them guessing and unprepared.

Let's say you're planning to acquire a company. You don't want competitors, regulators, or even the public to know you're behind the move. Maybe it's part of a plan to dominate a market, or you want to avoid spooking shareholders. Hidden ownership lets you pull off the acquisition discreetly, without anyone tracing it back to you. The method is simple: you use intermediaries, shell companies, proxies, or trusted insiders to create a web of entities that shield your identity. On paper, it looks like others are leading the acquisition.

Here's how it works: you set up or buy shell companies across various jurisdictions. These companies officially own the assets, but you remain in control from behind the scenes. Even if someone starts investigating, they'll run into dead ends or find intermediaries who legally "own" the business. You remain safely hidden behind layers of corporate complexity.

Why go through the trouble? Hidden ownership offers deniability. If things go wrong whether it's a business scandal, financial collapse, or legal trouble you stay insulated. Your name never gets dragged through the mud because, officially, you had no involvement. Even if the company is found liable for wrongdoing, you walk away untouched, while others take the blame.

It's also a powerful tool in the competitive landscape. Want to control an industry without drawing attention? Spread your ownership across multiple entities to create the illusion of competition. You can control pricing, supply, and influence market conditions while rivals remain oblivious to your true dominance. It's like controlling every piece on the chessboard, without anyone realizing you're the one making the moves.

Then there are the tax advantages. By hiding ownership through offshore entities, you can shift profits globally, reducing your tax burden in high-cost jurisdictions. It's a legal gray area, exploiting loopholes in international tax laws, and governments are left scrambling to catch up.

If you're feeling particularly strategic, hidden ownership can be weaponized. Want to destabilize a competitor? Slowly acquire shares through various entities, staying under the radar. Once you've built up enough influence, you can push for changes that suit you or orchestrate a hostile takeover without anyone realizing you were behind it until it's too late.

Shell Companies: Perfect Disguise

Shell companies are one of the most effective tools in corporate maneuvering. They allow you to shift money, hide ownership, or conduct business behind the scenes with minimal scrutiny. Essentially, a shell company is a legal entity that exists on paper but doesn't engage in actual business activities like producing goods or services. Its main function is to act as a financial and legal shield, giving you the ability to move assets or obscure your involvement without leaving a direct trail.

The advantage of a shell company lies in its simplicity. All it takes is a registration fee and an experienced attorney, and you've got a fully operational entity that can own property, move funds, or sign contracts.

To anyone examining the paperwork, it looks like a legitimate business. In reality, it's a carefully constructed front, keeping you safely hidden behind a network of corporate structures.

Imagine you've got funds that you'd prefer to keep out of sight, perhaps for tax reasons or simply to protect them from prying eyes. A shell company is the ideal solution. You route the money through the shell, moving it into a jurisdiction with lenient tax laws and confidentiality protections. Now, that money is clean, sitting offshore, and fully under your control. Or maybe you want to conceal your ownership in a business. The shell company becomes the official owner, and your name never appears on the documents.

One of the most effective uses of shell companies is to create complex layers of ownership and transactions. By routing money through multiple shell companies spread across different jurisdictions, you create a paper trail that is almost impossible to untangle. By the time anyone tries to figure out where the money went, they're left following a confusing path through multiple countries, each with its own rules and secrecy provisions.

Shell companies are also useful when you want to manipulate market perceptions or inflate the value of assets. For example, you can set up several shell companies to bid on a property, driving up the price and making it appear as though there's high demand. In reality, you control all the entities involved. Once the price reaches your target, you can sell it off at a profit, leaving someone else to handle the fallout if the market corrects itself.

Then there's fraudulent invoicing, a classic shell company tactic. You set up a shell company to provide "services" to your main business, invoicing for work that was never done. Your main company pays the shell, and the money cycles back to you, often tax-free. To outsiders, it looks like a regular business expense, but it's just a method for moving profits off the books.

Using shell companies does come with risks. If your activities are too obvious, or if regulators notice a pattern of suspicious transactions, they may start asking questions. That's why it's crucial to use shell companies carefully. Layer them, route funds through multiple jurisdictions, and always maintain plausible deniability. If anyone does investigate, you can point to the complex corporate structures and claim you had no direct involvement.

Offshore Accounts: Hiding

When it comes to shielding wealth and minimizing taxes, offshore accounts are still one of the best financial strategies. They're not just a place to store assets; they offer privacy, protection, and insulation from the kind of scrutiny that would raise eyebrows back home. Offshore accounts are the go-to for those looking to keep their financial affairs well out of reach from tax authorities and regulators.

Imagine you've accumulated a significant sum of profits from smart (or sneaky) business practices, income that you'd rather not declare, or gains that came through a few too many loopholes. You don't want that money sitting in a domestic account where it's easily accessible to tax collectors. Instead, you send it offshore to a country with favorable financial laws. These jurisdictions, often referred to as tax havens like the Cayman Islands, Luxembourg, or Switzerland offer minimal tax rates and strict privacy protections, allowing you to keep your wealth intact and far from prying eyes.

The appeal of offshore accounts isn't just about saving on taxes. They provide privacy and protection through privacy laws. In these havens, your assets are effectively shielded from public view, and in many cases, it's near-impossible to link the funds back to you. Whether you're a high-profile individual or a business looking to hide assets, offshore accounts ensure that your financial dealings remain discreet.

They also enable more than just tax minimization. These accounts are key to moving money around the globe quietly and securely. Need to funnel funds through a shell company or shift assets between various jurisdictions? Offshore accounts make it happen without triggering alarms. You can set up offshore trusts or foundations, which hold your wealth on paper but leave you firmly in control. It's a way to maintain influence over your assets while your name remains absent from official records. This system allows you to manage your finances without attracting unwanted attention.

Then there's the rise of cryptocurrencies, which offers a new form of offshore-like anonymity. Digital currencies, like Bitcoin, provide the promise of decentralized financial transactions beyond government reach. At least in theory, they offer the same benefits as an offshore account: protection from oversight and the ability to move money quickly and discreetly. But there's a catch: despite Bitcoin's reputation, its transaction ledger is public, and many exchanges that facilitate the conversion between crypto and traditional currencies share data with authorities. So while cryptocurrency offers potential, it's far from bulletproof when it comes to staying truly anonymous.

Of course, there are risks involved. Governments worldwide are cracking down on tax havens and demanding transparency from financial institutions. But savvy players know how to stay ahead of these efforts by layering their transactions through multiple entities and obscure jurisdictions. By staying flexible and playing the game carefully, you can still reap the rewards of offshore accounts while minimizing exposure.

Exploiting Bankruptcy Laws: Falling Upwards

When your financial empire starts to teeter, bankruptcy laws can be a strategic lifeline rather than a sign of failure. Instead of seeing it as a desperate last resort, you can use bankruptcy as a tool to reorganize, shed liabilities, and protect your assets all within the legal framework.

Bankruptcy laws are designed to give businesses a fresh start, but if you know how to navigate them, they can do much more. Filing for Chapter 11 bankruptcy, for instance, allows you to restructure your debts, keep the business operational, and even renegotiate unfavorable terms. It's not about going under; it's about staying in control while buying time to rebuild and stabilize.

During this process, bankruptcy can serve as a mechanism for getting rid of bad deals or obligations that have been weighing down the company. Whether it's dissolving toxic contracts, discontinuing underperforming business lines, or rejecting leases, bankruptcy gives you the legal means to reset your obligations. Giving you a leaner, more focused operation, free from the burdens that were dragging you down, while your creditors are left holding the bag.

The real advantage comes when you've safeguarded your assets before filing. By moving funds to protected areas offshore accounts, trusts, or shell companies you ensure that the bulk of your wealth is untouchable by the courts. While the bankruptcy clears out your debts, your hidden assets remain safe, allowing you to start fresh without losing what's most valuable to you.

Bankruptcy can also be used as a bargaining chip. The mere threat of filing can push creditors, suppliers, or even lenders to the negotiation table. No one wants to get pennies on the dollar in bankruptcy court, so they may be willing to offer better terms or extend deadlines just to avoid the hassle of a lengthy legal process. In this way, your financial struggles become leverage in securing more favorable terms.

In many cases, top executives have severance packages or bonuses written into their contracts that shield them from the financial fallout. Even as the company goes through the bankruptcy process, they land softly, prepared to move on to the next venture while others deal with the mess.

In the end, exploiting bankruptcy isn't about failure; it's about seeing the system as a way to reset and gain an advantage. With careful planning and a clear understanding of the laws, you can use bankruptcy as a tool to emerge stronger, leaving your competitors, creditors, and employees dealing with the aftermath while you move forward.

Asset Stripping: Take the Gold

When a company's value lies more in its assets than its operations, asset stripping becomes the go-to strategy. Instead of trying to save a failing business, the focus shifts to extracting everything of worth and moving on. It's about leveraging the valuable pieces whether it's real estate, equipment, or intellectual property while leaving the rest to wither.

Here's how it plays out: you acquire a struggling company, not for its business potential but for its hidden assets. Maybe it's sitting on prime real estate, expensive machinery, or valuable contracts. The business itself might be in decline, but those assets are worth gold. Once in control, you start liquidating. The real estate goes up for sale, the equipment gets auctioned off, and any intellectual property is monetized through licensing or sales. The aim is simply to get as much value as possible without bothering to fix the underlying problems.

For instance, you buy a manufacturing company that's bleeding cash but owns a valuable plot of land. Instead of trying to turn the company around, you offload the real estate, pocket the proceeds, and leave the company to deal with its mounting issues. Employees and creditors are left scrambling, but you walk away with a hefty profit.

A common tactic is spinning off profitable divisions. If the company has one part that's doing well amidst the chaos, you separate it into a standalone entity, letting the rest of the company sink under its operational challenges. You've stripped out the good part and left the struggling business to fend for itself, owning the valuable new entity outright.

Asset stripping can also involve exploiting intellectual property. Whether it's patents, trademarks, or proprietary technology, these non-physical assets can be sold or licensed for a quick return. You don't have to deal with the daily grind of running a business; you're simply cashing in on what already exists.

Perhaps the most ruthless form of asset stripping is when you go after cash reserves or even pension funds. By draining the company's financial resources or tapping into pension money earmarked for employees, you leave the business unable to recover while padding your own pockets. Employees and retirees are left empty-handed, but by then, you've already moved on.

This strategy leaves wreckage in its wake, employees lose their jobs, creditors go unpaid, and the company's left in tatters. But asset stripping isn't about building for the future; it's about extracting value as quickly and efficiently as possible. The goal is to walk away with profit, leaving the aftermath for someone else to deal with.

Ponzi Schemes: Get in Quick

In the world of financial schemes, Ponzi schemes have got to be the most notorious. At their core, they're simple: you attract investors by promising high returns, then use the money from newer investors to pay off the earlier ones. The whole operation hinges on constantly bringing in fresh money. As long as the flow continues, the scheme survives but when it dries up, everything collapses.

Here's how it works: You start by offering impressive returns far above what most people could expect elsewhere. The business pitch doesn't even need to hold water; what matters is the promise of quick and easy money. The early investors receive their returns, paid from the funds of newer investors, creating the illusion that the scheme is successful. As word spreads, more people rush to invest, and the cycle keeps repeating itself until it inevitably breaks down.

The power of the Ponzi scheme lies in its self-sustaining nature. As long as you can keep attracting new participants, the scheme rolls on, with earlier investors happy to see their returns and new investors eager to join the action. But the moment new money stops flowing in, the scheme collapses. By then, though, if you've played your cards right, you've already secured enough for yourself, and the fallout becomes someone else's problem.

It's important to note that Ponzi schemes, in their pure financial form, are illegal in most jurisdictions. However, schemes can be dressed up with products to skirt legal boundaries. Some multi-level marketing (MLM) setups operate on a similar model, where participants sell products but also recruit others, earning a percentage from those sales. While these systems might still carry the hallmarks of a Ponzi scheme, they often operate within the law by tying their structure to a physical product.

The trick to a good Ponzi scheme is making it look legitimate. You'll need to set up shop like a bona fide investment firm, complete with glossy reports and convincing presentations. It's about creating the illusion of a thriving business, even if that business doesn't actually exist. Keep everything just opaque enough that no one digs too deep, and if they do, smooth them over with half-truths or a small payout to keep them quiet.

The success of these schemes relies heavily on greed and the fear of missing out. Investors, seeing others reap the rewards, are desperate to get in on the action. This creates a cycle of increasing investment and buzz. But no Ponzi scheme lasts forever. Eventually, new investors stop showing up, or existing ones want their money back faster than you can provide it. When the collapse begins, you've either stashed away enough to disappear or position yourself as an innocent party who was just as blindsided as everyone else.

For those looking to push the limits, there's even the double Ponzi running multiple schemes at once. If one starts faltering, you pull funds from another to prop it up temporarily. It's a dangerous game, but the goal in a Ponzi scheme isn't longevity, it's about extracting as much as possible before the inevitable collapse.

There's also the pyramid scheme variation, where participants recruit others, creating a layered structure. Each new level of recruits feeds into the one above, all thinking they're advancing, but in reality, they're simply supporting the shaky system. The more people you can rope in, the longer the scheme can sustain itself, and the bigger your payday.

Ponzi schemes are a high-stakes con. The collapse is certain, and when it comes, there will be consequences, lawsuits, investigations, and potentially criminal charges. But if you've played the game right, you'll be long gone, far removed from the chaos, living off the fortunes you siphoned from your unwitting investors.

Summary

This chapter outlines the strategies for mastering legal and financial manipulation, emphasizing that corporate rules and regulations, in the right hands, are flexible tools to be shaped as needed. Techniques like underreporting income and inflating phantom expenses allow business owners to adjust financial realities whether it's reducing tax liabilities, avoiding financial scrutiny, or fending off potential competitors. These tactics can be applied discreetly or boldly, depending on the situation. Tax mitigation, for example, isn't just about minimizing taxes, it's about understanding different jurisdictions, structures, and how to use them to your advantage without crossing legal lines.

Further, insider trading and kickbacks demonstrate the power of information and incentives to drive outcomes in your favor. Manipulating financial reports, creating fraudulent contracts, or employing hidden ownership structures enables control without direct accountability, allowing you to influence from behind the scenes. Tools like shell companies, offshore accounts, and strategic use of bankruptcy laws are methods designed to protect assets, maintain cash flow, and avoid scrutiny.

More aggressive tactics, such as asset stripping and Ponzi schemes, exploit system weaknesses for significant short-term gains, often leaving others to face the fallout. Always check the laws and seek financial advice. These concepts are worth understanding no matter where you operate, but it doesn't mean these strategies are available or legal in your jurisdiction.

Chapter 10

Sabotage and Subterfuge

Sabotage and subterfuge are powerful, behind-the-scenes tools used to derail competitors without direct confrontation. Whether it's blocking key resources, tampering with products, or spreading false allegations, sabotage allows you to quietly undermine others while keeping your hands clean. It's important to note that while these tactics may be presented for their strategic value, they can also cross legal and ethical boundaries. Always ensure that you're operating within the law and seek professional advice before engaging in any business strategy that could have serious consequences.

Sabotage isn't about grand gestures, it's about small, subtle actions that create significant disruption over time. By attacking key resources, disrupting communication, or even undermining the trust between colleagues, you can quietly destabilize projects and careers without anyone suspecting your involvement. In this chapter, we'll explore various techniques of sabotage and subterfuge, focusing on how to weaken competitors without leaving a trace. But again, proceed with caution: these strategies can lead to serious repercussions, so always stay on the right side of the law.

Blocking Key Resources: Starve the Project

This approach allows you to undermine their success without direct confrontation. If they lack the necessary tools, time, or support, their projects are destined to fail, and you can remain above suspicion.

Resource blocking operates discreetly. When a project fails due to insufficient resources, it appears to be a result of poor planning or bad luck, not sabotage.

Consider the budget. If you control the finances, you can ensure a project struggles by making strategic cuts. By trimming essential funds while promoting other, less critical expenses, you can create delays that jeopardize timelines and tarnish reputations.

If you don't control the budget, you can still create obstacles through delays and miscommunication. If a team relies on data from another department, you might suggest postponing their inquiry, diverting attention and stalling progress without any direct interference.

Withholding personnel is another effective tactic. When key team members are needed, ensure they are "unavailable" due to other commitments or vacations, leaving the project understaffed at crucial moments.

Information access is equally critical. By controlling the flow of important data like market research or performance metrics you can prevent teams from making informed decisions. Simply forgetting to share vital reports can result in missed opportunities.

Physical resources, particularly in tech environments, can be just as important. Delays in hardware orders or misrouting essential equipment can halt progress.

You can also obstruct access to decision-makers. If an executive approval is needed, make sure that executive is tied up with other matters, pushing reviews further down the line and creating mounting pressure on the team.

This strategy often goes unnoticed, as people attribute setbacks to logistics or red tape rather than deliberate action. When you observe a rival project gaining traction, consider quietly restricting their access to vital resources. By the time they realize what's happening, it may be too late to recover.

Deliberate Overloading: Drowning Your Target

Deliberate overloading is another effective strategy for undermining a colleague's success. By piling too many responsibilities onto someone, you create an environment where they are likely to fail, all while appearing to support their growth.

Start by casually suggesting additional tasks, framing them as opportunities for development. For example, ask a colleague already managing client onboarding to also handle the quarterly report. Each new request should seem minor, but cumulatively, it becomes overwhelming.

To heighten the pressure, introduce last-minute urgent tasks. When these requests come from senior executives, it's even harder for them to say no. Before long, they're working late and struggling to keep up, while you position yourself as the supportive teammate.

Complexity matters too. Assign tasks that require frequent shifts in focus like managing client calls, financial analysis, and software deployment all in one day. This constant switching can be mentally exhausting and significantly impact their performance.

Maintain a sense of urgency around every task, ensuring they feel the pressure to deliver on multiple fronts. Remind them that everything is a top priority, which can lead to mistakes and missed deadlines. Encourage them to handle tasks independently, suggesting they show initiative. This isolates them and ensures they lack support when they need it most. Over time, burnout becomes inevitable.

When their performance slips, the blame won't fall on you. You'll appear to be a helpful colleague, while they look incapable of managing their workload. If you offer to help later, it reinforces the perception that they can't keep up, making them even more vulnerable.

Undermining Projects: Saboteur Within

Undermining a project doesn't require overt sabotage; it's about subtle actions that lead to failure over time. The aim is to introduce delays, create confusion, and cause errors, all while maintaining plausible deniability.

Delays are a key tactic. Instead of halting a project, create a series of small setbacks. Miss a meeting or "forget" to send important documents. When asked about progress, frame it as a delay caused by others. The longer these minor issues persist, the more they accumulate into a major problem.

Another effective strategy is to divert attention to other projects. Suggest that urgent matters take precedence, pushing deadlines further back. This gives the impression that you're simply prioritizing work, while the original project languishes.

Errors can also be useful. Provide incorrect information or miscommunicate details to throw the team off course. A small misunderstanding can lead to significant wasted effort, creating chaos without you having to do much at all.

Fostering friction among team members is another way to undermine a project. Encourage misunderstandings about roles or responsibilities, which can lead to conflict and inefficiency. A divided team is far less effective.

You can also slow decision-making by prompting unnecessary debates over trivial issues. This wastes valuable time and creates a sense of urgency as deadlines approach. Your role can appear to be one of caution or thoroughness, masking your true intent.

Passive resistance is another tactic. By showing up late to meetings or being slow to respond to requests, you force others to compensate for your lack of engagement. This can create frustration and lower morale, further hindering the project's progress.

The key to this approach is to ensure that each action can be easily justified. Any misstep can be explained away, making it difficult for others to see your influence. Undermining a project in these subtle ways, you create a scenario where the team struggles to keep up.

Sabotaging Relationships: Breaking Bonds

Targeting someone's relationships is an effective way to undermine their career. A strong network can be an asset, but it can also become a liability if you know how to dismantle it. Sabotaging relationships involves creating distrust and spreading subtle rumors to make colleagues drift apart.

Consider two colleagues who work well together. Their strong bond poses a threat to your interests. To break them apart, introduce small doubts. Casually mentioned to one, "I overheard someone say John wasn't thrilled with how you handled the last presentation." This plants a seed of doubt about John's loyalty.

To escalate this, drop hints over time to create misunderstandings. Tell John that Sarah has been working late without him. "She's probably just trying to catch up, but it seems like she's been pushing ahead without keeping you in the loop." Such nudges will prompt them to notice things that weren't there before, fostering insecurity.

If you want to be more direct, spread a rumor, such as suggesting that one might be interviewing elsewhere. "I heard Sarah's been looking at opportunities with a competitor." This will make John question her loyalty and could lead to further distrust.

You can also share concerns with a higher-up. If a boss relies heavily on an employee, approach them with, "I've noticed something off with Jake's attitude lately." This can create suspicion about Jake while positioning you as a concerned colleague.

In high-pressure situations, leverage crises to escalate tensions. If a project is behind schedule, imply that one colleague is blaming the other. "I think Sarah's been saying it's John's fault." This shifts focus from collaboration to blame.

By strategically weakening these bonds, you can undermine rivals without direct confrontation. This method is subtle yet effective, allowing you to remain undetected while achieving your goals.

False Allegations: Destroy Reputations

If you want to take someone down, a well-placed false allegation can be incredibly effective. It's not about direct confrontation but creating just enough suspicion to make others question their integrity. The key to this tactic is to make the allegation believable but vague enough that it can't be easily dismissed or disproven.

Start by choosing your target and the type of accusation. It needs to be something plausible, like financial misconduct or unethical behavior. For example, "I've heard Sarah has been spending a lot of time alone with the boss lately. Not saying there's anything going on, but it could raise some eyebrows." With a simple comment like that, you've planted a seed of doubt. People start talking, and soon, Sarah's integrity is under quiet scrutiny.

The strength of a false allegation lies in its subtlety. Even without evidence, the suggestion of wrongdoing is often enough to damage someone's reputation. The target will waste time and energy trying to defend themselves, while the rumor continues to spread.

One way to escalate this is by filing an anonymous complaint or raising a "concern" to HR. Something minor like, "I heard Jake might have fudged some numbers on the quarterly report. It's probably nothing, but worth looking into," can trigger an investigation. Even if nothing is found, the fact that Jake was being investigated will linger in people's minds, tarnishing his credibility.

As the rumor spreads, the target's reputation begins to erode. Colleagues may distance themselves, and management might become hesitant to involve the person in key projects. Even if they clear their name, the stigma often remains.

You can also leverage others to spread the rumor. Casually mentioned to a few people, "I heard multiple folks talking about Jake being under investigation for financial discrepancies." By the time it reaches the wider office, the rumor will feel like common knowledge, even if it started from nothing.

A well-timed false allegation can have a lasting impact, especially if your target is on the verge of a promotion or leading an important project. A subtle suggestion of misconduct or cutting corners could be enough to sideline them at a crucial moment.

The lasting power of a false allegation isn't in proving someone guilty; it's in planting doubt that sticks with them. Even after the accusation is disproven, people will still remember that something was off, and that doubt is often all it takes to undermine someone's career.

Fake Documents or Records: Rewriting Reality

Few tactics are as effective or discreet as creating or altering documents. This isn't about big, flashy lies, it's about subtle changes that shift perception, shape reality, and give you control. By tampering with records, you can undermine careers, disrupt projects, or protect yourself, all while keeping your hands clean.

Take a simple fake email, for instance. Want to make someone look incompetent? Fabricate an email thread where they agreed to an unrealistic deadline or admitted to an error. "Just confirming you agreed to have the report by Wednesday..." Even if they never made that promise, the email says otherwise, leaving them scrambling to explain. It's a quiet, effective way to make them look disorganized or dishonest without any direct confrontation.

Financial reports are another prime target. Small adjustments to the numbers can turn a project from profitable to problematic. Imagine subtly changing a budget line to make a successful department look like it's overspending. When the numbers don't match up, it's their credibility on the line, and with the altered documents in hand, you've got the upper hand in any dispute.

Another effective move is to create confusion. Maybe your competition for a promotion submits a key report. You quietly swap it with an error-filled version and then raise concerns. "I think we got the wrong version. Dave's report is full of mistakes." Now Dave is left trying to fix a problem he didn't cause, while his reliability is questioned. You, of course, remain the helpful colleague pointing out the issue.

Document tampering isn't just for attacking others it's also a great defensive tool. Let's say you've been cutting corners or making questionable decisions. A quick tweak to meeting minutes or backdated approval emails can cover your tracks. Didn't get sign-off on a risky move? No problem just adding it to the records after the fact. Need to make it look like you foresaw a project's failure? Edit the meeting notes to show you raised concerns months ago. People trust records, and no one's going to remember every detail from past discussions.

Want to go further? Forge a glowing recommendation from a senior leader or tweak your performance review. If a promotion's on the line, these small adjustments can make all the difference. Even a fake LinkedIn endorsement can give you an edge over rivals relying on legitimate feedback.

Fake documents hold so much power because of how hard they are to disprove. In corporate environments, written records are treated as fact. By the time anyone notices something's off, the damage is done. Whether you're trying to sabotage a competitor, cover your mistakes, or boost your own reputation, altering documents allows you to control the narrative from the shadows without leaving a trace.

Planting False Evidence: Framing Rivals

Planting false evidence is about setting up a situation where someone appears guilty of something they didn't do, and letting the fallout take care of the rest. The beauty of this approach lies in its subtlety: you don't need to directly confront your target. You let the evidence speak for itself, while you stay far from the blame.

The key to planting false evidence is to make it believable, yet just damaging enough to raise doubts. Take small steps. Let's say you're aiming to make someone look incompetent. You can alter a report they're responsible for, inserting a mistake that will catch the eye of their boss. Perhaps a financial discrepancy or a missing key detail is something subtle but noticeable. When they're questioned, they'll have no idea how the error slipped through, but it will still reflect poorly on them.

Another method is slipping sensitive information where it doesn't belong. Say your target is responsible for handling confidential client data. By placing that data in an unsecured location, like an email or a shared drive, you make it seem like they were careless. When a breach is discovered, they're the one who looks irresponsible, even though they never made the mistake.

Expense reports offer another opportunity. You could add a few extra charges to their account: a fancy dinner, a trip that wasn't approved, or duplicate expenses. When accounting flags it, they'll be caught off guard. The suspicion alone can be enough to damage their credibility, regardless of whether they eventually clear their name.

If you want to create real chaos, frame someone for a larger offense. You could fabricate emails that suggest they've been leaking confidential information or meeting with competitors. Forward sensitive documents to them and then claim they shouldn't have had access. When questioned, they'll look like they've been playing a dangerous game, even if they can't explain how it happened.

For an added layer of protection, involve others. Drop an incriminating document into a shared folder or public space where it will inevitably be found by someone else. When the discovery is made, you're just another bystander, far removed from the incident.

One classic example is using personal devices against company policy. Plant sensitive company files on their personal phone or laptop. When IT runs an audit, they'll find evidence that the person was using personal devices for business, a serious violation in many companies. Even if they try to argue they didn't do it, the evidence will be hard to refute.

Another variation is creating a false trail of negligence. Alter safety or compliance reports to make it seem like your target missed deadlines or failed to address important issues. Even if they can eventually prove the records were tampered with, the damage to their reputation will be done.

Finally, consider framing someone for unethical behavior. Plant emails or texts that suggest they've been inappropriately communicating with a competitor or violating insider trading rules. The goal here is not to prove wrongdoing, but to create enough suspicion that their reputation takes a hit.

The advantage of planting false evidence is that it forces your target to defend themselves against something they didn't do, while you remain out of the spotlight. Even if they manage to clear their name, their reputation will still be tarnished, and their credibility weakened. In the end, it's not about proving guilt, it's about creating doubt. And once that doubt is there, it's almost impossible to erase.

Data Tampering: Corrupting the Core

Data is the backbone of decision-making. Manipulating that data can destabilize projects, disrupt operations, and undermine reputations without leaving any obvious trace. The key to data tampering is subtlety and small changes that compound over time, causing chaos without raising immediate suspicion.

Start with minor tweaks. Let's say your target is managing a project, and everything is running smoothly. A small adjustment to financial data moving a decimal point or misreporting costs can make their budget projections fall apart. The goal is to introduce small errors that aren't immediately noticed but build up, leading to delays and confusion.

Another tactic is shifting project timelines in subtle ways. Alter deadlines in the project management tool by just a day or two, creating an illusion of missed targets. Team members start blaming each other for dropped balls, and the project slowly derail, all while the data changes remain unnoticed.

Tampering with key performance data can also be a powerful tool. For instance, if your rival relies on sales forecasts or market research, small adjustments to those metrics can lead to faulty decisions. Skewing the data just enough ensures that they're basing their strategy on flawed information, setting them up for failure without them ever realizing why.

Inventory management offers another opening. By altering stock levels marking key items as out of stock or over-ordering non-essentials you can disrupt supply chains and drive up costs. No one will suspect sabotage, as it looks like incompetence, system glitches or vendor errors.

Corrupting historical data is another effective strategy. Alter past performance metrics to make current results look worse in comparison, or inflate past achievements to set unrealistic expectations. Either way, your target ends up looking incompetent as they scramble to explain the discrepancies.

In highly technical fields, tampering with data used for algorithms or AI can lead to devastating results. A slight change in the training data for a model could result in inaccurate predictions or poor decision-making. The consequences might not be felt immediately, but when they do, they'll be far-reaching.

A classic tactic is causing key data files to go missing or become corrupted at critical moments. A major report due? Ensure the file can't be accessed or becomes riddled with errors just before submission. Your target will waste time scrambling to recover or recreate the data, often missing deadlines in the process.

Tampering with audit trails or compliance records is especially damaging in regulated industries. By altering key records, you can make it appear as though your target has missed important regulatory steps or engaged in unethical behavior. Even if they catch the error, the damage to their credibility can be hard to reverse.

Data tampering works because it's invisible. Most people will assume discrepancies are due to system errors or human mistakes, not sabotage. By the time they realize something's wrong, the damage is done.

Technological Sabotage: System Failure

Technology has always been essential to keep corporations running smoothly. That makes technological sabotage a powerful tool to cause disruption without direct confrontation. The key to effective sabotage is small disruptions that accumulate over time, making it look like technical glitches or bad luck rather than intentional sabotage.

Start by introducing minor bugs or glitches into key systems. A software tool that crashes occasionally, or a project management system that shifts deadlines slightly, can cause delays without raising alarms. Your target will waste time troubleshooting issues, while progress slows.

Exploiting existing system vulnerabilities is another effective tactic. If a company uses outdated software or weak security, you can manipulate it to corrupt databases or delay key processes. For example, causing critical data to go missing right before a big presentation will leave your target scrambling to recover, making them look disorganized.

Network slowdowns are another way to create widespread frustration. Overload the network by injecting extra processes or flooding it with traffic, causing delays in emails and other communications. No one will immediately suspect sabotage; instead, they'll blame IT or external factors, all while the company's productivity drops.

Targeting email systems is a classic move. By rerouting or delaying key emails, you can cause your target to miss important deadlines or appear unresponsive. "I never got the email," they'll say, but by the time they recover, the damage is done.

For deeper sabotage, consider planting spyware or keyloggers. These tools let you monitor your target's activities, giving you access to sensitive information or allowing you to anticipate their next move.

If you're willing to take a bigger risk, unleash malware or ransomware. Timing this before a major event like a product launch can cripple operations. The company scrambles to restore systems while deadlines loom, and you remain out of the spotlight.

Corrupting backups and recovery systems is another powerful method. When the company tries to recover from a crash or breach, they'll find their backup systems disabled or compromised. Without a safety net, recovery becomes a drawn-out, costly process.

Disabling security protocols is another option. Leave a backdoor open or lower firewall settings, allowing external attacks or breaches to occur. It looks like an IT failure or external threat, but you orchestrated the vulnerability.

Even hardware sabotage can be effective. Slowing down or disabling key devices like printers or computers creates frustration and hinders productivity. It looks like malfunctioning equipment, but in reality, you've ensured the constant disruptions.

Finally, disrupting communication channels like Zoom or Teams at key moments can derail meetings or prevent effective collaboration. When messages don't go through or video calls fail, confusion reigns, and progress stalls.

Technological sabotage allows you to create chaos from behind the scenes. Small disruptions gradually build into major issues, all while keeping you far from suspicion.

Disrupting Communication: Cutting the Lifeline

Disrupting communication is an incredibly effective way to sabotage someone or a project. The key is to create small delays and confusion without drawing attention.

Start by delaying important emails or misrouting messages, ensuring critical information doesn't arrive on time. Even a missed deadline or delayed response can derail plans and cause frustration. Miscommunicating meeting times or creating scheduling conflicts for key people also throws projects off track.

Technology provides easy opportunities. A "glitch" during a video call or a file that fails to upload at a key moment can undermine even the most prepared colleague. These issues seem like technical problems, but the impact is real delayed progress and damaged credibility.

Excluding someone from important email threads or meetings cuts them off from vital updates, leaving them out of the loop. Over time, this makes them appear unreliable or unorganized. Socially, you can prevent key players from having informal conversations where important decisions happen, further isolating them.

Conflicting information is another effective tactic. Send mixed messages to create confusion about priorities, which results in wasted time and frustration. This subtle erosion of communication creates inefficiencies, weakens leadership, and undermines credibility all without leaving a trace.

By carefully controlling the flow of information, you can slow down your target, create delays, and make them look ineffective all while remaining in the background, unnoticed.

Equipment Sabotage: Grinding the Machine to a Halt

Well maintained equipment is essential for smooth operations. A small malfunction at the right time can disrupt entire projects, delay production, and cost millions. Equipment sabotage uses subtle tweaks to disrupt tools and machinery, creating chaos without drawing suspicion.

Start small with computers. If your rival is preparing a critical presentation, tamper with their laptop, slow it down, corrupt a file, or disable the internet connection. They'll be scrambling to fix the issue while their reputation takes a hit.

Shared equipment, like printers or servers, are prime targets. A "broken" printer or software failure can delay entire teams. These small interruptions lead to missed deadlines, frustration, and costly delays.

In industries reliant on heavy machinery, tampering with a critical component a loose wire or missing bolt can bring operations to a halt. Intermittent malfunctions are particularly effective, making it difficult for technicians to diagnose the problem. The result? Endless troubleshooting, wasted time, and increasing costs.

Infrastructure sabotage works too. Imagine tampering with the HVAC system during a heatwave productivity plummets as employees struggle to work in discomfort. Or, disrupt the lighting in key offices, causing distractions that impact focus and efficiency.

Even tampering with office supplies can create small but meaningful setbacks. A printer that jams at the worst moment or a broken coffee machine during a busy day these minor inconveniences erode efficiency over time.

For high-impact moves, target security or backup systems. Disabling cameras or access control systems at key moments can lead to data loss or security breaches, all while appearing to be a technical failure. Sabotaging backup power systems ensures that when the lights go out, operations come to a standstill.

Equipment sabotage strikes at the core of what keeps a company running. Calculated disruptions cause delays, increase stress, and weaken your rivals' performance all while looking like harmless technical issues.

Destroying or Stealing Intellectual Property: Valuable Asset

Intellectual property (IP) keeps corporate ideas safe and is often more valuable than physical assets. Whether it's software, research, or strategic plans, IP represents a company's future. Sabotaging or stealing it can cause irreparable damage. The key is precision in targeting the core of what makes your rival valuable.

Deleting or corrupting critical files can have a devastating effect. Imagine a company losing months of research because key documents were erased or designs were subtly altered. A faulty prototype or flawed launch can cost time, money, and reputation before anyone realizes the root cause.

Corrupting version control systems is equally damaging. By mixing up file revisions, you can introduce confusion that derails projects and makes it impossible for teams to recover the correct data. Suddenly, they're working with incorrect information, leading to costly mistakes.

If destruction isn't your goal, stealing IP offers even greater rewards. Slowly siphoning off key data like algorithms, marketing strategies, or prototype designs allows you to quietly collect valuable information without raising suspicion. Forwarding documents to yourself "by accident" or saving files to a USB drive are easy ways to access IP without setting off alarms.

If direct access isn't an option, enlisting third parties like hackers or disgruntled employees can give you what you need without implicating yourself. Once stolen, IP can be sold, leaked, or used to give you an edge in the market. Leaking details of a competitor's new product ahead of its release can destroy their competitive advantage, leaving them scrambling to respond.

Targeting IP during development is particularly effective. Stealing source code or altering software during the design phase can lead to costly fixes later, or worse, flawed products hitting the market. Subtly inserting errors can ensure that the project is doomed to fail without anyone realizing why until it's too late.

Sabotaging or stealing intellectual property is a strategic way to cripple your competition. Whether you destroy it, take it for yourself, or leak it to damage their plans, intellectual property sabotage is one of the most effective ways to undermine a rival's future.

Product Tampering: Success into Disaster

Product tampering is another effective way to sabotage a company by targeting its core revenue stream and reputation. The goal isn't just to disrupt production but to ensure the product fails in the market, damaging credibility with customers. When executed carefully, tampering can cripple a business without leaving any trace.

Start with manufacturing. If you have access to the production process, subtle changes like using lower-quality components can cause products to fail after they reach consumers. For example, tampering with a tech product's battery or wiring might cause it to overheat, leading to recalls, refunds, and negative reviews. By the time the company realizes there's a problem, the damage is done.

Quality control is another weak spot. Allowing faulty products to pass through unnoticed can wreak havoc once they're sold. A batch of electronics with defective parts or food products containing contaminants can lead to safety recalls, lawsuits, and a PR crisis. By making sure only some items are affected, the problem looks like an unfortunate error rather than sabotage.

Inconsistencies in product performance can be just as damaging. Imagine a smartphone that randomly drops calls or a fitness tracker that provides inaccurate data. When some units work and others don't, customers lose trust in the product and the brand, leaving the company scrambling to fix the issue.

Tampering doesn't have to stop at the product itself. Packaging mistakes or delivery errors like switching labels can lead to confusion, missed sales, and frustrated customers. Safety seals on sensitive items like baby formula or medication can be compromised, causing a consumer panic and forcing the company to recall products and investigate, all while dealing with the negative press.

For digital products, tampering with software or firmware updates can disable entire product lines. Introducing bugs in the update process can cause devices to malfunction or lose functionality after an update, leading to consumer frustration and loss of confidence in the brand.

Timing is everything. Sabotaging a product just before a major launch can turn a high-profile event into a disaster. Early reviews filled with complaints about faulty performance can turn excitement into a PR nightmare, ruining the product's potential and damaging the company's reputation.

Product tampering is effective because it causes long-term damage. The company must deal with recalls, lawsuits, lost trust, and a tarnished brand. It often looks like a manufacturing issue, leaving no trace of your involvement. In the world of corporate sabotage, product tampering is one of the most devastating tools you can use, hitting a company where it hurts the most their relationship with their customers.

Summary

This chapter delves into the subtle yet highly effective tactics of corporate sabotage. Sabotage doesn't require bold, overt actions; discreet interference is more than enough. Whether you're blocking key resources to stall a project, tampering with a company's core products, or quietly manipulating data to steer decisions off-course, the goal is to weaken rivals while maintaining plausible deniability.

One of the most effective ways to undermine success is by restricting access to critical resources. By controlling or delaying the flow of money, personnel, or information, you can cripple a project's momentum without raising suspicions. Similarly, overloading a colleague with responsibilities and pushing them to the breaking point is a powerful way to force them into failure while appearing to support them.

Other tactics, like tampering with intellectual property or planting false evidence, strike at the heart of a competitor's value and credibility. Whether corrupting crucial files or framing someone for misconduct, these methods introduce doubt and confusion, leading to costly errors and missed opportunities.

Finally, product tampering offers a particularly destructive form of sabotage. By subtly compromising the quality or functionality of a product, you can inflict long-term damage on a company's brand, customer loyalty, and bottom line, often without anyone realizing it was sabotage.

Throughout the chapter, the key message remains: small, calculated acts of sabotage can have outsized impacts, disrupting operations and reputations while keeping you in the clear. But remember, crossing legal lines can have severe consequences, so try to stay within the bounds of the law.

Chapter 11

Offensive and Defensive Strategies

Offensive and defensive strategies are the basis for all corporate warfare, whether you're dealing with rivals, internal threats, or unexpected crises. The most successful people understand that these strategies aren't just reactionary tools; they're preemptive strikes, carefully crafted plans designed to keep you ahead of the game.

You can't build an empire standing alone. You need loyalists, people who are as invested in your success as you are, individuals willing to defend your interests and execute your plans without question. But even loyalty isn't enough. You need to be one step ahead, embedding your allies in key positions within your organization and even your competitors' ranks. By doing so, you control the flow of information, dictate the narrative, and steer the course of events from behind the scenes.

When subtlety isn't an option, there's nothing quite like the shock and awe of a massive, well-timed offensive. Whether it's a surprise restructuring, an unexpected acquisition, or a sudden shake-up of leadership, these moves strike fast and hard, leaving your competitors reeling and unable to mount a defense. The element of surprise is your greatest weapon, but preparation is key. As Sun Tzu wisely said, "He will win who knows when to fight and when not to fight." The moment you decide to act, everything must already be in place planned, prepared, and ready for execution.

This chapter explores the tactics necessary to win, from building a trusted inner circle to mastering strategic strikes. Every strategy is about control whether it's controlling the people around you, the flow of information, or the perception of power.

Building a Loyal Inner Circle: The Trusted Few

Never stand alone, in a cutthroat environment, a loyal inner circle is more valuable than any number of high-level connections. You don't need a crowd behind you, just a few handpicked loyalists who are as invested in your success as you are. Think of them as your personal buffer zone, ensuring that the heat never touches you directly. They'll catch the incoming fire, deflecting, defending, and occasionally launching an offensive of their own when needed.

A loyal inner circle isn't just about blind loyalty, anyone can find a yes-man. What you need are individuals who understand their role in the game. They aren't just followers; they're co-conspirators. These are people who benefit when you win and lose when you fail, meaning their self-interest aligns with yours. Give them just enough power to feel important but never enough to challenge your authority. Keep them dependent on your success, and they'll be more than willing to go down with the ship if it ever comes to that, ideally, they'll be throwing everyone else overboard first.

While you're building this circle, remember to keep a few of them in strategic positions. You want eyes and ears everywhere, but more importantly, you want people who are ready to act on your behalf when things get ugly. Whether it's running interference or playing the heavy, their loyalty ensures that you stay one step removed from the messier parts of corporate warfare. Just make sure they don't get too comfortable, remind them that their survival is tied to yours, and loyalty can shift when power does.

Infiltration: Among Us

Opposition is so much easier to predict and manage when you place one of your own inside their ranks. Infiltration is one of the slickest ways to gain an advantage, gather intelligence, disrupt operations, or sabotage plans. A well-placed mole can achieve more than any boardroom negotiation or hostile takeover ever could.

Years ago, I had a situation where a mainframe software supplier was bleeding us for millions more than they should have. I had a loyal, enterprising team member who managed to get himself invited to their staff Christmas party. The party was in their office, and when things started to quiet down, he slipped away and stole their manuals and documentation. He spent the entire weekend poring over them and booked a meeting with me first thing Monday. Impressed doesn't even begin to cover it. His little stunt saved the company a good couple of million over the next year. I made sure his salary doubled that year and was set to do it again the next.

You want your infiltrators to blend in so seamlessly that no one questions their motives. They shouldn't be obvious about their loyalties. They should be pros at playing the part whether that's as a mild-mannered accountant, a trusted project manager, or even a member of the board. Their job is to keep their head down, do their work well, and report back to you. Bonus points if they can also subtly sabotage key initiatives or steer decisions in your favor without raising suspicion.

Infiltration isn't just for your competition. It works just as well within your own organization. Maybe there's a department that isn't playing by your rules or a team that's pushing back. Send in one of your loyalists to stir the pot, identify the dissenters, and keep you informed of any brewing insurrections.

Done right, infiltration gives you the insider edge. Your rivals may think they have everything under control, but all the while, you're three moves ahead, just waiting for the right moment to strike. When the time comes, you've already got a man on the inside ready to flip the switch.

Controlled Transparency: Through the Looking Glass

Transparency is a buzzword that gets thrown around a lot, but from my experience true transparency rarely exists. Controlled transparency, on the other hand, is everywhere, showing just enough to keep everyone satisfied while someone holds their keys.

You release select information, curate the narrative, and let others feel like they're getting the full picture. They're not. But they don't need to know that. Controlled transparency allows you to shape perception, maintain trust, and avoid scrutiny, all while keeping the real levers of power firmly in your grasp.

You share information that makes you appear open and cooperative, but you carefully withhold the details that could cause you trouble. It's not lying; it's strategic omission. You're creating a façade of honesty while keeping your agenda intact. This approach is especially useful when dealing with stakeholders, higher-ups, or even the public.

Controlled transparency also serves as a shield. If you're too secretive, people start asking questions and poking around in places they don't belong. By offering a curated glimpse, you're giving them just enough to keep their curiosity at bay. It's a diversion, a sleight of hand. They think they've seen it all, but in reality, they're only seeing what you want them to see.

The benefit of controlled transparency is that it lets you manipulate the flow of information to your advantage. You're in control of what people know, and by extension, what they believe.

Plausible Deniability: What?

Nothing says "power player" like being able to walk away from a disaster with your hands clean. That's the magic of plausible deniability: creating just enough distance between yourself and the dirty work so that, when the house of cards collapses, you can shrug and say, "Who, me?" It's a safety net, a get-out-of-jail-free card for when your schemes blow up in someone else's face.

The key to mastering plausible deniability is keeping everything indirect. You never give orders explicitly. You never leave a trail. Instead, you hint, you suggest, and you surround yourself with people who understand the unspoken rules. They know what you want without you having to say it, and more importantly, they know how to cover their tracks while doing it. Always plan an alibi, things go sideways, eventually, something will need a solid excuse. You can feign ignorance with a straight face because technically, you never told anyone to do anything shady.

It's all about insulating yourself from the fallout. Use intermediaries, buffer layers of loyalists who handle the dirty details. They execute the plans while you stay far enough removed to deny any involvement. The beauty here is that even if someone tries to point the finger at you, they can't. The chain of responsibility is broken, the paper trail non-existent, and all that's left is a lot of finger-pointing in every direction except yours.

Remember, plausible deniability is especially crucial when dealing with anything that could tarnish your reputation or lead to legal trouble. Whether it's a financial scandal, a corporate sabotage, or a questionable "favor" done for you behind the scenes, you always need to be in a position where no one can prove you had anything to do with it. You can play the role of the concerned leader, swooping in to clean up the mess someone else made, someone who definitely wasn't acting on your behalf.

Let others do the dirty work, and when the time comes, you're free to act surprised, disappointed, or even outraged. It's the classic move where your hands stay clean, and the blame won't follow you.

Stonewalling: Nothing to See Here

Sometimes, the best defense is doing nothing. When you find yourself backed into a corner whether it's a wave of criticism, an inconvenient investigation, or uncomfortable questions the answer isn't to engage. It's to stonewall. Refuse to answer, delay indefinitely, and watch as the pressure shifts from you to the frustrated people trying to get a response.

Stonewalling is simple, you don't just sit in silence; you need to bury the opposition under a mountain of bureaucracy, misdirection, and polite deflections. "I'll have to check on that," "We're looking into it," and "I don't have that information right now" are your best friends. Each vague response buys you more time and, more importantly, frustrates the hell out of your critics. They'll start spinning their wheels while you quietly carry on with your agenda, undisturbed.

One of my favorite aspects of stonewalling is that it plays into people's natural tendencies. People hate dead ends, but they hate being ignored even more. By offering just enough engagement to keep them thinking you'll eventually cooperate, you keep them on the hook while giving them absolutely nothing of substance. It's a slow-burn tactic that grinds down anyone attempting to hold you accountable. The longer they have to wait for answers, the more likely they are to give up or move on to something else.

If someone accuses you of stonewalling it's another example where feigning innocence works. "I'm doing everything I can," you say, with a sympathetic smile, all the while knowing that you've created an impenetrable wall of delay tactics that would take a bulldozer to break through. If done right, stonewalling doesn't just buy time, it wears down your opposition until they're too exhausted to keep pushing.

Stonewalling isn't about solving the problem; it's about outlasting it. Critics will get tired, investigations will lose momentum, and eventually, people will move on. All the while, you've kept your position intact, avoided uncomfortable admissions, and made sure the real issues never saw the light of day. Slow and steady wins the race.

Strategic Leaks: Drink Then Leak

Sometimes, the best way to control a narrative is to let the right piece of information "accidentally" slip out. Enter the art of the strategic leak, a popular strategy used by politicians. When done right, a well-timed leak can shift perceptions, destabilize your rivals, and solidify your power all while keeping you safely in the shadows.

A strategic leak is a weapon disguised as transparency, often passed off as virtue signaling. It's about releasing just enough truth to make it believable, but with a twist that serves your agenda. Maybe it's confidential information that exposes a competitor's weakness, a bit of insider gossip that paints a rival in a bad light, or a damaging report that somehow finds its way into the hands of the right people. The trick lies in indirectness. You didn't come out swinging, you just took the moral high ground and let the "truth" do the dirty work for you.

You don't want to release something so explosive that it blows back on you, but you do want it to be significant enough to create ripples. Sometimes, a small piece of information can cause a chain reaction, leading others to dig deeper, ask the right (or wrong) questions, and eventually uncover a scandal you've been quietly nudging them toward.

Strategic leaks are also incredibly useful for managing your own image. Let's say there's a rumor about you that's getting a little too close to the truth. Instead of waiting for it to blow up in your face, you leak a version of the story that makes you look better. Maybe you admit to a minor misstep while downplaying the more serious accusations. You control the fallout by controlling what people know.

Leaks work best when they come from "anonymous" sources, or when they're traced back to someone far removed from you. Always have a middleman, a layer of plausible deniability, so that when the leak causes chaos, you're the one offering calm, reasonable explanations or just sitting back and watching the carnage from a safe distance.

The ability to orchestrate a strategic leak is a useful skill to have. Done right, it lets you set the stage for your enemies to self-destruct, while you walk away looking like the only adult in the room. Just be careful not to overplay your hand. Leaks should feel like accidents, not obvious plays. Otherwise, you risk exposing the puppet master behind the curtain.

Aggressive Lobbying: Join my Cause

When charm and persuasion just aren't cutting it, it's time to bring out the big guns' and aggressive lobby. This isn't your quiet chat in a pub, where you wine and dine decision-makers and hope they'll see things your way. Aggressive lobbying is about bending the will of the powerful to serve your agenda, using whatever means necessary. If they won't play nice, you'll make sure they play anyway.

At its core, aggressive lobbying is about leveraging pressure. You're not asking for favors, you're demanding them. Whether it's through relentless persuasion, strategic alliances, or outright intimidation, your goal is to make it impossible for key decision-makers to say no. You turn up the heat until they realize that agreeing with you isn't just in their best interest, it's the only option they have left.

One effective tactic is to mobilize other influential players who are already on your side. Create a coalition of voices that all echo your demands, making it clear that resistance isn't just a matter of personal inconvenience it's a career-ending mistake. Use the media to your advantage, planting stories that subtly (or not so subtly) push your narrative. If public pressure doesn't do the trick, you can always dangle the prospect of financial backing or, conversely, the threat of withdrawing support.

Lobbying requires persistence, relentlessly pushing your agenda until the decision-makers are worn out, overwhelmed, or convinced that fighting back will cost them more than it's worth. Make sure they know that you won't take no for an answer, and if they don't play ball, there's always another way to get what you want whether that's through legal means, corporate influence, or political leverage.

Done right, aggressive lobbying leaves the victim looking like the bad guy if they refuse. You're not the villain here, you're just someone with a vision, someone who knows what's best. You've done the work, rallied the support, and presented a clear path forward. If they're standing in the way, well, it must be because they're selfish, out of touch, or protecting their own interests at the expense of everyone else. Frame it that way, and suddenly the pressure on them multiplies.

Create a scenario where saying yes is the only option left. Whether you're influencing legislation, securing a lucrative contract, or manipulating a key business decision, aggressive lobbying ensures that those in power know exactly what's at stake and that defying you is a gamble they can't afford to take.

Preemptive Strikes: Did we Start?

Don't wait for a threat to materialize, crush it before it even gets off the ground. That's the philosophy behind the preemptive strike. It's about neutralizing your enemies before they've even realized they're in a fight, making sure they never have the chance to challenge your position. In a world where the first mover often wins, taking the offensive early can mean the difference between staying in control and watching someone else take your throne.

Preemptive strikes aren't about reacting to problems; they're about creating solutions before the problem even exists. Got a competitor who's getting a little too ambitious? Undermine them before they can gather any serious momentum. Heard whispers of someone gunning for your position? Make sure they never get the chance to follow through.

By acting first, you dictate the terms of engagement. Your opponent is left scrambling to respond, often without even fully understanding what's happening. While they're trying to recover, you've already moved on to the next phase of your plan.

A preemptive strike isn't always about open confrontation. Sometimes, it's a quiet word in the right ear, a carefully timed leak (see how these strategies come together?), or even a subtle sabotage. The key is to make sure your rival never sees it coming. They can't retaliate if they don't know who hit them. Even if they do figure it out, by the time they're ready to act, you've already solidified your position.

This tactic works especially well in political and corporate environments, where reputations and alliances are fragile. A little rumor here, a well-placed piece of misinformation there, and suddenly your opponent is dealing with a PR nightmare, internal chaos, or an unexpected crisis.

As always, preemptive strikes come with risks. Act too soon, and you might tip your hand. If done correctly, you eliminate the threat before it even becomes a problem, maintaining your dominance without ever having to get into a real fight. Think of it as snuffing out the spark before it becomes a flame. You don't want a full-blown fire, you want to make sure there's never even smoke.

Character Assassination: Did you Hear?

Sometimes, the easiest way to deal with an opponent isn't to fight them directly, it's to destroy their reputation so thoroughly that they're left powerless, even if they're still standing. Character assassination is a nasty dirty trick, a way to eliminate rivals without ever having to lift a finger in open combat.

Character assassination done right is all performed in the shadows. You don't need to shout from the rooftops; a quiet whisper can be just as effective. The goal is to plant seeds of doubt, small, seemingly innocent remarks that slowly eat away at your target's credibility. "I've heard some things about him lately," or, "Did you know she's been struggling with...," is often all it takes to start the ball rolling. People love gossip, and once you've lit the fuse, the rumor mill will do the rest of the work for you.

But don't mistake character assassination for mindless slander. It's a strategic, targeted attack, designed to hit where it hurts most. If your rival's strength is their moral integrity, chip away at that. If they're known for their expertise, create just enough doubt to make people question their competence. The trick is to find their Achilles' heel and drive the knife in not too deep at first, but deep enough that they can't pull it out.

Timing is everything here. You want your attack to land when it's most devastating, when your target is either on the rise or in the midst of a high-stakes situation. That way, the fallout will be swift and brutal. Once the cracks start to show, others will pile on, and soon your rival will be drowning in accusations, forced to spend all their energy defending themselves instead of advancing their position. By the time they realize what's happening, it's too late. The damage is done.

Plausible deniability plays a key role in character assassination. You never want to be directly linked to the rumors. Use intermediaries, anonymous tips, or even a carefully placed leak to get the ball rolling. The more distance between you and the actual attack, the better.

Character assassination is about removing your rival from the playing field without having to engage them directly. Once their credibility is shot, they'll have no choice but to step down, back off, or retreat in disgrace. Done right you're left untouched, the silent victor.

Counterattacks: Return Fire!

When you're under fire, sitting back and taking hits is a poor option. A well-executed counterattack turns the tables on your critics, detractors, or rivals, shifting the narrative from you being the target to you being the aggressor. The key is speed, precision, and ruthlessness.

A counterattack is solving a defense problem with a quick offense. It's about going after your opponent with such force that they regret ever coming for you in the first place. The goal is to not only shut them down but to make them the new target, leaving you standing tall as they scramble to recover from your response.

One classic tactic is to discredit your attacker. Are they really in a position to throw stones? Highlight their own flaws, past mistakes, or shady dealings. Better yet, use their attack as an opportunity to expose them for the hypocrite they are. Make it clear that their accusations are nothing more than a smokescreen to distract from their own shortcomings. If they're attacking your ethics, maybe it's time to dig up some skeletons in their closet. If they're calling out your performance, show how their numbers don't quite add up.

Another effective method is to play the victim while simultaneously throwing punches. Position their attack as unjust, unfounded, and part of a larger conspiracy against you. This not only casts doubt on their claims but also rallies sympathy and support from those around you. Make it seem like they're the bully, and you're just defending yourself, all while dealing them a knockout blow in the process.

Timing is crucial. You can't wait too long to strike back or you risk appearing weak. Don't rush, either take a moment to assess their weak points, plan your move, and then hit them where it hurts the most. The goal is to make your counterattack feel inevitable, like they walked right into a trap of their own making.

Remember, a counterattack doesn't have to be direct. Sometimes, it's more effective to undermine them from the shadows leaking damaging information, planting doubts, or rallying support from key allies who suddenly question your rival's motives. If you're lucky, your opponent will be too busy fending off these new challenges to even remember they started a fight with you.

A good counterattack flips the power dynamic. Suddenly, your opponent is the one on the defensive, scrambling to explain themselves, while you're back in control. The best counterattacks not only neutralize the original threat but leave your opponent looking weaker and more vulnerable than before.

Litigation as a Weapon: I'll Sue!

Litigation isn't just for resolving disputes; in the right hands, it's a precision-guided weapon aimed straight at your opponent's resources, reputation, and sanity. Using litigation as an attack means leveraging the legal system not to win in court, but to drain your rival dry before they even get to trial. The goal is to exhaust them financially, emotionally, and mentally long before a judge or jury even hears the case.

A well-timed lawsuit can wreak havoc on your opponent's life, regardless of whether your claims have merit. The mere act of filing a lawsuit forces them into an expensive, time-consuming, and reputation-risking process. Legal fees pile up, their focus gets divided, and before they know it, they're spending more time in courtrooms and depositions than on their actual business.

The advantage of using litigation as a weapon is that you don't even have to win to achieve your goal. In fact, winning isn't the point dragging them through the mud. You can file for baseless claims, knowing full well the case will likely get thrown out or settled, but by the time that happens, the damage will already be done. Your opponent will have spent a fortune defending themselves, their reputation might be bruised, and they'll think twice before crossing you again.

One particularly nasty tactic is to go after something personal whether it's a defamation suit that questions their character or a breach-of-contract claim that undermines their professional reputation. Even if they win the case, they lose the time, money, and focus that could have been spent elsewhere. There's always a chance that the mere existence of a lawsuit could scare away investors, clients, or business partners.

Litigation as a weapon isn't limited to civil suits, either. Get creative. Use intellectual property claims to block their products, antitrust complaints to stall their mergers, or labor disputes to disrupt their operations. The legal system is a labyrinth, and the more complicated you can make their life, the better. If you can bury them under mountains of paperwork, motion after motion, and endless delays, they'll eventually cave not because they're wrong, but because they simply can't afford the money or effort to keep fighting.

You can always settle or drop the case. But only after the damage is done. Where there is smoke there is fire and that's often enough. Offer them a way out that feels like a victory for them when, in reality, you've already achieved what you set out to do. Whether it's weakening their position, draining their resources, or forcing them into a costly distraction, the end result is the same: they're left wounded, and you're free to move forward without a scratch.

Don't think of litigation as a legal strategy, think of it more as a psychological one. It's about using the weight of the legal system to press down on your opponent until they crack.

Hostile Takeovers: It's Mine Now

Why build when you can simply take? Hostile takeovers are fun, ruthless, efficient, and often devastating for the target. This isn't about negotiation or finding common ground. A hostile takeover is about forcibly gaining control of a company or department or team, whether they like it or not. It's a raid, plain and simple, and when done right, it leaves you holding the reins while your rivals are left wondering what the hell just happened.

The trick to a successful hostile takeover is finding the right target: vulnerable, mismanaged, or simply underestimating you. Maybe the leadership is weak, maybe their shareholders are disgruntled, or maybe they're just too complacent to see the storm coming. Whatever the case, your goal is to exploit their weaknesses and seize control before they even know they're in a fight.

One classic method is to quietly buy up shares, slowly gaining enough control to influence or outright dictate the company's direction. By the time they realize you're a threat, it's already too late. You've got enough stock to force your way into the boardroom, and suddenly, you're calling the shots.

Shares aren't the only way to execute a hostile takeover. Sometimes, it's about destabilizing from within. Plant your loyalists in key positions and slowly erode the current leadership's authority. Create enough chaos that the board has no choice but to look for new leadership and conveniently, you've already got the perfect replacement in mind: you. Whether you're doing it with money, manipulation, or a combination of both, the goal is the same: seize control before they can mount a real defense.

Hostile takeovers can also happen in smaller-scale settings. Maybe you're eyeing a department within your own organization, or a competitor who's losing ground. The tactics are the same: destabilize, divide, and conquer. Sow distrust, isolate leadership, and rally support for your cause. Before long, the current regime will be too weakened to fight back, and you'll be left holding the crown.

Once you've secured control, you can reshape the organization how you see fit. Out with the old guard, in with your loyalists. Slash jobs, restructure divisions, or strip the company for parts if that's what suits your agenda. By the time you're done, the company or department will be unrecognizable, and all anyone will remember is that you're the one who came out on top.

Shock and Awe Tactics: Bang!

Never underestimate a good shock and awe campaign. This is the corporate equivalent of dropping a bomb delivering such a sudden, overwhelming blow that your opponents are left stunned, scrambling to make sense of what just happened. Destabilize, disorient, and crush your rivals before they have time to regroup.

Shock and awe tactics are all about the element of surprise. You hit fast, hard, and with enough force that resistance feels pointless. This could be an aggressive merger, a mass layoff, or a sweeping restructuring that no one saw coming. The key is to overwhelm your target with the sheer scale of your action, leaving them reeling and unable to fight back effectively. By the time they recover from the initial impact, you've already moved on to phase two solidifying your control.

As Sun Tzu said, "He will win who knows when to fight and when not to fight." In other words, don't start a war unless you know you can finish it. Everything must be pre-prepared plans, contingencies, and escape routes. When you pull the trigger, you want the whole thing wrapped up and done within hours. This strategy only works if you overwhelm them and move fast. Anything less than total domination gives them room to regroup, and that's the last thing you want.

Take, for example, a company-wide restructuring announced on a Monday morning. No one knew it was coming, but suddenly entire departments are merged or dissolved, key executives are out the door, and the power dynamics have shifted overnight. The shock leaves everyone scrambling to figure out where they stand. The new structure is already in place, it's too late.

Another powerful shock and awe move? Firing a key figurehead or longtime leader without warning. Whether it's a CEO, a department head, or a key team member, removing a lynchpin figure sends ripples throughout the organization. It creates chaos, but chaos that you control.

You seize the narrative, stepping in as the steady hand while everyone else is left trying to make sense of the new normal.

Shock and awe comes with risks. You need to be certain that you can maintain control after the initial strike. If you lose your grip, the chaos you've created can spiral out of control, potentially turning on you. But when executed correctly, it's one of the most powerful strategies in your arsenal leaving your rivals too stunned to do anything but watch as you take over.

Creating a Crisis: Fire Alarm Again?

Often, the best way to seize power is to manufacture the conditions that demand it. Creating a crisis is a classic strategy for consolidating control, eliminating competition, and forcing people to rally behind you. When chaos reigns, people will look for stability and conveniently, you're the one who offers it.

Creating a crisis isn't about total destruction, after all, you want to emerge from this with more power, not less. It's about engineering a situation where the existing order can no longer function, and you're the only viable solution. This can take many forms: financial instability, a sudden operational breakdown, or a carefully timed scandal that forces leadership to step down. The key is to create just enough chaos that it destabilizes your rivals without burning down everything you've worked for.

Let's say there's a project or department you want to take over. Start by highlighting existing issues, exaggerating problems, drawing attention to inefficiencies, and quietly ensuring that nothing gets fixed. As things spiral, you present yourself as the savior, the one with the vision to pull everything back from the brink. By the time anyone realizes the crisis was orchestrated, you're already in control, and they're too busy thanking you for saving the day to ask how it all started.

Financial crises are another powerful tool. Leverage mismanaged budgets, overspend in key areas, or quietly push a risky investment that's bound to fail. When the money runs dry, you step in with a plan to save the company or at least the parts of it that matter to you. Everyone else gets cut loose.

Creating a crisis can also be useful when you want to remove a rival. A well-timed scandal or "accidental" leak can force them into a corner, distracting them with damage control while you quietly take over. The beauty of a crisis is that it forces people to act quickly, often without fully understanding what's happening. In the confusion, you can move in, make decisions, and seize opportunities while everyone else is too panicked to see the bigger picture.

Of course, crises can be unpredictable, and you'll need to manage the fallout carefully. The trick is to make sure you're always one step ahead, with a plan in place to contain the damage. Done right, creating a crisis leaves you in complete control, with your rivals in disarray and the organization begging you to take charge.

Summary

Whether you're playing offense by launching preemptive strikes and orchestrating hostile takeovers, or defense by building a loyal inner circle and creating plausible deniability, every move you make must be calculated, deliberate, and with one goal in mind: maintaining control.

Infiltration, controlled transparency, and strategic leaks aren't just tactics, they're your insurance policy, ensuring that you stay several steps ahead of anyone who might threaten your position. When used effectively, these strategies turn you into an invisible puppet master, pulling the strings while others are left to scramble in the chaos you've engineered. Don't forget the importance of timing knowing when to strike is just as critical as knowing how to strike.

Corporate power doesn't come from sitting back and waiting for opportunities to present themselves. It comes from creating those opportunities, positioning yourself as the calm in the storm while your rivals are too busy putting out fires you've started. By mastering both offensive and defensive strategies, you ensure that you're always the one holding the cards, dictating the rules, and calling the shots.

Chapter 12

Ethical Defenses and Maintaining Integrity

Shortcuts and ethical flexibility are often rewarded, Maintaining integrity is a deliberate choice that requires constant vigilance and a clear set of principles. While it's tempting to focus solely on profits, building a foundation of ethical behavior is not just good for business; it's essential for long-term success. Ethical defenses are more than just policies written in a handbook they are the actions and decisions made daily by individuals and leaders alike.

This chapter delves into how companies can arm themselves with ethical defenses, from creating robust Codes of Conduct to fostering a culture where ethical decision-making isn't just encouraged but ingrained. It highlights the importance of ongoing ethics training, clear conflict-of-interest policies, and building a strong, loyal leadership that embodies integrity at every level. The strategies in this chapter provide the tools and mindset necessary to maintain integrity, protect reputations, and ensure that ethical behavior isn't a burden but an asset.

Ethics Training: Knowing What's Right

Where corner-cutting often feels like the fastest route to the top, creating a culture that values ethics over expediency is the long game. It starts with a well-crafted Code of Conduct, a blueprint for behavior that everyone from the boardroom to the breakroom is expected to follow. A piece of paper with lofty ideals won't magically turn people into paragons of virtue.

The purpose of ethics training is to take that glossy Code of Conduct and translate it into real-world actions. It's not just about showing employees the difference between right and wrong; it's about making them realize that doing the right thing can actually be to their advantage.

Take this scenario: Jill in accounting knows that approving certain vendor payments might slide by unnoticed, even though they don't technically align with company policy. With robust ethics training, Jill isn't just aware that approving these expenses would violate the code she's equipped with the confidence to stop it and the knowledge of exactly how to escalate the issue without fear of retaliation.

The key to effective ethics training is making it engaging, not a mind-numbing slog through a PowerPoint filled with legal jargon. Real examples, interactive scenarios, and even role-playing exercises can turn an otherwise dry subject into something that is fun and sticks. Instead of just telling employees, "Don't accept bribes," show them a situation where a vendor offers an all-expenses-paid trip to close a deal, and walk them through the ethical and career-preserving way to handle it.

It's crucial that ethics training is not a one-off event. A single afternoon workshop won't keep people from making sketchy decisions months later. Ongoing training, refresher courses, and incorporating ethics into everyday discussions can solidify it as part of the company's DNA.

The goal is to shift the mindset from ethics as a limitation to ethics as an opportunity to build trust, enhance the company's reputation, and create a workplace where people feel empowered to act with integrity.

Clear Conflict of Interest Policies: When to Declare

The lines between personal gain and professional duty can blur faster than a handshake under the table. Having clear conflict of interest policies in place is like having a spotlight that follows those who play in the murky waters. It's not just about ensuring that employees don't dabble in shady side deals; maintaining trust and credibility in every decision that's made.

A well-crafted conflict of interest policy doesn't need to read like a legal manifesto. It should be straightforward, defining what constitutes a conflict whether that's hiring your cousin for a major contract or investing in a competitor's stock while sitting on sensitive company information. They can be a challenge to enforce. It's not enough to just have a policy in the corner that gathers dust.

Imagine Dan, a senior project manager, has been offered a board seat at a tech startup that happens to be a subcontractor for his current company. Dan might convince himself that it's just networking, that the role won't affect his objectivity. Without a clear policy in place, Dan's colleagues and even Dan himself could start questioning whether his decisions are really in the company's best interest or just greasing the wheels for his side gig.

This is why declaring conflicts of interest has to be second nature, not an afterthought. Employees should know that if they're ever in doubt, transparency is the only option. Whether it's disclosing personal relationships, financial interests, or outside employment, bringing potential conflicts to light is the first step in maintaining integrity.

What happens when someone does the right thing and discloses a conflict? The policy must also outline how these situations will be managed. It could involve removing the person from decision-making in that area or even having a third party review major decisions where conflicts could arise.

Take, for example, a vendor selection process. Without conflict policies in place, employees could find themselves pressured into picking suppliers based on personal relationships, leaving the door wide open for favoritism or kickbacks. A solid policy ensures the selection is based on merit and company needs, not backroom deals.

Having clear conflict of interest policies isn't just about keeping people honest it's about setting a standard where personal gain never clouds professional judgment. It's a way of ensuring that when decisions are made, they're driven by what's best for the company and not what's best for someone's wallet or Rolodex.

Encourage Ethical Leadership: Reward the Good

Ethical leadership is setting the tone from the top down, showing that doing the right thing isn't just a guideline it's a mandate. If the leaders of an organization are cutting corners or playing fast and loose with the rules, you can bet that behavior will trickle down to the rest of the organization.

Encouraging ethical leadership means promoting those who demonstrate integrity, not just results. Sure, a CEO who boosts the bottom line looks good on paper, but if that success comes from trampling on ethics, the cost will eventually outweigh the gains. Look at any number of corporate scandals where profits were prioritized over principles. The fallout isn't just financial, it's reputational, and reputations are much harder to rebuild than balance sheets.

Imagine this: Lisa, a middle manager, consistently hits her targets, but she also regularly overrides internal controls to close deals faster. Her leadership might appear successful, but underneath, it's a time bomb waiting to explode. If Lisa's behavior is rewarded, she becomes a model for others to follow. Before long, you've got an entire department engaging in sketchy shortcuts because that's what got their boss ahead.

By contrast, ethical leadership prioritizes not only what gets done but how it gets done. A strong leader asks questions like, "Are we following our values?" and "Will this decision stand up to scrutiny?" They ask these questions even when nobody's watching. Ethical leadership isn't performative; it's the genuine article.

The trick is fostering an environment where integrity is rewarded. You promote leaders who don't just lead by example but make ethics part of the everyday conversation. Whether that's recognizing employees who flag potential issues or encouraging managers to ask for feedback on their ethical behavior, the focus should always be on creating a culture where doing the right thing is as important as profit.

Consider Alex, a team leader who takes the time to mentor his employees, not just on performance but on making ethically sound decisions. He openly discusses dilemmas, creating a safe space for employees to ask tough questions without feeling like they'll be penalized for hesitating over a gray area. Alex isn't just leading his team; he's cultivating an ethical mindset that will permeate long after he's gone.

This isn't just about moral high ground ethical leadership has tangible business benefits. It reduces the risk of lawsuits, improves employee satisfaction, and builds trust with customers and stakeholders.

Encouraging ethical leadership means choosing leaders who are as accountable to their moral compass as they are to their quarterly reports. It's about promoting those who don't just manage people, but manage integrity, setting a standard that echoes throughout the organization.

Transparency and Open Communication: Broadcast Depth

Transparency and open communication are critical for any ethical organization. In a world where half-truths and selective disclosure are often the norm, fostering a culture of honesty can feel like swimming upstream. But it's not just about avoiding scandal, it's about building a foundation of trust that can weather even the most challenging storms.

Transparency no matter the company, there are countless decisions being made behind closed doors, some necessary, others just convenient for those holding the power. A commitment to transparency means pulling back the curtain whenever possible, ensuring that employees, stakeholders, and even customers know what's going on and why. It's the antidote to the "need-to-know basis" mentality that often breeds distrust.

Example: A company announces a major restructuring. Instead of keeping employees in the dark and letting rumors spread, a transparent approach would involve clear communication about the reasons behind the decision, the timeline, and what it means for everyone involved. Not every piece of information can be shared. Some things are legitimately confidential but being as open as possible shows that the company values honesty over damage control.

Open communication. It's not enough to be transparent from the top down; communication needs to be a two-way street. Employees should feel empowered to speak up, ask questions, and share concerns without fear of retribution. A culture of open communication means encouraging dialogue, whether it's in team meetings, performance reviews, or even casual check-ins.

Consider John, a mid-level employee who notices a potential compliance issue with a vendor contract. In a company that values open communication, John wouldn't hesitate to raise the issue with his manager. He'd trust that his concerns would be taken seriously, not swept under the rug or met with retaliation. The problem with many organizations is that they pay lip service to open communication but, in reality, make employees feel like they're walking on eggshells whenever they bring up a sensitive issue.

Creating an environment where open communication thrives requires more than just an "open door policy." Leaders need to actively engage with their teams, soliciting feedback and addressing concerns in real-time. It's about showing that no issue is too small and no opinion is unwelcome. This isn't just good for morale, it's good for business. Problems get identified early, solutions come faster, and trust builds across the board.

Let's say your company faces a crisis, maybe it's a product recall or a data breach. In an environment where transparency and open communication are the norm, leadership immediately communicates the issue to employees and stakeholders, explains what's being done to fix it, and sets clear expectations. Employees, in turn, are more likely to stay calm and focused, trusting that leadership has their back and the situation is under control.

In contrast, a company that thrives on secrecy and closed-door decisions will find itself scrambling. Employees don't know what's going on, stakeholders feel blindsided, and the rumor mill fills the vacuum left by poor communication.

Ultimately, transparency and open communication aren't just feel-good ideals, they're practical tools for creating a company that people want to work for and do business with.

Building a Speak-Up Culture: Whistleblowers

In most workplaces, the idea of speaking up when something feels off is great in theory but often translates to nervous glances, whispered complaints, and a whole lot of "I don't want to rock the boat." A true speak-up culture means more than just having a hotline for complaints; it's about creating an environment where employees genuinely feel safe raising concerns without fearing backlash. It's the difference between telling people they can speak up and showing them that it actually pays off when they do.

Let's take a look at what happens in a company without this culture. Say an employee, Sam, notices that a manager is inflating sales numbers to make the department's performance look better. He's uncomfortable with it, but he's also seen what happens to people who question authority, cold shoulders, lost opportunities, maybe even subtle forms of retaliation. So, Sam keeps quiet, and the unethical behavior continues unchecked.

Eventually, when the inflated numbers come to light, it's not just the manager who looks bad it's the entire company. The damage is done.

Now imagine the same scenario in a company that's built a strong speak-up culture. Sam knows his company takes concerns seriously and has seen colleagues speak up without consequence. Instead of staying silent, he reports the issue through the proper channels, confident that the company will investigate fairly. Not only is the problem addressed before it becomes a scandal, but Sam also feels valued for protecting the company's integrity.

This is where a speak-up culture shows its real power. It's not just about catching bad behavior, it's about empowering employees to take ownership of the company's ethical standards. When employees feel they can speak out without risking their careers, they become guardians of the company's integrity. A speak-up culture turns potential crises into opportunities for improvement, and it shows employees that their voice matters.

Building this culture isn't as simple as plastering "We value your input" on the breakroom wall. It requires active work from leadership. Management needs to visibly support employees who raise concerns and be crystal clear that retaliation won't be tolerated. This can involve everything from public recognition for those who speak up, to creating anonymous reporting mechanisms, to providing regular training on how to spot and report unethical behavior.

For example, a company that implements a monthly "Ethics Spotlight" meeting where employees are encouraged to bring up any issues or suggestions related to ethical behavior. These meetings are framed positively, not as a place to complain but as a space for improvement and proactive problem-solving. Leadership attends, listens, and takes action. Over time, employees see the direct impact of their input, and speaking up becomes just another part of the job, not a risky act of defiance.

The benefit of a true speak-up culture is that it promotes accountability at every level of the organization. Employees feel responsible for maintaining ethical standards, and leadership is held accountable for responding swiftly and fairly. This kind of environment doesn't just prevent unethical behavior, it actively discourages it from the start. When people know they can't get away with bad behavior because anyone, from an intern to a senior executive, might call it out, the temptation to cross that line fades fast.

Building a speak-up culture isn't about giving employees a place to vent, it's about creating a system where everyone feels empowered to protect the integrity of the organization. It's the corporate equivalent of a self-cleaning oven: employees keep things in check, leadership listens and responds, and the whole company runs more smoothly as a result.

Confidential Reporting Systems: I Heard Something

Even in the most open and transparent companies, there are times when speaking up openly feels risky. That's where a confidential reporting system steps in as a safety net for employees who need to raise concerns without putting themselves in the spotlight. It's a vital tool in any ethical organization because, let's face it, not everyone feels comfortable marching into the boss's office to report shady behavior, especially when that shady behavior might be the boss.

A well-designed confidential reporting system offers employees a secure, anonymous way to flag misconduct, unethical practices, or even just concerns about how things are being run. But for this system to work, it needs to be more than a suggestion box in the corner of the breakroom. Employees must trust that their identity will be protected, that their reports will be taken seriously, and that the company will act on their concerns without hesitation.

Imagine you work in a department where a senior executive is pressuring employees to manipulate financial data to make quarterly targets look better. Speaking up directly feels like career suicide after all, this executive holds power over promotions, raises, and the general office atmosphere. This is where a confidential reporting system can save the day. It gives employees an outlet to raise the issue without fear of retaliation, knowing their concerns will be investigated discreetly.

Take the case of a large corporation that implemented an anonymous whistleblower hotline. Employees were able to report issues related to fraud, harassment, and violations of company policy without fear of being identified. Over time, the company saw a drop in misconduct, not because people stopped doing shady things, but because they knew there was a high chance they'd be reported by someone who didn't have to reveal their identity. The system helped create a culture of accountability, where wrongdoing became a high-risk game.

A confidential reporting system is only as good as the trust employees have in it. If they believe that reporting anonymously will still somehow lead to retaliation, or if they think their concerns will be buried under paperwork and ignored, the system won't work. The company needs to clearly communicate how the system works, what steps will be taken when a report is made, and, most importantly, that retaliation will result in serious consequences.

Confidentiality should extend beyond just the reporting stage. Once a report is made, the company needs to ensure that the investigation is handled with discretion. It's not just about protecting the person making the report, it's about maintaining trust in the system. If employees see that reports are mishandled or used as gossip fodder, faith in the entire process crumbles.

Consider a company that faced a series of reports of unethical behavior in its procurement department. Employees used the anonymous system to flag issues like kickbacks and personal favoritism. Thanks to the confidentiality of the process, the reports were thoroughly investigated, and the guilty parties were removed without ever exposing who made the complaints. The result? Not only was the company able to clean up its act, but employees felt empowered knowing their concerns were taken seriously without having to risk their jobs or reputations.

A confidential reporting system is about creating a channel for accountability without fear. It's a way to keep the organization honest, even when power dynamics or personal relationships might make it difficult for employees to speak up openly. When done right, it's a vital part of building an ethical workplace, one where people know that even if they have to stay silent in the office, they can still make sure their voice is heard.

Whistleblower Protections: You Are Safe Now

Creating a system where employees can report wrongdoing is great, but it's only half the battle. The real test comes when those whistleblowers step forward. Are they protected, or do they get steamrolled by retaliation, demotions, and whispered accusations? A company can have the best reporting system in the world, but if whistleblowers aren't protected, it's all for nothing. Fear of retaliation can silence even the most principled employees.

Whistleblower protections are essential because they send a clear message: "If you speak up, we've got your back." These protections must go beyond promises in an employee handbook; they need to be embedded in the company culture and backed by serious consequences for anyone who dares retaliate. Whether someone reports financial misconduct, harassment, or safety violations, they need to know that their career and reputation won't be on the line for doing the right thing.

Let's consider Jane, an employee who uncovers a widespread pattern of expense fraud within her department. She reports the issue through the appropriate channels, but without strong whistleblower protections in place, Jane finds herself ostracized. Suddenly, she's no longer getting invited to important meetings, her projects are reassigned to others, and her promotion track mysteriously stalls. Even if no one outright says, "We're punishing you for speaking up," the message is clear: whistleblowers aren't welcome here.

Contrast that with a company that has robust whistleblower protections in place. In this company, Jane's report triggers not only an investigation but also a series of checks to ensure she faces no retaliation. Her performance is evaluated fairly, she's kept in the loop on key projects, and her career trajectory continues as if nothing had happened. Better yet, she's confident that if anyone does try to retaliate, they'll face serious consequences up to and including termination. The difference is night and day, and it's the kind of environment where ethical behavior thrives.

Effective whistleblower protections don't just benefit the individual they benefit the entire organization. When employees see that whistleblowers are protected, it creates a ripple effect. People feel safer reporting misconduct, knowing they won't be left out in the cold for standing up for what's right. Over time, this helps build a culture where transparency and accountability aren't just buzzwords; they're practiced daily.

A key part of these protections is ensuring anonymity when possible. If a whistleblower doesn't want their identity revealed, the company should go to great lengths to honor that. When that's not feasible, say, in smaller teams or highly specific reports whistleblower protections still need to ensure that the person reporting is shielded from any backlash.

Take a manufacturing company with a strong whistleblower protection program. When a group of employees reported safety violations that could have led to serious accidents, they were initially worried about retaliation from their supervisor, who had a reputation for making life difficult for "troublemakers." However, thanks to the company's clear, enforced whistleblower protections, the employees were able to report the violations without fear. Not only were the safety issues addressed, but the supervisor was quietly reprimanded for previous retaliatory behavior.

The result? A safer workplace and a culture where employees knew they wouldn't be punished for speaking out.

Whistleblower protections can't just be a reactive measure. Companies need to be proactive in creating a culture where employees know they're protected. This includes regular reminders about the policies in place, training sessions on how to report concerns, and clear examples of how whistleblowers have been protected in the past. When employees see that protection in action, they're much more likely to come forward.

Whistleblower protections aren't just about shielding individuals, they're about protecting the integrity of the entire organization. When people feel safe to report, the whole company benefits. Misconduct gets exposed before it becomes a scandal, and employees trust that doing the right thing won't lead to career suicide. That's a company people want to work for, and one that can weather any storm because its foundation is built on transparency and trust.

Ethical Mentorship Programs: Sharing is Caring

Ethical behavior doesn't just happen by accident; it's cultivated, often through the influence of those around us. That's where ethical mentorship programs come into play. In a corporate environment, mentorship is usually all about climbing the ladder, networking, and building career skills. But an ethical mentorship program takes it one step further. It's about fostering integrity alongside ambition, ensuring that tomorrow's leaders don't just know how to win but know how to win without losing their moral compass.

An ethical mentor is more than just a guide to corporate success; they're a role model for doing things the right way, even when cutting corners might seem easier. These mentors help mentees navigate tricky situations, not by offering shortcuts, but by showing how ethical choices are not only possible but also smart. It's about teaching that integrity isn't a luxury, but a requirement for long-term success.

Take Emma, a rising star in the marketing department. She's ambitious, smart, and driven, but she's also new to the unspoken rules of corporate culture. Her mentor, Paul, is a seasoned executive who's seen it all. Over lunch one day, Emma asks Paul how he handled a situation where a major client subtly hinted at wanting to receive "special favors" in exchange for continued business. Paul doesn't sugarcoat it. He explains how he carefully navigated the conversation, kept the company's reputation intact, and, most importantly, maintained his integrity. Emma walks away not just with career advice, but with a concrete example of ethical decision-making in action.

In an ideal ethical mentorship program, this isn't just a one-off lunch meeting. It's an ongoing relationship where ethical dilemmas are discussed as they arise, and mentors share their experiences both the successes and the mistakes. The idea isn't to create a perfect image but to show that ethical behavior is a constant, evolving choice that needs to be made repeatedly in the face of various pressures.

One major benefit of ethical mentorship is that it helps bridge the gap between company policies and real-world application. It's one thing to sit through an ethics training session; it's another to have a trusted mentor who can help you apply those lessons in the messy, complicated situations that don't always fit the textbook examples. A mentor can help employees see how sticking to their values can pay off, even when it seems like the harder path.

Consider this scenario: Mike, a mentor in the finance department, guides his mentee through a situation where they're asked to "massage the numbers" a bit to make the quarterly earnings report look more favorable. Mike doesn't just say, "Don't do it." He walks the mentee through the potential long-term consequences regulatory scrutiny, damaged credibility, even criminal charges. He then helps brainstorm ways to address the pressure without compromising integrity, showing that there's always a way to meet goals without bending the rules.

Ethical mentorship doesn't just for the benefit of the mentee. It reinforces the mentor's own commitment to integrity, reminding them of their responsibility to model ethical behavior. After all, it's one thing to talk about values in an abstract sense, but when you have someone looking up to you, it raises the stakes. The mentor is accountable not just for their own actions but for the example they set.

A successful ethical mentorship program also breaks down silos within the organization. By pairing employees from different departments or even different levels of the company, it encourages a broader perspective on ethics. An employee in sales might gain valuable insights from a mentor in legal or compliance, learning how their decisions can have ripple effects throughout the company. It's about creating a web of accountability and shared values, where ethics isn't just a box to tick, but a fundamental part of how the organization operates.

Ethical mentorship programs ensure that integrity isn't left up to chance. It creates a formal structure where the next generation of leaders is guided not just by the desire to succeed but by the understanding that true success never requires sacrificing one's principles. It builds a culture where ethics are passed down, not just in policy manuals but through personal connections, real stories, and practical advice.

Practicing Ethical Decision-Making: Practice Makes Perfect

Ethical decision-making sounds easy enough in theory, just do the right thing, right? But in the real world, decisions often come wrapped in shades of gray, conflicting interests, and pressures from all sides. The reality is, ethics requires practice, just like any other skill. And the best way to develop that skill is by creating an environment where employees aren't just expected to make ethical decisions but are actively guided through the process of how to do it.

Practicing ethical decision-making starts with a shift in mindset. Instead of treating ethics as a final check something to think about after the decisions are made it becomes the starting point. It's about asking the right questions at every stage: "Is this the right thing to do?" "How will this affect others?" and "Would this hold up under scrutiny?" Companies that want to foster ethical decision-making don't just encourage these questions, they make them part of the fabric of daily operations.

For example, a product development team that's under intense pressure to get a new launch out the door before the competition. The engineers know that the product isn't fully ready, and releasing it prematurely could lead to safety issues. The ethical dilemma here is clear: delay the launch and risk losing market share, or push it forward and hope the problems don't escalate. An ethical decision-making culture would empower the team to say, "We're not launching until it's safe, no matter the pressure." Importantly, they would feel supported by leadership in that choice.

One of the most effective ways to build this culture is through scenario-based training. Instead of abstract lectures about ethics, employees are given realistic situations where they must make tough decisions. These scenarios can range from handling conflicts of interest, to navigating financial reporting pressures, to responding to unethical behavior from a superior. By walking through these situations in a controlled environment, employees build the muscle memory to make ethical decisions when real stakes are involved.

Consider a training exercise where a manager is faced with cutting costs on a project by skimping on quality. During the scenario, they're encouraged to weigh the long-term effects of customer dissatisfaction, potential safety issues, damage to the company's reputation against the short-term savings. The exercise doesn't just show them what the right decision is; it shows them how to think through it, step by step, so they're prepared when a real-life version comes knocking.

Another key to practicing ethical decision-making is to embed it into the company's performance reviews and decision-making processes. If ethical considerations are left to an afterthought, employees will feel pressured to prioritize profits or productivity above all else. But when leadership consistently asks how decisions were made, not just the outcomes but the process itself employees start to realize that how they achieve results is just as important as the results themselves.

A sales executive, Steve, is encouraged to close deals aggressively, but he also knows some of the clients he's targeting may not benefit from the product he's pushing. In a company that emphasizes ethical decision-making, Steve isn't just judged by how many deals he closes; he's evaluated on whether those deals are in the best interest of both the client and the company's long-term reputation. Steve knows that pushing a product just for the sake of numbers could backfire and damage trust, so he opts for a more measured, ethical approach. When his performance review comes around, leadership recognizes and rewards that foresight.

The final piece of the puzzle is creating a culture where employees feel safe to challenge decisions that don't align with their values. Ethical decision-making isn't always popular. Sometimes, the right call means slowing things down, questioning authority, or pushing back on deadlines. If employees feel that raising these concerns could hurt their career, they'll stay silent and unethical decisions will slip through the cracks. A company that practices ethical decision-making encourages its people to voice concerns and engages in open, respectful dialogue when dilemmas arise.

Think of it as the difference between having a "yes man" culture versus a "why man" culture. In the former, employees nod along and let ethical concerns slide to meet short-term goals. In the latter, they feel empowered to ask "why" something is being done and to speak up when they think it's wrong.

Practicing ethical decision-making isn't just about avoiding scandals or regulatory issues; it's about building a business that thrives on trust, sustainability, and long-term relationships. When ethical choices are second nature, they become part of the company's DNA, leading to decisions that not only look good on paper but actually stand the test of time.

Documenting Everything: Paper Trail

A paper trail is like an insurance policy, it protects, clarifies, and ensures accountability. When it comes to ethics, documentation isn't just helpful; it's essential. Whether you're dealing with internal audits, compliance issues, or potential disputes, documenting decisions, communications, and actions is the one thing that can cut through the noise and get to the truth.

The idea of "documenting everything" can feel tedious, but it's less about paperwork for paperwork's sake and more about creating a system of accountability. When ethical decisions are documented, it becomes a lot harder for anyone to backtrack, rewrite history, or blame-shift.

Take this example: Sarah, a mid-level manager, notices irregularities in a supplier's billing. She raises the issue in an email to her supervisor, outlining her concerns and suggesting an internal review. Her supervisor brushes it off, saying, "Don't worry about it. Just sign off on the invoice." Sarah knows this could become a problem later, so she documents everything: her emails, the supervisor's responses, and the irregularities she's flagged. Months later, when the discrepancy comes to light, that documentation saves Sarah from being implicated. She has a clear record showing she did the right thing.

In situations like this, documentation isn't just a safeguard for the person raising concerns, it's a company's best defense against accusations of negligence or misconduct. Without proper records, it's one person's word against another's, and that's a slippery slope. With documentation, facts take center stage.

Documentation isn't just for the big-ticket items like fraud investigations or compliance audits. It's for every decision, every meeting, every approval. Let's say a project is delayed because of a key client's indecision. If there's no record of those delays, the team working on the project might get blamed for missing deadlines. If every communication with the client, every change request, every email exchange is documented, the team has the evidence to show exactly why the project didn't move forward as planned.

It's not about covering your tracks; it's about clarity. It's about making sure that, in a world full of moving parts and conflicting agendas, there's always a clear record of what was decided and why. This becomes especially important when ethical dilemmas arise, and the right decision might not be the easiest one.

Consider a scenario where a company is offered a lucrative contract, but accepting it would mean cutting ethical corners. The team that makes the decision to reject the offer documents every part of the process discussions around the risks, the ethical concerns, and the final decision. Later, when questioned about why they didn't take the money, they have a detailed, documented rationale showing that their decision was grounded in the company's ethical values, not just fear of a bad deal.

Documentation also protects employees from the fallout of retaliation. In cases where an employee reports unethical behavior, having a clear record of what was reported, when, and to whom can make all the difference. It prevents situations where a whistleblower's concerns are conveniently "forgotten" or distorted over time. This record-keeping ensures that the issue was raised properly and that any future retaliation can be addressed head-on with proof.

Documentation isn't just about defense. It's also about clarity. Let's say a company has clear, documented processes for how ethical dilemmas should be handled. Those documents can be referenced when new situations arise, giving employees a framework to follow. It makes ethical decision-making less about guesswork and more about consistency.

Take an organization that regularly faces complex ethical questions, maybe a financial firm handling client investments. If they document each time they've had to weigh the ethics of a particular strategy, they create a bank of knowledge that future teams can reference. They'll know what questions were asked, what outcomes resulted, and how those decisions impacted both the firm and its clients. This is documentation as a tool for growth, not just protection.

Documenting everything is about more than just protecting yourself in case of a dispute. It's about creating transparency, accountability, and a record of ethical decision-making that speaks for itself. It ensures that, no matter how chaotic things get, the truth is always there, written down, accessible, and untouchable by memory's distortions.

Independent Audits: Big Brother

Independent audits are more than just having a second set of eyes on your business. These eyes don't care about your bottom line, your office politics, or how much pressure you're under to deliver results. They only care about one thing: are you playing by the rules? When it comes to maintaining ethical standards, independent audits are crucial for keeping everyone honest, from the C-suite down to the front lines.

The key word here is "independent." Internal reviews are important, sure, but they often come with inherent biases. Whether it's a desire to protect reputations or a tendency to overlook "minor" infractions in favor of bigger priorities, internal audits can be swayed by the company's internal dynamics. Independent audits, however, offer an outside perspective, free from any influence. They see what's really going on, not what leadership hopes is going on.

A manufacturing company that performs internal safety audits every quarter. Everything looks fine, no major issues, just a few minor adjustments. But when an independent audit team comes in, they uncover a systemic issue with equipment maintenance that's putting workers at risk. The internal team missed it because they were too familiar with the day-to-day processes and didn't think to look deeper. The independent auditors, with their fresh eyes and lack of internal biases, caught the problem before it led to a serious accident.

Independent audits are especially important when dealing with financial or regulatory compliance. Imagine a financial services firm that handles large client accounts. The firm might have internal teams to ensure that transactions and investments are above board, but the potential for conflicts of interest or cutting corners under pressure is always there. An independent audit team can step in to review the firm's books, making sure that everything is not just legal, but ethical too. If there's a pattern of risky or borderline behavior, an independent auditor will spot it and they won't be afraid to call it out.

Let's say you're running a startup. You're focused on scaling, hitting revenue targets, and keeping investors happy. Ethical concerns? They're on your radar, but they might not be your primary focus. Enter the independent audit. A good auditor isn't just going to give you a financial check-up; they're going to examine whether your company's processes align with ethical best practices. They might flag issues like incomplete documentation, potential conflicts of interest, or areas where compliance is lacking. They'll tell you what's working, but more importantly, they'll tell you what could go wrong if you don't fix it now.

Independent audits hold everyone accountable, even leadership. When the board of directors commissions an independent audit, it signals that no one, not even the CEO, is immune to scrutiny. This creates a culture where cutting corners isn't just risky, it's guaranteed to be caught.

Consider a large multinational corporation facing rumors of shady labor practices in its overseas factories. Internally, the company insists everything is fine, pointing to internal audits and compliance reports that show minimal issues. But after pressure from stakeholders and the media, an independent audit is conducted. The findings? Widespread violations of labor laws that internal audits either missed or chose to ignore. The independent audit didn't just expose the issues, it forced the company to confront them head-on, leading to real changes and better protection for workers.

Independent audits don't always find massive scandals. Often, they simply highlight areas where a company can tighten its processes, ensuring compliance and ethical behavior before things go wrong. They can serve as an early warning system, spotting potential risks and giving companies the chance to correct course without public fallout.

One of the biggest advantages of independent audits is the trust they build with stakeholders. Investors, customers, and employees want to know that a company isn't just paying lip service to ethics they want proof. When a company voluntarily submits to independent audits, it sends a clear message: "We have nothing to hide, and we're committed to doing things the right way." That transparency builds credibility and trust, which can be just as valuable as a clean balance sheet.

Independent audits are about more than just compliance; they're about creating a culture where ethics are front and center, not an afterthought. They're a safeguard, a way to ensure that the company's actions align with its values, and that no one is cutting corners when it comes to integrity. Whether they uncover hidden issues or simply confirm that everything's on track, independent audits are an essential tool in keeping companies honest, accountable, and on the right side of ethics.

Third-Party Oversight: Review Committee

Third-party oversight takes the concept of accountability to the next level by bringing in an impartial, outside perspective to oversee decisions and operations. While internal teams may have good intentions, they can sometimes be too close to the situation, overlooking critical issues or getting caught up in company politics. A third-party overseer doesn't have that problem; they don't answer to the internal hierarchy or care about office politics. Their job is to ensure that decisions are fair, compliant, and most importantly, ethical.

Third-party oversight works best when companies understand that outside experts can help them see blind spots. Whether it's for regulatory compliance, conflicts of interest, or even just basic decision-making, having an external perspective ensures that decisions aren't being made in a vacuum. The purpose of third-party oversight is to prevent potential ethical missteps before they turn into full-blown scandals.

Consider a scenario where a company is deciding which vendor to choose for a multi-million dollar contract. Internally, the team might be tempted to go with a familiar face, a vendor they've worked with before, or perhaps one with close ties to leadership. While this may seem like a good idea to the team, it could raise serious ethical red flags, especially if there's a conflict of interest involved. A third-party overseer could step in to evaluate the vendor selection process, ensuring that it's based on merit, not favoritism or backroom deals. By providing an impartial analysis, they prevent any appearance of impropriety, protecting both the company and the individuals involved.

In highly regulated industries like finance, healthcare, or pharmaceuticals, third-party oversight isn't just a nice-to-have, it's often a legal requirement. Regulatory agencies often require companies to have independent auditors, compliance officers, or legal advisors review decisions to ensure they meet ethical and legal standards. For example, a pharmaceutical company developing a new drug might bring in an independent ethics board to oversee clinical trials, ensuring that patient safety isn't being compromised in the rush to market.

Third-party oversight can also be a powerful tool for maintaining trust with employees, customers, and investors. When a company invites an outsider to scrutinize its decisions, it sends a message of transparency. It says, "We're willing to be held accountable, even if it means exposing flaws." That kind of openness builds credibility, particularly in industries where trust is paramount.

Imagine a tech company known for its innovative but controversial data-collection practices. Privacy concerns are constantly swirling, and stakeholders want assurance that the company is handling user data responsibly. By bringing in a third-party data ethics committee, the company can demonstrate that it's not just policing itself, it's allowing an external body to monitor its practices and keep it in check. This kind of oversight builds trust with users who may otherwise be skeptical of the company's motives.

Third-party oversight can also help resolve conflict of interest in ways that internal teams can't. Let's say an executive sits on the board of another company that does business with one of their own. Even if the executive swears they'll remain impartial, the conflict of interest is clear, and internal teams may struggle to address it fairly. A third-party oversight body, however, can step in to make objective decisions about the relationship, ensuring that no undue influence is exerted and that the company's ethical standards remain intact.

Another key benefit of third-party oversight is that it provides a level of expertise that internal teams may lack. Complex ethical dilemmas often require specialized knowledge whether it's in legal compliance, financial integrity, or data privacy. A third-party expert brings a depth of understanding that ensures decisions are not only ethical but also legally sound. This expertise can help a company navigate tricky situations with confidence, knowing they're operating within the bounds of both the law and good ethics.

Consider a multinational corporation dealing with labor rights concerns in its overseas factories. Internally, they may believe that their labor practices are ethical, but a third-party human rights organization can provide a more objective assessment. They might conduct audits, interview workers, and assess whether the company's policies are truly protecting employees or just ticking compliance boxes. Based on their findings, they can recommend changes, ensuring that the company's operations align with global human rights standards.

For third-party oversight to be effective, it needs to be more than just window dressing. Companies can't simply hire outside experts and then ignore their advice. The overseers need real authority, and their findings must lead to actionable steps. If the third-party oversight committee flags a potential issue, leadership needs to be prepared to act on it, even if it's uncomfortable or inconvenient. This is where the real value of oversight lies ensuring that ethical concerns are not only raised but addressed.

Third-party oversight isn't about relinquishing control, it's about enhancing accountability. It's about recognizing that no matter how well-intentioned an internal team might be, outside perspectives can offer valuable insight and objectivity. When used effectively, third-party oversight ensures that ethical standards are upheld, risks are mitigated, and trust is maintained.

Ethical Crisis Management

Most companies don't think about crisis management until something goes horribly wrong. Ethical crisis management isn't just about dealing with a disaster; it's about how you handle the situation when your integrity is on the line. In a crisis, decisions are made fast, under pressure, and often in a fog of uncertainty. Without a plan that prioritizes transparency, accountability, and ethics, the rush to contain the damage can lead to even worse mistakes, making a bad situation catastrophic.

An ethical crisis management strategy ensures that when things go south, your company's response isn't just about survival, it's about doing the right thing, even when it's difficult. The first rule of ethical crisis management? Own the problem. It's tempting to downplay the issue, shift blame, or hide the full extent of the problem, but these tactics almost always backfire. A company's reputation often suffers more from the cover-up than from the crisis itself.

Consider a famous case: in 2015, A certain European car manufacturer was caught manipulating emissions tests to make their cars appear more environmentally friendly than they actually were. The initial response was denial and deflection, which only worsened the fallout when the truth emerged. Had the company immediately acknowledged the problem and committed to making things right, the damage to its reputation and its bottom line could have been far less severe.

The ethical approach to crisis management starts with transparency. If something's gone wrong, whether it's a product failure, a data breach, or a financial scandal, communicate it openly and honestly, both internally and externally. Employees need to know what's happening so they can respond appropriately, and stakeholders deserve the truth about how the company is handling the crisis.

Take a data breach, for example. The unethical approach would be to bury the information, hoping it doesn't leak out, or to provide a vague, sanitized version of the truth to customers. But in the age of social media and instant information, bad news doesn't stay hidden for long. The ethical path is to alert affected customers as soon as possible, explain the scope of the breach, outline the steps being taken to resolve it, and offer support to those impacted. Sure, the company will take a hit in the short term, but in the long run, customers appreciate transparency and are more likely to stay loyal if they believe the company is handling the crisis responsibly.

Ethical crisis management means not only admitting there's a problem but also taking responsibility for it. This is where many companies stumble. Leaders fear that accepting blame will invite lawsuits, regulatory scrutiny, or worse. But failing to take responsibility usually makes matters worse. An ethical crisis management plan includes a clear process for assessing what went wrong, who was involved, and how accountability will be assigned. It's not about throwing people under the bus, it's about ensuring that mistakes are owned and corrected.

Let's take an example from the food industry. A company discovers that one of its suppliers has been using substandard ingredients, resulting in a widespread recall of its products. The unethical approach would be to blame the supplier entirely and avoid taking any responsibility. The ethical approach, on the other hand, would involve acknowledging the company's role in not catching the issue sooner, taking full responsibility for any harm caused, and ensuring that corrective measures are put in place to prevent a recurrence. In doing so, the company not only addresses the crisis but also demonstrates a commitment to doing better in the future.

Ethical crisis management also involves a commitment to corrective action. A company can't just issue a mea culpa and hope the problem goes away. There must be concrete steps taken to resolve the issue, prevent it from happening again, and make amends with those affected. This could mean overhauling internal processes, making leadership changes, or compensating customers or stakeholders who were harmed by the crisis.

Look at the well known large pharmaceuticals company handling the paracetamol tampering crisis in the 1980s. After several people died from taking cyanide-laced paracetamol capsules, the company immediately recalled 31 million bottles of paracetamol, worked with law enforcement, and developed tamper-resistant packaging. Their swift, transparent, and ethical response not only helped them recover from the crisis but also set a new standard for product safety in the industry.

A critical element of ethical crisis management is empathy. In the middle of a crisis, it's easy for companies to get lost in damage control, protecting the brand, managing PR, and safeguarding the bottom line. But what about the people affected? Whether it's customers, employees, or the public, ethical crisis management prioritizes the human element. That means not only apologizing but offering real solutions that address the harm done. This could involve compensating customers, providing free services or products, or offering genuine support to those impacted. It's not just about minimizing losses; it's about making things right.

An ethical crisis management plan includes learning from the crisis. Once the immediate fallout has been handled, the company should conduct a thorough review to understand how the crisis happened and what can be done to prevent a recurrence. This review should be transparent and involve multiple levels of the organization to ensure that the lessons learned are integrated into future policies and practices.

Ethical crisis management isn't about avoiding blame or minimizing the impact, it's about turning a negative situation into an opportunity to demonstrate integrity, accountability, and responsibility. A crisis handled ethically can even strengthen a company's reputation, showing that when the chips are down, the company is willing to do what's right, not just what's convenient.

Summary

In this chapter, we explored the importance of building strong ethical defenses within an organization. A well-crafted Code of Conduct and effective ethics training ensure that employees understand not only what is right and wrong but also how to apply these principles in real-world scenarios. Establishing clear conflict-of-interest policies, practicing transparency, and encouraging open communication help create a culture where integrity is not just expected but celebrated.

We also discussed the role of ethical leadership in setting the tone from the top, showing that success should never come at the cost of integrity. By fostering a speak-up culture and providing whistleblower protections, companies can empower employees to report unethical behavior without fear of retaliation. Confidential reporting systems and independent audits further strengthen ethical defenses, ensuring accountability at every level.

Ultimately, maintaining integrity in a corporate environment is not just about avoiding misconduct, it's about creating an organization that thrives on trust, responsibility, and long-term sustainability. The strategies outlined in this chapter are designed to build a culture where ethical behavior is both a strategic advantage and a cornerstone of success.

Final Thoughts

We've journeyed through the darkest bits of the corporate world, peeling back the layers to expose the tactics that many use but few openly admit to. The goal of this book wasn't to glorify unethical behavior or to turn you into a corporate sociopath. Instead, it was to arm you with knowledge. Knowledge that, when used wisely, can help you navigate the treacherous waters of office politics, manipulation, and power struggles.

It's important to remember that understanding these strategies doesn't mean you have to adopt them. Power isn't just about being ruthless; it's about knowing when and how to use the tools at your disposal. True strength lies in balance. Sometimes, the best move is not to play the game.

The corporate world can be harsh, unforgiving, and, at times, really unfair. But now you're equipped with the insight to see through the smokescreens, to understand the real motives behind actions, and, most importantly, to make informed decisions. Whether you choose to rise by playing the game or by staying true to your principles, you now know the rules.

In the end, the path you choose is yours. There's a huge difference between knowing how to be nasty and actually being nasty. Understanding corporate sociopathy is just one part of the puzzle; how you decide to apply that knowledge is a question for your personal ethics.

Remember: the climb to the top doesn't have to come at the expense of others but it does require awareness, resilience, and strategy. Good luck, and may you find success not just in your career, but in every aspect of your life. How you navigate the corporate world is just one chapter; how you choose to live is the entire story.

www.ingramcontent.com/pod-product-compliance
Lightning Source LLC
Chambersburg PA
CBHW031504270326
41930CB00006B/240